This edition, issued in 1958, is for members of the Companion Book Club, 8 Long Acre, London, W.C.99, from which address particulars of membership may be obtained. The book is published by arrangement with the original publishers, Cassell & Co. Ltd.

THE WAY BACK

"A blessed companion is a book"—JERROLD

THE
WAY BACK

**THE STORY OF LIEUT.-COMMANDER
PAT O'LEARY, G.C., D.S.O., R.N.**

*

VINCENT BROME

THE COMPANION BOOK CLUB
LONDON

Made and printed in Great Britain
for The Companion Book Club (Odhams Press Ltd.)
by Odhams (Watford) Limited
Watford, Herts
S.458.ZTD.

ILLUSTRATIONS

Pat O'Leary in Korea, 1951   *facing page* 64
Lieutenant-Commander Patrick O'Leary, R.N.   65
Jean de la Olla and his wife   96
Robert Leycuras   96
Mario Prassinos and Gaston Nègre   97
Pat O'Leary in Marseille   97
Hugh Woollatt and Airey Neave in Louis Nouveau's
    flat in Marseille   160
Canet-Plage   160
Banyuls and the hills near the frontier   161
Tom Groome   192
Airmen on the Line, September, 1942   192
Pat O'Leary at Baden-Baden, 1946   193
"We keep in touch"   193

FOREWORD

DR. ALBERT MARIE GUÉRISSE—alias Patrick O'Leary—is a man of middle height with an explosive quality in some of his movements as if a tremendous force lay dormant in his personality. There are two deep furrows between the eyes, the mouth is set and the hair thinning at the temples. It is a tense, disciplined face. Everything about it suggests energy canalized to specific ends. Savage marks beneath the eyes and a certain pallor are the last visible signs of Dachau.

Sometimes talk flows away in a torrent, full of subtle gesture, driven home with great emphasis; sometimes he is quiet, watchful, non-committal, as a secret agent should be. He smokes, drinks, does not like dancing, never goes to a cinema, loves the music of Chopin and Mozart, and reads, for preference, history. By birth a Belgian, he can radiate a charm which endless people in his life have found irresistible.

Now a man of forty-five, he has crowded three careers into those years—soldier, doctor and secret agent—and on those dress occasions when he can be persuaded to wear all his decorations, he bears some resemblance to a full-scale general. He holds from Britain the G.C. and D.S.O., from France the Legion d'Honneur and Croix de Guerre, from Belgium high national orders and the Croix de Guerre, from America the Medal of Freedom, the Korean D.S.C., and many others, totalling some twenty awards.

Sitting upon a lamplit terrace, dipping down towards the lake of a beautiful German country club outside Cologne, Dr. A. M. Guérisse began, one autumn evening, to tell me his story. We drank considerable quantities of whisky. Night settled, the plains around Cologne became black and impenetrable; one by one the lights in the club went out, voices around us ceased talking and the face of the man opposite me was lost in recovered memories of another world.

At one o'clock we paused. A small cold wind had begun to stir. At two o'clock we ordered the last whisky. At three we went to bed. When we parted Patrick O'Leary was still talking in the same vivid, torrential fashion, drawing inexhaustible energy from some unidentified source. He rarely gets to bed before two in the morning, and never seems tired.

Our meeting in Cologne was part of a long pilgrimage which really began when I went to Menton, Nice, Marseille, and across the Camargue to les Saintes Maries de la Mer, Arles and Perpignan, unaware that I was following a trail later to become so familiar. Presently the trail took me to Germany where I met Patrick O'Leary, brought me back to England to Paula and Francis Blanchain, Costa Dimpoglou, Leoni Savinos, Whitney Straight, and Wing-Commander Higginson; carried me on to Paris where twenty-five of the men and women who were agents in Organization Pat pieced together fresh parts of the present book. To the droll Jacques Wattebled with his brilliant command of dialect English, to Robert Leycuras, Jean de la Olla, Fabien de Cortes, Bernard Gohon, Norbert Fillerin and his indomitable family, and to Paulette Gastou, I owe a lot.

For detailed and extensive documents I am indebted to Jean de la Olla, Robert Leycuras and Jacques Wattebled; to Costa Dimpoglou, Paula and Francis Blanchain, and Leoni Savinos, many hours of patient analysis of complicated points; to Patrick O'Leary, the diffident understatement of a story which you must now judge for yourself.

I gratefully acknowledge permission to use certain material in Chapters IX to XII from Airey Neave's book *They Have Their Exits* published by Hodder and Stoughton. Nor must I forget the fluent aid in three languages from Sylvia Guérisse, Dr. Guérisse's wife, who time and again unravelled difficult mazes. It should also be noted that for various reasons it has been necessary to alter certain names, places and identities.

For the rest, full-scale books could be written about

every one of the two hundred people involved in Organization Pat and there are many people I have no more than touched upon. It is sad that justice cannot possibly be done in a single volume to more than a small fraction of those involved. To Robert Leycuras, in particular, I owe apologies for the scant attention he receives, remembering the magnificent part he played. Primarily, this is the story of Patrick O'Leary, and if it neglects so many others, I hope they will understand the difficulties, and try to forgive me.

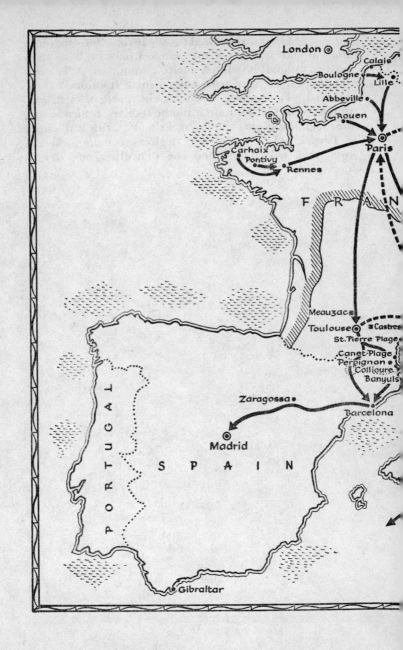

POLAND

GERMANY

Brussels
BELGIUM

CZECHOSLOVAKIA

Saarbrücken

Vienna
Linz   Wiener
Neustadt

Natzweiler

Dachau
Bad Tölz   Munich   Mauthausen

HUNGARY

AUSTRIA

C   E

SWITZER-
LAND

Geneva

YUGOSLAVIA

Lyon

I

St.Hippolyte
Nimes

La Turbie
Nice

T

Marseille

A

L

Y

TO GIBRALTAR

////// Demarcation line

■ Fortresses   ═══════▶ Escape routes

▪▪▪▪▪▪▪▪▶ Pat O'Leary's route through French
prisons and German concentration camps.

I⊤ WAS a cold April night in 1941 with a fresh sea running,
a few clouds coming up, the barometer falling and away in
the darkness the coastline of German-dominated Europe,
waiting. At midnight, the heavy old lifeboat with its 5-h.p.
engine was swung out from the Q-ship H.M.S. *Fidelity* and
six men climbed silently aboard with bicycles, luggage and
radio set. Lieutenant-Commander Langlais kissed each
man good-bye—Ford, an N.C.O., the French Lieutenants
Fergusson and Rogers, Aromatic an ancient Maltese, a
Polish agent and especially Lieutenant-Commander
Patrick O'Leary. Once a military doctor in the Belgian
Army he had escaped to Britain determined to continue
the fight against Germany and now, a fully trained agent,
with a French-Canadian background "manufactured" for
him in London, was launching into his first mission.

H.M.S. *Fidelity* lay shrouded in darkness two miles off
the south coast of France, her engines silent, every light
extinguished. The lifeboat groaned down into the sea, the
engine spluttered to life, hands were waved and the boat
headed shorewards. Fergusson, very young, smiling and
completely unperturbed, sat at the tiller, familiarity with
the coastline breeding a certain contempt for its dangers.
In the bows, the radio transmitter between his legs, sat
Aromatic, known by that name because of a certain odour
he distilled and now lost in deep Oriental communion.
In command was Patrick O'Leary, endless memories
stirring as he approached the land of sunshine, cypresses,
vineyards and long blue Mediterranean days.

Twenty minutes later, nearing the coast, speed was
reduced, the note of the motor muted. Presently they were
rowing, hands ready on revolvers as the boat eased towards
the sand. The sea was getting up and suddenly Pat decided
that they would keep a little offshore in case the boat

stuck in the sand. Fifteen yards away they strained their eyes into the darkness. Deserted sand dunes stretched away on either side with no sign of life, no light, no sound of any kind. Just the wind, whipping sand from one crest to another and mysterious, unseen slitherings.

Two men stepped out to steady the boat, the Polish agent made his own way ashore and O'Leary waded off with Aromatic and the radio set carried high on his shoulders. It seemed even darker as they reached the shore, a pitch black darkness almost tangible to the touch. Whispered farewells over, they were back in the boat again, and pushing off, when suddenly a hushed cry came from the shore. It was Aromatic. He was saying in a fierce subdued whisper: "You've put us on an island!" The deceptive range of sand banks extending into the sea produced false coastlines. They returned at once, the agents were taken aboard again and they moved farther down the coast.

The sea was still rising, the wind showing every sign of becoming strong. Again they put inshore and this time everyone left the boat to make certain that the agents had reached the mainland proper. When the crew returned the boat was firmly stuck in the sand. In unison they heaved and tugged for five minutes but the keel of the lifeboat was deeply embedded and she did nothing more than heel over with a groan. All ballast was thrown overboard. The lead weights which held her steady in rough seas were jettisoned, the heavy mast flung on the sand, the spare sail dragged out and abandoned. Once more in unison they heaved and tugged and at last she slid away into the sea.

They set course for Collioure. There remained the second part of their mission, to pick up twelve Polish officers, hidden by the French Resistance and waiting to be taken off. A whole hour had been lost, the clockwork precision necessary to such operations wrecked. Theoretically they should have reached Collioure before the dawn, but the sky was already lightening and the sea steadily worsening as they completed the first mission. The boat chugged through heavy seas, the 5-h.p. engine spluttering and straining. No one said very much. Dawn was coming up as they moved past Canet-Plage, sighted the tiny stone jetty of Collioure and pulled in towards it, every eye watchful. A handful of quiet fishing vessels, a sleeping deserted street and a few nets spread along the sea wall gave at first no sign of life. Then they picked out the small figure wearing the understood red scarf, sitting at the end of the jetty.

The engine down to dead slow, the boat nosing very cautiously, a quick survey for anything suspicious and then, with that over-casual air of fishermen trespassing in fields to which they did not belong—"Hi! What course for Montpellier?" "Don't know!" the red-scarfed figure returned. "I'm a stranger here myself."

It was the password—question and answer. Somewhere behind the figure on the lonely jetty, a network of Resistance men had informed London of the twelve Polish airmen waiting to be taken to safety, and on this stormy April morning a ship had at last come from far-away England.

"Where are they?" O'Leary called softly.

"We thought you were coming last night. They are still asleep in the hotel."

Pat swore softly to himself. "How long will they be?"

"Not long. Don't worry. I know everyone in the village. Nice people. We're all right. Come into the harbour."

O'Leary hesitated. It was getting steadily rougher and the calm of the harbour looked very inviting. He scrutinized the sea wall, the sleeping village, the scalloped tiles of the roofs beginning to glow dull red, the empty streets, the café with its Dubonnet advertisement, and knew the sense of complete security to be illusory, but slowly he nosed the boat into the harbour.

The man on the jetty smiled and waved.

"How long will they be?" O'Leary called softly.

"Fifteen minutes."

"Tell them it's too long. Ten minutes at the most."

In the rapidly lightening sky, clouds massed and scurried across the horizon and the wind rose. The waves dashed at the jetty, the rigging of the moored boats moaned, but the harbour remained at peace. Striking the attitudes of men fishing, they were aware of that hushed expectancy which precedes the full dawn, and as the minutes dragged out it seemed impossible that some threat should not break in and wreck everything. Five minutes gone and no sign of anyone. Fergusson fidgeted with the silent engine. O'Leary stood, his eyes sweeping back and forth for any sign of life. Tension ran from one to the other in the boat.

"Bloody stinking hell! Where are they?" someone muttered.

O'Leary addressed the man on the jetty. "Four more minutes. If they don't come then—they've had it."

The boat rocked, the wind rose another point, the silent village remained blank and unyielding. And then something stirred at the end of a street, a man in uniform appeared, ran down the jetty and bellowed: "What are you doing there?"

"Just fishing," O'Leary said, but his heart was beating faster. This was a customs officer, and for all the Latin ease with which the French had once interpreted that office, this man clearly had a powerful sense of duty.

"Fishing? Fishing?" he said, peering unconvinced at the crew now seriously absorbed in watching imaginary bait. "Are your papers in order?"

"Perfect order," O'Leary replied, reflecting how much care had been given to them in far-away London.

"Come here and show them!"

"Oh, don't be difficult," O'Leary said. "You'll spoil the fishing."

The customs officer gestured: "If you're not here in five minutes, I shall telephone Port Vendres."

The exact nature of this threat was not immediately clear but did not remain in doubt very long. They stared at one another. Two minutes went by, the customs official gestured again and strode off. O'Leary at once nodded to Fergusson who started the motor, and the boat, with Rogers at the tiller, pulled out.

Beyond the harbour heavy seas were running. The boat dipped and rose, lack of ballast making her roll heavily at once. The engine stuttered uncertainly. The *Fidelity* lay three miles off out of sight, the wind presently reached *mistral* force and the boat bucketed and jumped like a frightened animal. Soon no one could stand up or sit down. They lay down and clung to the thwarts. The boat heaved and tossed, shipping water, but somehow Rogers managed to keep control of the tiller.

Fifteen minutes later the beach seemed far away and hopes of reaching the *Fidelity* rose. Then the smell of petrol seemed to grow very strong and suddenly the engine stopped. The boat was thrown in all directions. Staggering under the repeated blows, Rogers tried to examine the petrol feed pipe. The buffeting had broken the pipe and, unnoticed in the uproar, large quantities of petrol had poured into the bottom of the boat. Clinging desperately to the thwarts with his legs and feet, Rogers was flung about as he pulled the pipe together, tied his handkerchief round it, and somehow O'Leary poured part of two jerri-cans of petrol into the tank. The motor started, the mad bucketing settled to a steadier rhythm and once more they began to make progress.

At that moment they glimpsed, between the waves, a French cutter making towards them at full speed from Port Vendres. A series of heavy waves shook the boat from stem to stern, the petrol pipe burst again, and the engine stopped. The boat wallowed, dipped and twisted, as though desperately trying to plunge to the bottom. Five minutes later they knew that they were lost. Somehow their collection of hand-grenades and machine-guns were slipped over the side. As the French cutter came up a Naval gendarme pointed a sub-machine-gun and threw a rope. Taken in tow, slowly, ignominiously, the battered old lifeboat began the return journey to the coast, this time heading for Port Vendres. Thinking swiftly as the boat wallowed along in the wake of the cutter, O'Leary quickly evolved a plan. Huddled in the stern sheets he explained it in a throaty whisper to the three members of the crew. "Let me do the talking. We are French from the north of France, we have stolen this boat and we are trying to reach the Spanish coast to join de Gaulle." Had he but known how the French in Port Vendres then regarded de

Gaullists. Falsely reassured that the divided French must have some sneaking regard for those who continued the fight overseas, he felt that they might excite some sympathy and reasonable treatment by pretending to be Gaullists. Moreover, any check on their origins in the north must take considerable time and above all it was time that they needed to play for.

A soaked and battered quartet at last landed at Port Vendres. Cross-examination was carried out in a small harbour office by French and Italian Naval officers.

"Who are you?"

"We are Frenchmen from the north."

"Where in the north?"

"Lille—Calais—Amiens."

"What were you doing?"

"We were taken prisoners by the Germans—escaped—made our way back south. We're trying to join de Gaulle via Spain."

The French officer looked pensive. "I too am from the north," he said. "It is sad, but I must arrest you."

The Italian said: "Where did you get the boat?"

"I can't tell you that."

"You must."

"It was a Frenchman who understood us. We are not giving him away."

They were split into two parties and marched off under escort. O'Leary and Ford, the N.C.O., were taken down the main road by one gendarme towards a destination which they never discovered because O'Leary had already determined to escape. Presently he whispered in snatches to Ford—"I'm going to run for it—one or other will have a chance. He won't know which one to follow."

It turned out to be Ford's salvation, not O'Leary's. As O'Leary darted away the gendarme, thrown into complete confusion, first grabbed Ford and then rushed after O'Leary, shooting wildly into the air. Ford stood casually at the hilltop, watching the pursuit with interest, until he turned and made his way slowly back down the road. Eventually he reached Gibraltar and returned to England.

O'Leary was recaptured. Thrown into the huge old

Naval prison at Toulon he was subjected to a routine deliberately calculated to reduce prisoners to that spiritless state where all thoughts of escape were banished from the mind. What little light penetrated to his small, windowless cell came from the barred aperture at the top of the heavy wooden door with crossing steel bars which gave on to the corridor. In one corner stood a bucket, left in the cell all night, offering the crudest sanitation. Inevitably towards dawn the smell grew unbearable. One blanket covered a bare wooden bed, and for five days of the week there was no release at all from the cell. The two remaining days were broken into for one hour when prisoners were allowed to walk in a courtyard. Food was appalling. Ersatz coffee in the morning, lunch from artichoke soup, and a little bread and a few vegetables at night.

The first day that O'Leary was allowed in the courtyard among the other prisoners came as something of a shock. The men he saw about him were waxen in colour, listless in bearing and not interested in any activity which required the slightest initiative. Clearly prison life had undermined morale. Many of these men had been sentenced to five years imprisonment for Gaullist activities, and it suddenly became clear to O'Leary that pleading such a role himself had opened the way to long-drawn-out decay in this dungeon-like fortress where the sun never reached. Something must be done and done rapidly.

Walking in the courtyard for the second time, he was delighted to meet Fergusson and Rogers. Both looked untouched by what had happened. Fergusson's face was still round and smiling, if less rosy, and with his hands in his pockets he strolled about looking just as placid as he had been on board the *Fidelity*. Rogers remained his vivid Marseille self. They tried to talk. It wasn't easy, but they managed to agree that they must drop their French alibis and reveal their British origins, claiming, this time, that they were French-Canadians. In the next twenty-four hours O'Leary set up a continuous clamour for audience with the prison commandant. It was at last granted.

Forcefully, in very direct French, he demanded international rights for himself and his comrades as British prisoners-of-war. At first the commandant was unimpressed. Clearly this *volte-face* was a device to win privileges due to British prisoners-of-war for Gaullists taken in a part of France still not occupied by the Germans and theoretically neutral in international law. O'Leary now played his trump card. He had sent a message to the American Consulate in Marseille via a prisoner who left two days before, he said, and repercussions were likely within the week. Cross-examined, he refused to divulge the name of the prisoner in case of reprisals. At that the commandant said, "Well—we'll see." It was all done, on O'Leary's part, with that assurance which characterizes a man telling the truth.

Two days later O'Leary, Fergusson and Rogers were summoned for fresh interrogation at the hands of a local magistrate. They were taken to the French Naval barracks and there, in a large, simply furnished office sat a sallow-faced, middle-aged man, who spoke with conscious ease and authority, explaining that he was the local *juge* and would like to hear their story. He listened politely while O'Leary talked and ironically remarked at the end that it seemed a little far-fetched.

O'Leary at once burst into protest. He had seen the treatment which Frenchmen meted out to prisoners of their own race in Toulon prison and it appalled him. He could not understand why patriotic Frenchmen had to be treated like that, but whatever they did to their own people, they had better treat a British officer correctly or the consequences might be unfortunate.

"The trouble is," said the magistrate, "I don't believe a word you say." There followed a battle of wits in which the magistrate, well informed about London, set one trap after another, and O'Leary with equal skill refused to fall into any of them.

"Whereabouts in London is Green Park?" asked the magistrate.

"It runs beside Piccadilly, beginning at the Ritz and ending towards Victoria," O'Leary answered.

"And why in such a peaceful country, are policemen armed?"

"They are not armed."

"Why is it that books of tickets on London's Underground are so much more expensive than on the Paris Metro?"

"There are no books of tickets," O'Leary said.

"You say you know Cardiff well?"

O'Leary agreed. He was then subjected to a series of questions which revealed so intimate an acquaintance with the city on the part of the magistrate that O'Leary, who had spent several months there under training, was driven to express his admiration. As he listened to the detailed answers which his questions brought, the magistrate in turn was moved to some astonishment. The case seemed to be assuming different proportions. There remained, as the magistrate remarked with an ironical smile, one major difficulty. It was possible for one to have visited all these places, to know them intimately and still remain unalterably French-Canadian—providing, of course, one hadn't a Belgian accent.

But two days later the miracle happened. All three were transferred from the *Prison Maritime* at Toulon to Fort Lamalgue and everything changed. In Lamalgue there were sheets on the beds, mattresses, reasonable food, cigarettes and even books. Typical of several forts along the coast Lamalgue had massive, crumbling walls, deep-set rooms, dungeons below ground level and a courtyard where the prisoners were permitted to walk every day. On the third day the commandant summoned O'Leary, Fergusson and Rogers to his office, obviously very interested to meet a group of alleged British officers.

"You are lucky," he said, after a few polite preliminaries.

"Lucky?" O'Leary echoed.

"Your life means something—you are still fighting—you have a purpose. Life means nothing to me."

The commandant was a tall, thin, aristocratic Frenchman with the restrained bearing of an old-world gentleman.

Sensing someone sympathetic to the Allied cause, O'Leary said: "I met Free Frenchmen in England. They were still fighting, and with a purpose."

23

The commandant stiffened: "I didn't mean that kind of purpose."

"May I ask what kind of purpose you did mean?"

"I hope one day to fight against England—and against you!"

"I see," O'Leary snapped back. "You have your country, I have mine. All right!" At thirty, young, handsome, dashing, he often spoke with that vigorous directness which later experience was to inhibit. For the moment he was afraid of nothing.

The interview with the commandant closed abruptly. Over the next few days printed copies of all Marshal Pétain's speeches were sent by the commandant to the prisoners, and they found occasion to smoke rather more than usual to consume the mass of paper.

Years afterwards O'Leary remembered how little they then knew of where this was to lead, how far they were from realizing the steady sharpening of realities, how they might have hesitated and even turned back if they had known what a nightmare world of horror and brutality those Mediterranean shores were soon to reveal. But as the spring of 1941 became warm and beautiful, flowered terraces sprang to brilliant life beyond the fort, the vineyards burgeoned, the cypresses grew black against cloudless skies, it seemed impossible that there could be waiting, so short a time away, a world where all civilized values collapsed, men became animals prepared to fight one another for a scrap of food, and the single driving purpose of living was the avoidance of pain.

IT WAS in St. Hippolyte du Fort that the plan to escape
first became a serious reality. Transferred from Lamalgue
to St. Hippolyte, the three officers found their new home
more a barracks than a fort, with the entrance on a busy
main street. On the first floor were large rooms with heavily
barred windows destined to accommodate British officers,
and from the inner windows could be seen the courtyard
where 250 prisoners paraded every morning for roll call.
It was a brick building painted a dirty yellow, with walls
ten feet high and cells below ground level for solitary
confinement.

At this stage of the war the commandant interpreted his
duty towards prisoners with a beneficence quickly qualified
as one after another escaped, but there was no lack of
guards. Inside and outside they paraded day and night:
every main door had its guard and each floor a sprinkling
of soldiers. But to see what followed in perspective it must
be remembered that these were still the very early days
of prisoners-of-war in the south of France. There was still
a chivalrous interpretation of the captured soldiers' plight.

Among the 250 prisoners were three British officers,
Hewitt and Parkinson, infantry officers of the 51st Highland Division, and Milton, an R.A.F. officer. Pat quickly
got to know them well. Hewitt was a dark-skinned Scot
about twenty-eight years old, much quieter and calmer
than Parkinson, a young man of twenty, tall, thin, enthusi-
astic, and ready for anything. Milton looked out on the
world with a massive calm, accepted what happened to
him without complaint and was, like Hewitt, a man not
gravely inconvenienced by the loss of physical liberty.
They exchanged stories and with Fergusson and Rogers
plunged into plans for escape. The inevitable escape committee selected Pat, the senior officer, as its leader. Already

in St. Hippolyte, the name Ian Garrow was whispered as an English contact somewhere in Marseille, in touch with a network of guides capable of crossing the Pyrenees, but what the committee needed immediately was a collaborator inside the prison.

It was decided to probe the guards to see if there were any weak spots, and it quickly became evident that an officer called Maurice Dufour had possibilities. Slowly they won his confidence, and he admitted one night that he desired, above all things, to get to England. At whispered midnight conferences it was agreed that if he turned a blind eye to certain activities of theirs, they would put him in touch with Ian Garrow, and possibly the road back. Ten days later, while Dufour was on night duty, the figure of Fergusson, clad in a French Service uniform, slipped past him and away into the night without the alarm being raised. To give the situation ironic perfection, Fergusson, with his Marseille French, insisted at Nîmes station on getting the full 75 per cent reduction in his fare which his uniform permitted. He then boarded a train for Marseille and went first to the Seamen's Mission run by the Reverend Donald Caskie. A Scottish padre who had himself taken part in the mass flight from Paris, Caskie had reopened the Seamen's Mission at Marseille, and now concealed in its cellars any British soldiers who might be in need of refuge. Taken in one night at dusk, Fergusson was away again by three the next morning, escorted by a person then unknown to him, who hurried him into one of Ian Garrow's refuges, *en route* for the border.

The name Ian Garrow was to become tremendously important to O'Leary, but to those in the prison he was a ghost figure somewhere in Marseille who might assist in escapes from St. Hippolyte. Little was known of his methods or his men, but for the moment in St. Hippolyte they were deeply preoccupied with other matters.

At roll call on the morning following Fergusson's escape, someone tried to fake Fergusson's response but failed, a search was made and a furious commandant demanded an immediate revision of the whole security system. Both O'Leary and Rogers had given their word of honour not to try to escape, but the committee had already decided that Rogers must be the next to go. For some days it looked hopeless. Guards were freshly alert, privileges had been cut, severe penalties imposed and once a man withdrew his word, he was subject to minute scrutiny. O'Leary then conceived the idea of reporting with Rogers to the commandant, withdrawing their undertaking not to escape, and as they were crossing the courtyard back to their rooms, making a break for it. Instantaneous action after withdrawing their word would, O'Leary argued, take everyone by surprise. The commandant could reasonably expect a gentlemanly interval. If it sounded dubious, it was none the less worth trying. When they told the commandant that they no longer wished to be on parole, he made a wry face.

"You realize what this means?" he said. They knew quite well.

Walking back across the courtyard, O'Leary suddenly rushed to the wall, Rogers raced up his back, stood on his shoulders, gave his feet into O'Leary's hands, received a shove, and was half astride the wall. O'Leary grappled with the guard who came rushing up. Rogers took one long leap and was racing up the opposite street, snatching a bicycle and pedalling like a madman. On the ground a second guard was kicking O'Leary as a shot rang out and a flood of French blasphemy burst through the courtyard. Dragged off to the commandant, the interview which followed was ferocious. A plump, rosy-cheeked man, normally very polite, the commandant's threats were more ominous because delivered quietly, but above all, some sense of outraged morality drove him to say: "It just isn't fair."

"What's unfair about it?" O'Leary asked.

"The way you rushed off two seconds after seeing me."

"It's our duty to try to escape," O'Leary said.

"Not by a trick," snapped the commandant.

"It wasn't a trick, it was intelligence," O'Leary answered.

"We'll see about that," said the commandant.

Without another word O'Leary was taken off to solitary

confinement. The guards had not dealt lightly with him, and he was bruised and shaken, but in St. Hippolyte solitary confinement did not, at this stage, mean continual darkness and no food in a rat-infested cell. For ten days O'Leary saw only the guard who brought very sparse meals, did not leave his cell and was cut off from the life of the fort. In that time he worked out the plan for his own escape. Already the primitive techniques of rush, surprise and bluster were out of date. The commandant had effectively sealed off escapes of that kind. A completely new approach had to be made and step by step Pat evolved his plan. Once out of solitary confinement, work began.

First a British soldier with an artistic bent set to work on a spare piece of linoleum with a stolen knife, and diligently chipped and trimmed until he produced a rough and ready linocut of a French identity card. Some debate followed as to how O'Leary should be named, but it was the artist who decided: "I'll call you Adolphe—Adolphe Lecomte, a fine, rich name," and Adolphe Lecomte, by profession an engineer, he became. Several times the lino was inked with stolen prison ink and a copy run off. At first it blurred and smeared, but half a dozen attempts at last produced a reasonable copy. O'Leary was now equipped with an identity card and a profession.

As senior officer in the fort he was permitted to call occasional meetings to pass on orders and information from the commandant, and under cover of some small change in regulations, he held a quick and hurried conference with the men in a ground-floor room, explaining his plan to set up a complete escape organization once he himself was free. But he had first to escape and his plan depended on one thing. Somewhere at the back of the O.R.'s assembly room was a locked and disused chamber with a barred window giving on to the path of one of the sentries. Could they break into this and saw through one of the bars, carefully replacing it, making it look as if the bar were still intact?

Within forty-eight hours a key to the room was forged from old wire and successfully turned in the lock. From two French girls outside the camp came a small hacksaw which Maurice Dufour smuggled in one night. After the evening meal an N.C.O. and two men turned the forged key in the lock, slipped in, re-locked the door from the inside and with relays of men keeping watch outside, went to work. The room was pitch dark, low-ceilinged, smelling of damp and decay, and full of rusting old iron bedsteads. The dim light from the window made it possible to select the weakest bar and they sawed steadily in relays for two hours the first night. Progress seemed disappointingly slow. The cut in the bar was not more than an eighth of an inch deep, the screeching of metal on metal seemed to get worse as they penetrated deeper, and twice warnings from outside sent them scurrying into the darkest corner of the room. Worse still, barely three feet below them ran the sentry's path and it seemed impossible that he would not detect the noise as he paced up and down.

The second night they smeared margarine into the cut and began sawing more slowly to reduce the noise. Another eighth of an inch gave before their assault. When one cut had been carried right through the bar at one end, they reported that it was such a tough, thick bar of solid iron that it did not seem likely to yield to pressure and another cut at the opposite end would be necessary. Pat estimated that to cut the bar at both ends would occupy a week. He selected the day following its probable completion for his escape bid, and made elaborate arrangements with Hewitt and Parkinson. Zero hour would be 11.55, when the men queued up to get the midday meal in the main courtyard. Pat would use the faked key to lock himself in the room and at 11.55 Hewitt would give the signal to create a diversion of the most elaborate and noisy kind possible. A whole mass attempt to escape would be staged on the opposite side of the fort.

Night after night the sawing went on. As the cuts in the bar grew deeper it became necessary for the workers to conceal their handiwork from the guards on the pathway outside. They kneaded pieces of discoloured bread into dough and worked them into the cuts, spreading the dough like rust. On the seventh day Pat received a report that only a thin sliver of metal now held the bar in place. He went over every detail of the arrangements with Hewitt and Parkinson once more. Only one thing could give them away; the sense of expectancy in the atmosphere which always preceded any escape known to a mass of prisoners.

At 11.50 on the Friday morning Pat sat locked in the dank, dirty room, sitting on a fast decomposing iron bedstead, watching the guard through the window. A gentle test pull on the bar showed that it would give easily. He could hear the distant sound of feet, the usual clanging of heavy doors and the murmur of voices as the gendarmes talked amongst themselves. Outside, a thick-set soldier, his pistol very much in evidence, stood with his feet apart, hands clasped behind his back, staring towards the town. It was a beautiful day, the air crisp, the sun beginning to burn, and the sky brilliant blue. Everything depended on the reaction of that thick-set gentleman standing down there wrapped in contemplation. Taken sufficiently by surprise he might be thrown into confusion; given a chance to recover he might shoot at sight.

11.54. In the courtyard two hundred men were milling around, trying to form some kind of queue for lunch, when Hewitt looked at his watch, saw the minute hand creep to 11.55 and gave the signal.

Suddenly the mass of prisoners made a dash towards the outer wall, a dozen men climbed on the shoulders of others, a rope mysteriously appeared, was run up the wall, and a whole hysterical uproar of shouting and gesticulation began. It did not need much insight to detect the theatricality of the outburst, but every guard within sight rushed to the wall, fighting broke out and guns were levelled.

O'Leary had stared tensely at his watch. 11.53 . . . 11.54 . . . 11.55 . . . 11.56. . . . At 11.57 he reached up and dragged the bar inwards. As he saw the guard outside running towards the courtyard he took a flying leap out and down. The guard swung round and saw him: "Stop or I shoot!" Pat staggered to his feet and raced away. A swerving zigzag, the main street reached, the sound of shooting and he dived wildly into a side street. People pointed and tried to stop him. He crashed into and through a talking group;

a man tried to cling to his arm and he brushed him off, sending him sprawling. Suddenly an old house barred his path, the door wide open in the hot sunshine. Straight into the cool black shadows he leapt and before he could stop himself saw a long trestle table with old people eating their lunch, barring his way. Carried forward by his rush he had no alternative but to leap on to the table. He dashed down the centre, trying to avoid the soup and the plates, aware only of faces aghast, of cries, of chairs falling backwards. Off the opposite end and into a small dark kitchen, where an old woman and a young girl were washing dishes. This was a hospice for old people and the girl one of the nuns, very correct in her white apron and bonnet. Pat seized her by both hands and babbled— "British officer escaped from the prison—help me—where can I hide?" The nun blanched and muttered, "I'll fetch Mother Superior." O'Leary pushed himself into the darkest corner of the kitchen, the older woman standing paralysed, as he listened, tense, for the cries of his pursuers. A second later an imposing figure entered the room. Stout, very calm, and clad from head to foot in black, she said: "You are a British officer?" O'Leary began to explain, but she took him by the hand: "Come with me." Up one flight of stairs and then another; more stairs, with twisted landings and dark old timbers, the house growing quieter the higher they climbed. At last they came to a huge attic full of every kind of junk, and in the centre at least twenty-five chests and coffers of all shapes and sizes, as though a bankrupt undertaker had left his stock to rot. She opened one of the chests: "Get inside," she said. "I'll come back later."

In the oldest tradition of concealment O'Leary lay panting in the trunk. The footsteps retreated down the stairs and the house settled into silence again, with only the creaking of ancient timbers remaining to try his nerves. Ten minutes and the trunk had become stifling; its gold vestments, musty with age, distilled a powerful odour. He raised the lid, looked round, took several deep breaths and sank back again. Presently the trunk became intolerable and every five minutes he raised the lid for a breather, but the atmosphere in the trunk grew thicker and thicker. One hour went by and there was no movement, no sign of life from the house below. Pat thought of creeping downstairs again. But supposing the guards had occupied the hospice and were waiting, supposing the Mother Superior was under arrest and the whole house surrounded. Lying there without news, not knowing what had happened, was a torment.

Another half-hour went by before he heard footsteps on the stairs. He listened intently, trying to distinguish whether they were male or female. The steps came nearer. He pulled the vestments over his head and lay very still. Suddenly he felt the lid rising and a woman's voice said: "All right, but we must be very careful. Come with me." It was the Mother Superior. Climbing out, thanking her in whispers, O'Leary was at last told what had happened. The guards had raced in after him and she had admitted seeing him. "Yes, he was English and an officer—but he went clean through the house and out the other side." The guards had looked suspicious and the Mother Superior added: "In the sight of God, there is no Englishman here." Still suspicious, the guards had gone away but had thrown a cordon of soldiers round the entire hospice, in the belief that if they waited long enough, they would catch him. "But," said the big, composed figure in her nodding white bonnet, "there is still one way out." She showed no sign of alarm or even anxiety, and as she talked she walked steadily from the third to the second, and the second to the first floor. Quickly surveying the kitchen she hurried to the ground floor and down into a gloomy, musty cellar. There she went swiftly to a dark aperture at one side. "Follow me," she said. They entered a narrow tunnel and O'Leary suddenly realized where they were going. This was a tunnel running to the heart of a vineyard along which the harvest could quickly be gathered and brought to the house in former times. Everywhere the rich, heavy smell of grapes and the scent of wine permeated the earth, producing, in the confined space, an atmosphere heady to the senses. A great stillness and silence settled, the air grew thick, little trickles of earth ran down the walls as the tunnel narrowed, and presently they were walking bent

32

double, and everything was black. Just the rustlings of the Mother Superior's habit, her deep breaths and the sound of her feet, sullen and heavy in the tunnel. Presently a dim light appeared ahead which strengthened and grew until Pat could see the sky, and a minute later the Mother Superior gestured to him to remain behind while she climbed out and reconnoitred. A hundred yards back she could see the guards. O'Leary came out of the tunnel behind the Mother Superior's skirts, went down on all fours as she walked towards the boundary of the vineyard, and crawled along in the shelter of her gown. Three minutes later a whispered farewell—and he was free.

THE sky was serene, the ships in the harbour silent, the mercantile life of Marseille a ghost of its peace-time self. Outwardly there were no great scars to mark the passing of the years of war. Inwardly, disguised Gestapo men kept watch, German agents mingled in the cafés, gendarmes served their new masters with varying degrees of loyalty and a swarm of counter-agents and Resistance men moved by stealth of night. Marseille was divided against itself. The mass of middle-class people now hated the English as they came to terms with their new masters. In the minority some were spies for the Germans, some neutral, some actively prepared to fight and die in one network or another which outwitted all attempts at suppression.

In the Old Town nothing could be trusted. The narrow streets honeycombed the hill, rising steeply in fantastic twists. Slant-eyed men jostled beside donkeys, Negro children played with white, black passages led into blacker alleys, the houses seemed drawn together as they rose until nothing but a narrow cleft revealed the sky, releasing mysterious stenches into the upper air. There were hide-outs for a multitude, rendezvous no one could check, a great filthy teeming warren which offended the German sense of hygiene and baffled its inquisitors. They rarely dared to venture into it after dark.

Not far from the Old Town in the last three rooms of a very large flat in the rue Roux de Brignolles, O'Leary sat talking to Ian Garrow. A big, powerful, moon-faced Scot, Captain Garrow was a survivor of the last stand of the 51st Highland Division at St. Valéry in the days after Dunkirk, who had set moving the beginnings of an escape Organization in Marseille.

He had heard details of Pat's escape, asked many questions about St. Hippolyte, and now he said: "I'm glad you've come. I need some help. I need someone who speaks French better than I do."

"But I am an officer in the Royal Navy," O'Leary said. "I have to report back for duty."

"Supposing we ask the Admiralty to let you stay?"

"How can you do that?"

Garrow shrugged. "There are ways and means."

O'Leary already understood something of the work which Garrow had begun in the south of France, with little money, no encouragement, and the handicap of a powerful English accent. Making his own way south with the remnants of the 51st Highland Division, he had seen scores of soldiers and airmen drifting towards the Mediterranean, a disorganized rabble in constant danger of arrest for lack of any systematic help. Hundreds were carried off to prison and prison camps. It seemed to him that a serious wastage was taking place. A Scot who reconciled dour determination with quick intelligence and immense reserves of strength, he set to work against hopeless odds. He could easily have made his own way to safety within a few days. Instead he chose to stay, even when Vichy France first reaffirmed the authority of the gendarmerie in the south, then tightened its controls, and finally admitted some curious liaison with their new masters which permitted Gestapo agents to move incognito in Marseille. Presently Garrow himself had agents scattered at certain points along the south coast and was in touch with Vidal, a Spaniard whose network of guides could cross the frontier undetected. Enormous difficulties remained.

In Patrick O'Leary Garrow saw the solution to some of his problems. "You have everything we need—training in underground work, perfect French, a Service background. I'll get a message through to London. I'm in touch with one of the embassies across the border."

"How long will it take?"

"I'll ask them to add a message on the B.B.C. news one night."

"But how long will it take?" Pat insisted.

"Oh, two weeks perhaps."

Pat thought a moment. "All right. Let's try."

They proceeded to work out a coded reply which the Admiralty could use if the plan met with its approval. "*Adolphe doit rester*"—"Adolphe must stay".

Garrow's method of communication with England was simple. He handed the message to one of the guides crossing the Spanish border and eventually it reached Gibraltar. From there it was passed on to London. The interval which followed seemed inordinately long. Night after night in the rooms at the end of the Marseille flat Pat listened hopefully to the B.B.C. news. A week went by and still there was no sign of that small trailer message at the end. In that time O'Leary came to know the owner of the flat which they occupied and more about the growing Organization.

Dr. Rodocanachi was an elderly, grey-haired, distinguished looking man who had lived in Marseille all his life. When France capitulated, America had appointed him its representative on a repatriation board which examined prisoners-of-war in the area and recommended repatriation for those medically unfit. Unknown to anyone, Rodocanachi had strong British sympathies and had already signed certificates for what he imaginatively described as borderline cases. His activities were steadily widening and he was to become an important member of the Organization. Already he had turned over three rooms in his huge twelve-roomed flat for Ian Garrow's use. Shut away at the end of the main flat where no one could penetrate without warning, they were, in effect, self-contained and soundproof. A practising doctor, Rodocanachi also offered the great advantage that numbers of people could file into his flat in surgery hours, and strangers passed unnoticed amongst them.

O'Leary quickly developed a deep respect for the doctor and his charming, cultured wife. He also became very familiar with every part of the heavy mahogany furniture, the Victorian curtains, the elderly maid, completely trusted by everyone, and the evening ritual which began at 9 p.m. precisely. With doors locked, windows shut, and the radio set muted, they listened to the B.B.C. giving news which never appeared in German broadcasts. But when two weeks had gone by and the news bulletin continued to tail off into silence with no sign of his small personal message, O'Leary began to wonder. Had the message ever reached London? Should he be trying to make his way back to England? In the third week he had given up hope, and was planning a return to Gibraltar when one night the news tapered to an end, and a deep voice said: "*Adolphe doit rester.*" O'Leary found it a little miraculous. Somewhere away in London a vast machine had turned and this tiny message had been projected across hundreds of miles especially for him.

The next few days were very active. First he changed his name. In the growing Organization he was henceforth to be known as Joseph Cartier. Then he plunged into work and Garrow quickly took him to another remarkable flat at the Quai Rive Neuve where Louis Nouveau lived. If Nouveau's flat was surprising, with its fine proportions, *objets d'art* and sweeping window giving a wonderful view over the Old Port, Nouveau himself was even more remarkable. A merchant stockbroker by profession, an Englishman by adoption and a well-known figure in pre-war Marseille, he was to be seen walking the boulevards in perfect Savile Row clothes and could so easily have stepped straight from the Athenæum into the Old Port of Marseille. His behaviour in the first World War was categorized, with British understatement, as brave, and the appalling cough which threatened to burst his lungs on occasion was the result of a gas attack in 1917. A man given to old-world charm, he knew nothing of espionage work until one day in December 1940 two Greek Gaullists invited him to tea to meet some British officers, among them Garrow, and he quickly found himself involved in activities which belonged to the pages of E. Phillips Oppenheim.

O'Leary—alias Joseph—had preserved with Garrow the French-Canadian personality built up at the espionage school in England, and now, one evening, settled in the luxury of Nouveau's flat, he sipped his wine and felt Nouveau scrutinizing him from head to foot. It was a shrewd examination. Tall, grey haired, with eyes very watchful behind his glasses, Nouveau looked at human beings as an artist might, and at Pat with a dash of suspicion.

"You speak with a Belgian accent," he said presently.

"Of course," Pat said. "My father mixed with a Belgian group in Quebec."

"I've always wanted to go to Quebec," Louis said. "What's it like?"

A man of wide culture, Nouveau was already familiar with the general layout of Quebec. Equally well-briefed himself, Pat answered at some length. Nouveau then pressed him about the slang terms used by French-Canadians for certain words and Pat felt his answers were less convincing. They talked on for some time. Slowly the atmosphere became more frank and friendly. They could not then know that their relationship would run on for so long or that they would become so important to one another.

At the outset Nouveau played a part in one of Pat's early missions. It concerned Philip Herbert, a twenty-year-old sergeant-pilot in the R.A.F., having the innocence and niceness of a boy of seventeen. Crashing into the sea in his aircraft he had been picked up by Vichy Frenchmen and transferred to Sainte Marthe Military Camp.

Locked in a hut one day, Herbert examined the windows, floorboards and walls in the hope that there might be some loophole for escape, but it was fruitless. Then, quite casually, he turned the handle of the door. It was open. Something had made the guard believe that he had locked the door, but astonishingly it was open, and Philip Herbert simply walked out—wearing the civilian clothes which had been given him when he left his dinghy. He idled down the path, nodded at the sentry and strolled towards a stationary tram. It took him to the centre of Marseille. There he made straight for the Seamen's Mission run by Donald Caskie who put him in touch with Louis Nouveau.

When he arrived at Louis Nouveau's flat in the Quai Rive Neuve, Philip Herbert was still in poor shape; lack of food had left him pale, thin and weak. He stayed in hiding at Nouveau's flat for twelve days, steadily regaining his strength, and then Nouveau escorted him one day to Marseille station where Pat, as Joseph Cartier, was waiting to pick him up. Pat examined the forged papers Nouveau had provided and gave last-minute instructions.

"On no account speak to anyone. If there is any talking to be done, leave it to me. Sit next to me and try to look as if you are asleep. When they come to check the papers I will tell you to wake up. Hand me the tickets and papers and I will give them to the guard."

When at last the two guards stood at the door of the carriage one of them took the papers and said: "From the north, eh?" He glanced at the photo and then at Philip Herbert. "I come from the north, too." Pat thought for a moment that he was going to sit down and begin reminiscing; then he said: "Times are bad in the north, messieurs," and went.

The seats were the hard wooden seats of a third-class coastal train in the south of France and the sun made the carriage unbearably hot. From Marseille to Perpignan is just over four hundred miles. The journey took nearly seven hours. At every stop there was danger. One never knew whether a gendarme, a *garde mobile* or a disguised Gestapo agent might not select the carriage and try to draw out the sleepy-looking man with the badly-fitting clothes who so ostentatiously did not want to talk.

At Port Vendres the ticket barrier offered fresh hazards. This was the border town and everyone came under the closest scrutiny.

Providence seldom deserted Pat in these early and very simple missions, and one July day he waved farewell to Philip Herbert, knowing that a white-booted Spanish guide would take him into the Pyrenees that night with a group of others.

If all went well he would be back in England within a week. It seemed impossible then to visualize any agent being beheaded for such small and polite deceptions.

★ 4 ★

SITTING with Ian Garrow one day in a café at Nîmes sipping ersatz coffee, Pat became aware that a man three tables away was watching them. Slightly built, dark, with shabby clothes and rather beautiful eyes, he seemed restless and presently he got up and came over to their table: "I am Jean de la Olla," he said, and at once was invited to join them. Already they knew something of this man, and his reputation stood high. It quickly transpired that he wanted to go to England to join the Free French forces, that he had heard of Ian Garrow's growing Organization and hoped it would get him across the Pyrenees. Garrow and Pat moved with the utmost caution. Neither admitted the existence of anything resembling an Organization, and the problems of reaching England were discussed with a detachment almost academic. Only later did Pat discover the extremities to which Jean de la Olla had been reduced in his attempts to reach them and serve the cause of Free France.

Originally a shopwalker in Algiers, de la Olla had entered the French Army, become an N.C.O., and when France fell was offered the job of chief accountant to the detachment in charge of British prisoners-of-war in the prison of St. Hippolyte. There he swiftly made himself indispensable to the prison authorities, simultaneously devising a method of "losing" men in his books for several days after they had escaped. A man with little small talk, de la Olla was sustained in the worst extremity by his Roman Catholic faith, and was known among his friends for a saint-like detachment from commonplace pleasures. Dissatisfied with the small contribution he had made from St. Hippolyte, he persuaded the military authorities to demobilize him and set out to trace someone connected with the underground movement of which there was so much talk and so little evidence. It was a bold move. A man with a wife, three children and no capital, he might easily have hesitated, but de la Olla was never a man to worry about money or the future. Day after day he sat at the café tables in Nîmes, searching for some point of contact with the cause he desired to serve, and no one took the slightest notice. His money ran out, food became scarce and presently there was little more than bread. On the last three days before he met Garrow and Pat he had one scrappy meal every twenty-four hours and the aperitifs he drank—just one a day—went to his head. Slightly drunk and uneasy, but still sustained by that extra-ordinary faith which was to preserve some degree of dig-nity in him even under the final horror of torture, he continued sitting at café tables until one day he suddenly saw the big bluff Englishman and the fair-haired man in dark glasses. Watching for a time he at last went across to them.

Now as he drank a second aperitif with Pat and Garrow he was clearly elated and his devotion to the Allied cause very plain. "We must meet again," Pat said. A period of reflection always followed the offer of services from any-one in order to overcome the first flush of enthusiasm. A few days delay gave the opportunity to check back on statements made, to meet people who knew the possible recruit. In Jean de la Olla's case, everything was shining clear, his genuineness quite without blemish and it seemed to Pat a complete mistake to think of sending such a man back to England. When they met again he said: "I have three men—Englishmen. I want someone to convoy them safely to the Spanish border. Spanish guides are waiting to take them across. Will you do it?" Unhesitatingly, Jean de la Olla agreed. Indeed, a light came into his eyes which warmed Pat's heart. This was indeed the type he required. Always the recruit was given an isolated job to do and told nothing of the general Organization. If he carried it out successfully and kept his mouth shut another step in his initiation might follow.

Recruiting new agents was one thing, getting money quite another. As first one and then another fresh agent was brought into the growing network, money troubles grew. Feeding escapees, taking flats, compensating peasants who concealed and fed prisoners for weeks on end, travelling from one end of France to another, all required money in abundance. Louis Nouveau and others had already contributed private money. Presently another and far bigger source began to pour regular contributions into their coffers.

They had discovered, living in the Perigord district, a certain Mr. Gosling, an ex-manager of the French factory Le Fil à la Chaine, owned by the British company M. & P. Coates. It was said that he had in his possession a sum approaching six million francs held on behalf of M. & P. Coates in London. Clearly if they could get direct reassurance from London that for every thousand francs transferred to the Organization an equivalent sum would be credited to M. & P. Coates in England, they might endlessly tap this reservoir. Louis Nouveau was deputed to put the proposition to Mr. Gosling.

He located him in the village of La Coquille, and estimated that it would take him fourteen hours to reach Gosling from Marseille. It was a long, tiring journey. He found Gosling living in a small country hotel with his wife, two daughters, and a secretary. Another man who had fled to Paris before the German advance, he had sought an obscure place where he could live anonymously until he decided what to do next. Confronted with the tall, elegant Louis Nouveau, somewhat travel-stained, but still preserving a Savile Row *savoir faire*, there were signs of suspicion. It was some time before he talked openly about the money and then he refused point-blank to hand over a single franc.

Before Nouveau left he had persuaded him to agree in principle to the plan for equivalent exchange from Britain, but Gosling said that he would need to see the actual telegram from London before he surrendered a penny. The telegram was to be camouflaged in everyday language. "Make your own decision," it would say, and that would be the signal for Gosling to begin passing the money in prearranged instalments.

Louis reported back to Marseille. They decided to press their case with the British Embassy at Madrid and sought around for someone who had business reasons for travelling across the frontier. Living on the same floor as Louis Nouveau at the block of flats in the Quai Rive Neuve was a certain Monsieur de Ricci and his wife, refugees from Paris who had been unable to bear the thought of living cheek by jowl with the enemy. De Ricci's business took him across the frontier and he agreed to call at the British Embassy. There was no reason on earth why Colonel Drummond Woolf, then military attaché to the embassy, should see yet another of the interminable row of people who were at that time crossing the frontier and pressing a variety of claims—some extremely dubious—on British help and generosity, but it so happened that on the day de Ricci arrived, the colonel was expecting a certain Mr. Ritchie, an Englishman, to call, and confusing the two names, at once admitted de Ricci, only to be confronted by a total stranger. He heard him out with great sympathy. He said it was very difficult—very difficult indeed—but he would see what could be done with M. & P. Coates in London.

Six weeks later Gosling wrote to Louis Nouveau. The telegram had arrived. The money began to flow.

Gradually the network widened. At Nîmes, Gaston Nègre, tall, easy-going, with a cigarette screwed eternally in the corner of his mouth, and a thick Marseille accent, performed black-market wonders with food, drink and escaped airmen. The Misses Morel, romantic young Frenchwomen, carried messages in the hems of their dresses, or hid pilots at home within shouting distance of St. Hippolyte prison. Leoni Savinos and Mario Prassinos were skilled Greek *convoyeurs* capable of travelling undetected from Paris through the demarcation line to Marseille. Dubina, at the Czech Consulate in Marseille, smuggled out papers covering Czech workmen which had the great advantage of explaining why English airmen carrying such papers did not speak French or any intelligible langage. In the north was Paul Cole, a soldier left over from the British Expeditionary Force, convoying airmen south from Paris and occupied territory. Also from the north were Robert Leycuras—known as Albert—and Guy Berthet, two police inspectors who had served sentences for organizing resistance among the Paris police, and had made their way south. Guy, tall, drooping, eagle faced, looked the part of the police inspector: Albert, dashing, quick-witted, presently undertook every kind of work, time and again slipping out of impossible traps.

The names, the people, the types multiplied. And so did the dangers. As one after another, prisoners and crashed airmen slipped through the hands of their guards, extreme penalties were widely publicized; as the Germans settled more securely in Europe and French hostility to England increased, strange men of indeterminate class, wearing light raincoats and pork-pie hats, began to circulate. The police became liable to quick shooting, and savage sentences were meted out to anyone connected with the Resistance. These were hazards of a kind. At the end of the long, tortured vista lay that act which somehow revived medieval brutality with great force—death by beheading. If every agent already lived in the shadow of these things, they did not at this stage take much notice. Indeed a certain slapstick humour and gaiety remained in much of the work. It was Paul Cole who first gave reality to the guillotine.

When Pat first set eyes on the tall, thin, red-headed man with the red moustache, instinctively he disliked him. It was difficult to say why. His eyes were too close-set and he talked too much, but these were superficialities which did not seriously condemn a man. It was some "feel" about his personality which made O'Leary question Paul Cole closely on his work in the north. The picture he drew was vivid, detailed, and full of every kind of adventure.

While Pat was away, Cole had brought down five out of six airmen at one stroke, weaving through every kind of trouble with remarkable skill. Travelling by train from Paris towards the demarcation line with six Englishmen, only one of whom spoke French, the inevitable "control"

44

on the train had led to trouble. Cole, sitting in the corner nearest the corridor, had collected the tickets from his six men, all pretending to be half asleep, and handed them to the two gendarmes. But the gendarmes were talkative. They tried one question after another on the airmen, and getting no response became suspicious.

They began to cross-examine Cole. Two minutes later the airmen were all under arrest and taken off the train at the next station. Suddenly—according to Cole—he grabbed one gendarme's pistol and forced both the guards back into the train as it was moving out. Dashing into the station yard the party then commandeered a charcoal-driven car and raced away. The charcoal ran out, they abandoned the car and set off across country on foot. It took them twenty-four hours to reach the demarcation line at the River Allier. Hungry, thirsty, they dare not trust anyone that side of the line, and waited for dark. At midnight they moved cautiously down to the water's edge.

Every few minutes a German patrol on bicycles with powerful headlamps came along the towpath, probing every inch of the bank and water. Cole calculated that the patrols passed at least every six minutes, which gave them approximately four minutes to cross once they were in the water. But they had to find something to float one airman—who could not swim—over the river. It took them half an hour to root out an old rubber tyre. As they were examining it, a beam of light began to creep towards them and another patrol approached. With nowhere to hide and running for it impossible, they lay flat in a small hollow with the tyre over them, and hoped that the beam would not probe too far. It crept towards the tyre, almost touched its circumference, wavered, waited . . . and turned away.

One minute later, when all seemed quiet again, they plunged into the water, but they were too quick. Hearing faint splashes, the last German pedalled swiftly back. It was a pitch black night, but he could just make out forms swimming in the water. A shouted challenge and he began firing. They abandoned the man on the rubber tyre and swam furiously for the opposite bank. Some mysterious current took the tyre and swept it diagonally downstream.

Three minutes later, six panting, exhausted figures crawled out of the water and flung themselves into the reeds. Then they heard a sound like a boat approaching, staggered to their feet and ran for dear life. They never knew what happened to the sixth airman on the tyre. Cole brought the remaining five into Marseille twenty-four hours later.

Some time after these details were recounted to Pat in the three rooms at the end of the Rodocanachis' flat, he said to Garrow: "You haven't any reason to doubt Paul Cole?"

"No," said Garrow. "Why?"

"I find it hard to believe that his work in the north is as elaborate as he says."

"Maybe it isn't—but it works."

"And you still pay him money?"

"Of course."

"He leaves for the north tonight, doesn't he?"

"He does."

Pat nodded and said no more.

That evening he went to dinner at a Marseille restaurant and there met a friend of a woman known to Garrow as Cole's mistress. Pat invited her to join him; they talked and drank and gradually Pat brought the conversation round to Paul Cole. Suddenly the girl said: "We're having a big party tonight with Françoise."

"Late tonight?"

"Yes."

"Will Paul be there?"

"Of course."

Immediately dinner was over Pat telephoned Garrow. "Did you understand that Paul was leaving for the north tonight?" he asked.

"Yes."

Pat then told him about the party. A furious Garrow said he would go to the party himself. One hour later he confronted Cole in the midst of considerable gaiety and asked for an explanation. Cole laughed: "Don't worry," he said. "There were one or two things I had to clear up.

46

I've only delayed a day and I shall leave tomorrow." And leave he did.

Presently every week men were coming down the "Line". Sometimes they were soldiers left over from the days of Dunkirk; sometimes crashed pilots; sometimes Resistance men for whom the chase had become too hot.

In October 1941, Sergeant Patrick Bell, Sergeant William Crampton, Flight-Lieutenant Barclay and Sergeant Kenneth Road were all spirited out of Occupied France to Marseille, over the Spanish border and away. Pilot-Officer Oscar Coen, of the American Eagle Squadron, also "passed through", giving an account of his adventures in slang American which richly rewarded his rescuers. He was the first of scores of American pilots. More important for the moment was the appearance of Flight-Officer Alex Nitelet, of 609 (Belgian) Squadron, R.A.F. Outnumbered in his Spitfire he had shot down one German plane and then himself suffered a series of direct hits, one bullet gouging away part of his right eye. He managed to crash land and found himself in the Fauquembergues area, near the village of Remy. In great agony he was eventually picked up by Norbert Fillerin, a man already active for the Organization in the St. Omer region. The legend of the Fillerin family was to become famous. Tall, blond, tough, Fillerin found a doctor, Dr. Delpierre, who treated Nitelet's eye, took him into his home and at great risk nursed him back to health.

From Fillerin, Nitelet was passed down the underground chain to Didery, then working with yet another key man, the Abbé Carpentier at Abbeville. Carpentier provided forged papers which carried Nitelet, now totally blind in one eye, down to Le Petit Poucet, a bar on the Boulevard Dugommier in Marseille.

This had become the receiving centre where "parcels" had to prove their identity before going into hiding. From Le Petit Poucet, Nitelet passed into the hands of Louis Nouveau, and remained in hiding under treatment from Dr. Rodocanachi for ten days. Presently, he too, took the train from Marseille along the coast to Arles, Montpellier,

Perpignan, and Banyuls, to be smuggled over the frontier by Spanish Republican guides *en route* to England, destined to play a bigger part in the developing Organization than he then knew.

Soon after Nitelet's departure, Pat's suspicions of Paul Cole hardened. He persuaded Garrow that he should make a brief check on Cole with an agent Dupré, in the far north at Lille. It meant crossing two demarcation lines, one to enter Occupied France and another at Amiens on the Somme, both heavily guarded by the Germans.

He left with Maurice Dufour, who was by now a full-time agent. Forged papers carried them uneventfully to the River Allier, and there, waiting for a dark night, they stripped and waded into the river at a point where it was said to be fordable. Moving slowly, step by step, with his clothes held above his head, Pat felt the current growing more powerful and the water rising above his armpits. There was always the possibility that a guard would break his routine and suddenly appear where he should not be, and Pat, still a comparative novice at inter-zone travel, wondered whether he dared risk swimming. The water came up to his chin, and the current was so powerful that he had to walk diagonally. Mud, stones and drifting rubbish gripped at his legs, the power of the swirling water became stronger and for a flashing moment he saw himself swept off his feet, and carried bodily downstream, a sitting target for the guards who patrolled so short a distance away. Frequently the beam of a powerful bicycle lamp came down the towpath, and a German guard, cycling along, searched every foot of the bank. Often a quick challenge was followed immediately by shooting.

But tonight all that happened was the water lapping over his chin and threatening to reach his mouth. He had not quite calculated how far the drag of the river would lengthen his crossing and take him off his course. Three minutes later the water dropped, the pressure eased and he slowed his pace still more as he gingerly approached the blackness of the bank. He and Dufour slithered out unnoticed.

48

The border-crossing at Amiens was far more difficult. Special passes were scrutinized by gendarmes with the utmost care and at this stage the Organization had not yet forged a good enough replica. Dufour knew the district well and they went to lunch at a certain café where Dufour talked to the patron, recalling many mutual friends. Presently he asked discreetly about crossing the line. The patron smiled and brought over to their table two railway employees. They were men of indomitable goodwill, beaming on the world with a geniality which not even the German occupation had diminished. Slowly the four, with infinite subtlety, the expense of many smiles and the broadest gestures, came together in close understanding on a plan which first gave O'Leary and Dufour tickets from Arras to Amiens.

Since Arras was the station they had to reach this seemed a contradiction, but all quickly became clear. Escorted by a ticket collector through the station, they carefully avoided the grey-green German uniforms and presently were shown a way across the lines at the back of the station which no one knew. Entering the station on the down line, they slipped into an empty train and hid themselves in a first-class carriage. There they remained until the train travelling north to south from Arras to Amiens entered the station. It drew up on the opposite side of the platform where they lay hidden. People poured out, O'Leary and Dufour slipped from their carriage, mingled with the crowd, made towards the ticket barrier and looked pained when the gendarme stopped them for *lack of a pass to the south*. Pat argued vociferously. His protests were swelled by other genuine travellers all lacking passes. In vain. Six people were first arrested and then put on a train returning north to Arras. Pat and Dufour sat among them in a second-class carriage reading copies of *Signal, bona fide* travellers to the north, completely without a pass.

When at last they reached Lille they made their way to Dupré's house. Mme. Dupré opened the door and said that her husband was out. A small, plump, fair-haired woman, she looked worried. Explaining his identity Pat saw fear on Mme. Dupré's face, and a moment later she said she simply did not know what he was talking about. He tried to reassure her, mentioning Ian Garrow and Paul Cole, giving one detail after another until he saw her weakening. Then suddenly she hardened again and the anxious look came back into her eyes. Clearly he might so easily be a counter-agent who had penetrated the Organization and knowing so much needed to know more. Never had the necessity of a password—preferably a double password—been more evident to Pat. Another five minutes passed in which he continued to give more and more details until at last he spoke of Cole with that distaste in his voice which he could no longer conceal. It was then that Mme. Dupré said, "I don't like that man", and at last the barriers were down. She spoke of Cole at some length and continually said, "I don't trust him. I don't trust him."

When at last Dupré came limping in he, too, eyed Pat with considerable suspicion. A middle-aged man with an artificial leg, he looked what he was, a partner in a successful family business. Suspicion quickly vanished and he talked freely. He shared his wife's view of Paul Cole and when Pat asked about the money which Garrow had paid Cole to pass over to Dupré, he burst out: "Money! I've never had a penny from him."

"According to Cole, you are quite an expensive item amongst our agents in the north."

"He's a liar."

"You never received any money at all?"

"Not a single sou. This is outrageous. I always distrusted the man, but I'm not going to have him going around telling lies about me."

"It may be worse than that," Pat said. "If he lies about this what else is he lying about?"

"What can I do?"

"The best thing would be to come down to Marseille and report personally to Ian Garrow."

After some hesitation and consultation with his wife, Dupré at last agreed. It meant leaving his business in the hands of his ageing father, but the urge to deal with Cole was overwhelming.

Three days later, back once more in the Rodocanachis' flat in Marseille, Pat was met by a very worried Madame Rodocanachi. She revealed the shattering news that Ian Garrow had been arrested. Mario Prassinos, the Greek agent, arrived a few minutes later; a very harassed, unhappy Mario, with a few bare details of the arrest. Garrow had been taken in the street shortly after keeping an appointment with a police officer thought to be loyal to the Organization.

In the three rooms at the end of Rodocanachi's flat, a council of war was held. Automatically, Pat, senior British officer, had taken charge of the Organization, to be immediately confronted with the problem of Paul Cole. Cole himself had arrived from the north shortly after Pat, and was at once ordered to report to the flat. It was a cold November day with the curtains drawn and the air thick with cigarette smoke from five men in varying states of tension. Four sat in the living-room and Dupré, unknown to Paul Cole, was concealed in a back room. In the armchair lounged a remarkable young man called Bruce Dowding—known in the Organization as Mason. An Australian by birth, he had lived for years in the south of France, spoke perfect French, combined a deep interest in music with the physique of a policeman, and had become one of the most active and daring members of the Organization. Opposite sat Mario Prassinos, charming and polished, his civilized sensibilities deeply shocked by anything resembling duplicity. A man who loathed violence, he was even more perturbed by the scene than Paul Cole himself, who lounged against the mantelpiece trying to look at ease. Cole drew hard on his cigarette and said: "Well, what are we going to do now?"

"Do now?" Dowding asked.

"Now that Garrow's gone."

"It's not Garrow I wanted to talk to you about, it's something else," Pat said. "Listen carefully, Paul. I've been to the north and I've found out one or two things which don't make me particularly proud of you."

"What on earth are you talking about?"

"I found out that you haven't paid the Organization's money to Dupré."

"Who told you that?"

"And I have reason to believe that you squandered it on yourself and women."

"I swear it's not true. I did pay Dupré."

"He says you did not."

"He's a liar!" Words began to pour from Cole. He worked up a fine indignation, throwing himself into the part with considerable effect until Pat walked to the door, opened it, and Dupré himself came into the room.

Paul Cole's sudden pallor was emphasized by his red hair. He literally staggered back a step or two, but what happened in the next few minutes remains somewhat confused. It is possible that Cole intended to escape and took a menacing step towards Pat. Whatever the precise nature of the provocation, Pat suddenly hit him and he fell to the carpet and lay there a moment, his mouth bleeding. Then he rose to his knees, tears came into his eyes and he began pleading, his voice broken. . . . "I've done something terrible—I admit it—terrible—it was a moment of weakness—I'm sorry—sorry—sorry. . . ."

There was silence. Dowding and Mario had come to their feet, Dupré and O'Leary stood guarding the door.

"We cannot trust you any longer," Pat said, controlling his fury. Cole crawled a pace forward on his knees, his hands in supplication.

"Oh, I know it's terrible—terrible—but I've done some good things too—I did bring men down from the north—you know that."

Again there was silence. Cole's babbling burst out afresh. He seemed utterly broken, and the spectacle emphasized his weakness to O'Leary, who had already determined that weak men were a danger to an Organization which must from now on be run with military precision.

"What do you think, Bruce?" he asked. Bruce hesitated a moment. Then he said quietly: "I think we should kill him." An extraordinary combination of æsthete and man of action, he knew, and the others knew, that the weakness

52

revealed in Paul Cole was a danger to them all. Quite clearly he meant what he said. Mario threw up his beautiful hands—"Oh no," he said, "we can't do that." Every civilized susceptibility was outraged.

Pat thought for a moment. "I could send him back to England and forget what he's done . . ." he said. "He'd be safely out of the way."

Unaware that Cole already had a criminal record in Britain they were surprised when he did not seize upon this, but began pleading all over again until Pat broke in abruptly. "Put him in the bathroom while we talk." The bathroom door was locked behind him and Bruce Dowding stood against it. The conference which followed was brief. There was no evidence that Cole had yet played the traitor and it seemed extreme to condemn him to death for a momentary burst of embezzlement, but releasing such a man as this armed with a detailed knowledge of the Organization and a considerable capacity for corruption was—well—unwise. Suddenly Dowding heard a noise from the bathroom. Swiftly unlocking it, he was in time to see Paul Cole stepping across from the minute bathroom window to a window opposite in the main building of the flat. Dowding rushed to the door, down the side corridor into the main corridor, and the front door slammed as it came into view. Hurling himself forward, he tore the door open and rushed down the stairs. Then he realized that a chase in the streets of Marseille, with a fight at the end, would bring the police, possible arrest and almost certain exposure. Slowly he turned back into the flat. Pat met him at the door. Uneasily they returned to the living-room and the conference continued. "In the first place, we must warn everyone Cole knew," said Pat.*

He left for the north with Bruce Dowding and Dupré the next day. Characteristically Dupré shrugged his shoulders when the full danger of Cole at large was made clear to him. It would be better, Pat said, if Dupré uprooted his family from Lille, travelled to the south,

* Donald Darling states that he had suspected Cole in mid-1941.

changed his name and became a paid agent of the Organization. Gosling's money now made it possible to employ people on a full-time basis. Dupré rejected the plan outright. He had his business, home and friends in Lille, and if Providence decreed that the Gestapo should get him, then so be it. It was not so much fatalism as the impossibility of breaking ties rooted for years in a certain district which literally condemned many agents to death in the long run.

For the Abbé Carpentier, living at Abbeville, it was different. He was one of the men they were now called on to warn. A slight, dark, bearded person, widely respected in the area, the Abbé hated the Germans with that kind of qualified hate inevitable to the true Christian. Pat told him that he must have nothing more to do with Cole, and introduced Bruce Dowding as his successor in the north.

"Don't open your door to Cole. Pretend you don't know him. Send him packing whatever approach he makes. We cannot trust this man."

The Abbé Carpentier nodded quietly. If there was a hint in his eyes that no Christian could accept quite such wholesale condemnation he did not put it into words. He gave them a simple meal. They talked of the Vichy Government with wrinkled noses, of life in the north, of the many Resistance networks now coming into the open.

Carpentier was a man who had served with the Army as an N.C.O. but after the fall of France had been demobilized immediately as a Roman Catholic priest. He took his work for the Organization as a matter of course. He did not regard it as in any way heroic. It was required of him. "I am here to serve my country," he would say, and he could use such phrases without false nobility. Concealing an iron courage behind his piety, his manipulations of a small printing press concealed in a drawer could produce on demand forged identity papers, passes into the forbidden red zones, demarcation-line cards and a whole variety of related documents. He had dummy passes, identity papers, photographs, engraving stamps by the dozen, all ready for adaptation to a given problem. In some senses he was a dedicated man.

Presently Pat and Bruce Dowding moved on. In these journeyings Pat came to know Dowding well. He combined every contradiction. He could look out of the train window entranced by the beauty of the countryside and simultaneously convey the impression that he was happy to live a dangerous life. He spoke little. His voice was soft, his cheeks rosy and freckled, his outer personality warm and friendly. But the more dangerous the job the better he liked it and he was completely devoted to the cause and Pat. Big and raw-boned, the Australian in him had been overlaid by French sophistication, but his love of music and the arts was qualified by that streak of controlled ruthlessness so necessary in a secret agent.

One after another they warned the French families who sheltered British airmen, and one after another the families refused to move. Steadily fresh contacts were made, new agents established, and Bruce Dowding repeatedly introduced as the new chief in the north. It was a long and arduous process. Only those people known for years to agents already active could be countenanced as candidates for the new network. At last they reached Lille in the far north and there, just across the border, lay Belgium.

It was nearly eighteen months since Pat had set foot in his own country. Communication with his parents in Brussels had been impossible and repeated Red Cross interrogations had left them quite unaware whether he was dead or alive. There was another reason why a swift skirmish across the border seemed justified. Pilots were being shot down in Belgium as well as France and the idea of extending the network into Belgium had often occurred to Pat. He made up his mind to cross the border, and for once it was a simple operation, with his Belgian accent at last becoming an asset. Brussels he found a tired, depressed city, with vigorous rationing, a black-out which seemed so much more extreme in a city accustomed to café life, and far too many German officers walking the boulevards with self-conscious restraint. Any incrimination of his family was impossible, and he went first to the bank where his father normally worked. There, at closing time, the familiar figure emerged, and it was a considerable shock to see him walking so much less briskly down the street. Following, Pat found his father moving in the direction of their old flat. Much later that night, when the streets were almost empty, Pat returned and knocked quietly on the door. His mother went very white when she saw him. "Albert—Albert—Albert," she said, kissing him and continuing to repeat his name.

They talked far into the night and his mother was deeply distressed to hear that he must leave in the morning. Where was he going? What was he doing? Why didn't he come back to Brussels, take up life as a doctor once more, settle to a civilized profession? He shook his head sadly and firmly. For the moment that way of life was closed, and he could not tell her in any detail what strange paths he trod. But they must not worry or despair. Already forces were beginning to gather which would challenge Hitler and all his conquests. It would come right in the end. These men would be thrown out of Belgium again. Pat was quite, quite sure of that. Somehow his confidence lightened their depression. But in the kitchen at two in the morning, over the last brew of ersatz coffee, they fell silent. They did not want him to disappear without trace all over again. At five o'clock, when the household was sound asleep, he slipped away into a cold, misty dawn.

5

WITHIN two months the news from the north was devastating. The Abbé Carpentier, Dupré and Bruce Dowding were all arrested. Pat felt a sudden chill. This was the first real breath of the enemy and what he could do. Momentarily there flashed into Pat's mind a picture of Bruce on that last train journey, leaning forward to absorb the beauty of the countryside, his face alight with pleasure. In the many disasters which followed there was always the antidote of action. Regret, fear, sympathy, even indignation were swept aside by the necessity to know, at once, the exact cause of the catastrophe.

Immediately Pat contacted Madame Voglicimacci, a hairdresser in Lille whose beauty had not only exercised a powerful fascination on Cole, but had aroused whatever in him was equivalent to the state of being in love, and in the long run was one of the few people he did not give away. She was able to approach one of the jailers at the prison where Dowding and the Abbé were held. At first the jailer, selected for his Catholic faith, seemed reluctant to have anything to do with it, but when he learned that a Catholic priest, bound to silence by his religion, was involved, he agreed to smuggle out any message which the Abbé might write. It took the form of a pencilled letter scrawled in semi-darkness on a few pages torn from an exercise book. The writing was not easy to decipher, the words were direct and blunt, but even in this message there remained a note of Christian tolerance. It came safely into Pat's hands. The story it told was appalling.

One November evening when Bruce and the Abbé were talking together in the room where the Abbé concealed his forged papers, there came a knock on the door and he went to answer it. Paul Cole stood there with three British airmen. Showing them into the drawing-room he returned to Dowding and they held a swift consultation. Was Paul Cole out to betray them, or was he simply resuming work to expiate his past? For two agonized minutes they debated what to do and then, while Dowding remained hidden in the back room, the Abbé went out to talk to Paul Cole again. Dowding at least must be free to escape if there was any trouble.

In the drawing-room one of the airmen spoke to the Abbé with an unmistakable English accent. It seemed proof enough. He decided that Cole was genuine. Listening in the next room Bruce heard the sound of a drawer opening, of papers being shuffled and then suddenly: "Put your hands up!" Immediately Dowding opened the French windows and ran for it across the garden. Back in the house two of the three airmen revealed themselves as disguised Gestapo agents. Extraordinarily the third man, who had first spoken, was a genuine British pilot and no one ever knew how he came to allow himself to play the part of dupe. The Gestapo turned the house upside down, took the seals, the photographs and the printing press, searched the cellars, terrorized the maid, but found no trace of Bruce Dowding. All that day he wandered alone from place to place, too distraught to speak to anyone. Then at last, galvanized to action, he set out to warn everyone in the area and that was precisely what the Gestapo expected him to do. On his third call they were waiting for him. Paul Cole had not only given away the Abbé Carpentier but ten other agents as well. The Gestapo knew their names, addresses and activities in detail.

A cold fury possessed Pat as he read the full story. If only he had followed Dowding's advice. If only he had killed Paul Cole, Dowding and the Abbé would still be safe. In his mind's eye he could see Dowding, big, raw-boned, sure of himself, humming something from Mozart and breaking off to say: "You know—I did once meet a good German." And the Abbé, the simple, pious Abbé full of his belief in the goodness of human beings, wanting every man to share the inward grace which had been granted him—what use was his God to him now, shut in a dungeon awaiting a horrible death? Where could Cole be traced? Pat thought. What would lure him into those hands which would joyfully twist his neck until he was dead? But vengeance took second place to sounding the alarm throughout the Organization.

Rafarrin on the Paris-Marseille express was at once warned. A fat, jolly, happy-go-lucky chef on the train, Rafarrin had become the courier between the north and south. He carried the latest news of Cole north within twenty-four hours. With him went Jean de la Olla, the one-time shopwalker from Algiers, to begin operations in Paris itself.

Pat followed them to the north the next day. Once over the Line, Germans were everywhere and liable to shoot a suspected man on sight. With that resilience inseparable from such work, Pat had quickly accepted one driving need above all others—the Organization must continue. Gaps in the north must be closed, compromised agents removed and replaced. The iniquity of traitors, the death and mutilation of friends, feeling itself had to be suppressed in a life disciplined to action above everything else.

One small concession Pat permitted himself. Travelling north he called upon one of Paul Cole's mistresses. He was very blunt. "I know," he said, "that you are Paul's mistress. I want to warn you. From the British point of view he is a traitor—we are all out to kill him. If you are a true French-woman you should beware." Then he tried to discover Cole's whereabouts and when he was next likely to call on Françoise, but she, near to tears, pleaded complete ignorance. Paul was erratic, ruthless, unreliable —she never knew when he might call next. Later Pat thought this visit foolish. She already knew too much and such a visit might not have gone unobserved by the Germans. Poor Françoise. Cole, who stopped at nothing, eventually gave her away to the Gestapo in a moment of pique, in order that he might visit her empty flat and take her money.

Back in Paris, Pat quickly fitted into its war-time life. He stayed first at the Hotel des Empereurs. Receiving and answering messages from north and south, helping to escort airmen, interviewing agents, arranging new hide-outs, continually thinking of ways and means of extending the Line, could not entirely banish Bruce, Ian Garrow and the Abbé Carpentier from his mind. Still tense, uneasy, blows seemed to be coming from all directions and no one could tell who would go down next. He took several fresh precautions. A new and perfectly forged set of papers—the best the Organization could offer—sub-stituted the old, but he was still known to a few close friends in the Organization as Pat and they still believed Patrick O'Leary to be a Canadian-born British officer.

Every morning now Pat was greeted in Paris by un-heated rooms, drank the ersatz coffee tasting of acorns, nibbled at the grey-brown bread. There was no butter and little margarine. Outside on the streets S.S. officers passed, their high riding-boots burnished, their peaked caps almost obscuring their vision, and somewhere in the course of the day walked those with a yellow star sewn on their clothing, the Jews branded by the Nazis as the cattle of mankind.

What a sad face beautiful Paris wore. By eleven at night the cafés were black, the outside tables stacked, the streets silent. By day motor traffic had almost ceased for lack of petrol, and only cars pulling towers of swaying metal, belching flames from gas-containers, broke the traffic silence. Bicycles were everywhere, and the velo-taxis—wooden trailers drawn by men indomitably pedalling bicycles—plied expensively like rickshaws. Most public cafés were unheated, shoes were soled with wood, ration cards for all basic foods and tobacco circulated on the huge black market; but a black-market meal cost 800 francs and the average worker's income was 2,000 francs a month.

The Café de la Paix, full of German officers, kept its charcoal braziers burning in the winter, the bookstalls along the Seine still confused rubbish with rare books and prints, and only at one point had the German occupation broken the æsthetic laws which governed the great squares and open spaces. Occupying the Hotel Crillon off the Place de la Concorde the Germans had simultaneously taken over the French Naval Ministry, and for convenience of communication had built a clumsy wooden bridge connecting the two above street level. It broke a century of æsthetic discrimination.

Grey-green uniforms were everywhere. Certain streets were for German use only. In the great black caverns of the Gare St. Lazare and the Gare du Nord the Feldgendarmerie were always waiting and watching. Everywhere the simple elements of trust had suffered.

Amongst it all Pat marvelled at the serenity of Jean de la Olla, now living a haunted life, moving from one flat to another, his austere routine unmarked by any of the vices common to secret agents. An almost saintly dedication overwhelmed all other interests. He went often to early morning Mass, to confession and the sparse ceremonies to which the war had reduced the splendour of the Roman Catholic Church in Paris, religion and the Organization filling his life.

Presently airmen and soldiers, disguised in shabby French clothes, began to pass through their hands on the way down the Line to the south. Sometimes they reached Paris by a series of the most fortuitous accidents; sometimes by design. Shot down in open country an R.A.F. man might be picked up by a friendly farmer who concealed him in his farmhouse for days. Disguised as a French peasant he often began working on the farm and the family might become so attached to him that they did not want to lose him. When the airman pressed his desire to return to England they went through the motions of making enquiries and gave him an extra special supper that night with a whole litre of wine. But presently something had to be done, and the farmer's son whispered his secret to a friend in the market at the nearest country town. His friend would shake his head sadly. *Résistance— Réseau-evasion*? They were beyond his comprehension. Life was hard enough without deliberately creating difficulties. Why not stick to the airman? At last, on a special week-end trip to a larger town, a man in a local bar would say that he might be able to do something, and carried the chain to a third man met at Sunday morning Mass. It was very dangerous, the third man said, but fifty miles away at another town in the Rue de la République there lived a man in touch with a *Réseau*—or so he thought. A month might elapse before the airman entered the underground network and began moving from one hideout to another; a second month before he at last reached Paris and Jean de la Olla or one of his assistants was warned and met him at the Gare du Nord.

More directly airmen were sent into Paris under escort by Norbert Fillerin from the St. Omer region, and Didery from the Lille area. Letters warning Jean or Pat of new arrivals always referred to "parcels"—"I am sending the shirt and trousers in two parcels which should arrive by goods train at the Gare du Nord on November 8 at 8.45".

Picked up at the Gare du Nord the parcels were hurried into hiding. There were soon many secret places in Paris where rescued airmen were taken in. Perhaps it was the flat of Dr. Schreider in the Rue Spontini, or Levêque's in the Avenue d'Orléans, or Gisele Gaudier's in the Avenue General Laperrine, all now parts of the network; or perhaps simply the Hotel des Empereurs.

The airmen might be very exhausted and need fresh papers, different clothes, or *convoyeurs*, when none were available. Sometimes it meant a week or ten days in hiding before they were escorted south to the demarcation line and on to Marseille. Sometimes it meant moving from one hotel room in Paris to another.

Pat himself perfected a method of convoying airmen from Lille to Paris, staying openly in Parisian hotels. He would walk boldly into the Hotel Massena in the Rue Tronchet and ask for a double room, while the Englishman stood in the background buried in a newspaper. Always they arrived late at night and Pat would say, "My friend is not very well. Can you send up a bottle of wine and some aspirins?" He then signed two false names in the register, and they went straight up. They knew that the Gestapo were liable to check the registers early in the morning. Always they left the hotel by seven to have breakfast—such as it was—out. No one in Paris questioned a visitor who left before seven without his breakfast. Only once did they observe the Gestapo entering an hotel before seven—one minute after they had left.

One day the growing group in the Calais area warned Jean that an English airman was waiting to be picked up and Jean quickly sensed from the information given that this was no ordinary case. He reported to Pat who asked him to convoy the man from Calais to Lille. Immediately Jean met him he knew that something was wrong. Back in Lille he settled the man at a certain Madame le Prêtre's and went off to report to Pat. "This is a very queer chap indeed—I cannot get any sense out of him. He doesn't answer when I speak to him in English."

Freshly alert to every sign of danger, Pat said: "Bring him to the Palais de la Bière. I'll talk to him there." When they met, there seemed to Pat something Germanic in the man's cast of feature. He was sullen and uncommunicative. Pat tried him in one language after another without success. His story seemed childishly, transparently false, and suddenly Pat became impatient. It was incredible that the Gestapo could have adopted a story quite so unconvincing in the mouth of such a naïve agent, but all manner of double deceptions were possible and Pat had learnt to suspect simple-mindedness. He tapped his side under his armpit and said in German, "I shall kill you if you have anything to do with the Gestapo. Now, come on, out with it—who are you?" The man hesitated. Pat broke into German again. Suddenly the man said: "*Ja .. Ja .*" and began talking fluently and eagerly. Pat's hand moved towards his gun, his mind flashing to one point and one point only. This man was a German, he had penetrated the Organization and he must die. The German was talking in a quick, hurried whisper: "I am a German soldier," he said. "I have deserted from the German Army. I had to pretend to be a shot-down pilot. No Frenchman would have helped me if he had known the truth." It might be the subtlest piece of deception. Each step in this absurd story might have been foreseen by Gestapo Intelligence before they released this man on his mission. Yet a German agent introduced into their midst fully informed about the growing Calais cell and so ingenuously pleading his origins . . what treatment could they possibly expect for him?"

"Come outside," Pat said, "and don't run or I'll shoot." Turning to Jean he whispered: "Make sure I am not followed."

Fear and confusion showed on the German's face as they left the café, but Pat wanted to see his papers in detail and he needed, in this network of suspicion, to be sure that they were not under surveillance from other German agents. Jean waited as Pat walked behind the German from the Palais de la Bière, down the Rue Nationale. They had gone a considerable distance and there was still no warning from Jean, when the German turned and said something. In the confusion of street noises Pat thought he heard the word Gestapo. His heart jumped, and he felt for his gun. "The papers!" he snapped. The German gave him some papers and with one eye fixed on his sullen, frightened face, Pat examined them. They were in perfect order; everything a German soldier needed to establish his identity was in the small leather case.

They walked on and Pat continued asking questions. Gradually one question after another was answered so spontaneously, with such a mixture of pleading and fear, that Pat became convinced the man was telling the truth; but resolving his doubts, he suddenly realized, did not help him very much. Here was a German at large amongst them who knew far too much and who had it in his clumsy power to become a second and far worse Cole. The death of a stray German broken away from his own people did not mean very much. It was an understatement to say that the ethics of murder relaxed in war. There was no certain dividing line between the necessity of taking life to serve the higher end of national survival and cold-blooded murder carried out for personal protection. The problem was to renew itself continually. For the moment Pat shelved it by deciding to send the German south down the Line under protective arrest. He chose an agent called Bortolia for the job without realizing into what complications this would lead. Bortolia was a short, swarthy, fast-

Pat O'Leary in Korea, 1951, after receiving the Chung Mu awarded him
by the Korean Government

Pat as a Lieutenant-Commander, R.N., second-in-command of *Fidelity*, 1941

speaking Corsican, as tough a breed as his ancestors of old, and given to the same displays of violent temperament. Instructed to provide papers for the German and to make his way to the Hotel du Paon at Nevers, it was arranged that he would be joined there by a convoy of British airmen brought down by another agent, Marcel Debaume, from Paris. Tougher if anything than Bortolia, Debaume was a small, blue-eyed, rosy-cheeked peasant of northern extraction, who loathed everything German. Pat arranged to leave Jean de la Olla in Paris and proceed to Nevers himself to join the *convoyeurs*. When it became evident that there might be friction between the two parties arriving simultaneously at the same hotel, Pat gave Bortolia permission to take the German off to some hotel at the other end of the town.

The proprietor of the Hotel du Paon, fat, easy going, unshakably jovial, arranged a champagne party for Pat and his friends on the night they arrived. Bortolia came late to the party, having lodged his German elsewhere. Presently Debaume was asking Bortolia about the stray German, and they fell into argument and tempers ran high. Debaume appealed to Pat: "Will you tell us what you are going to do with this German bastard?"

"I don't know yet," said Pat.

Debaume looked aggressive. "If I had to take him to the border, his body would be found somewhere on the Line."

Bortolia snapped: "He's a man like any other."

"No, he's not, he's German."

"They're not all bastards."

"If I happen to see him on the demarcation line I'll kill him."

"Not if I'm there."

"So you're going to stop me, are you?"

"Easy," said Pat. "Easy."

Debaume exploded: "He disgusts me—first because he's a German and second because he's a deserter."

"Quite right," said Pat. "But he's also a danger to us."

"That's a third reason for killing him."

"It's not for you to decide," Pat said.

"You're not going to protect this bastard, are you?"

"That's enough," Pat snapped, and there was strained silence.

The party ran on very late. By one o'clock feuds and quarrels had vanished in a cloud of champagne. By two, even Bortolia showed signs of sleepiness. Pat now arranged the complicated rendezvous for the following day. Debaume was to leave with the British airmen at 9 a.m. and Bortolia was to be met at the station at 8 a.m. and taken with his German to a point of contact with Debaume near the demarcation line.

Everything went wrong the following morning. Two agents came hurrying back to the Hotel du Paon at 8.45 to say that there was no sign of Bortolia. Pat told Debaume to wait and went straight to Bortolia's hotel to see what had happened. The porter said: "He left at seven with another man." Rushing back to the Hotel du Paon Pat told Debaume to leave at once. He would remain behind to clear up the mess.

"I'll try to join you at the demarcation line, but don't worry if I'm not there."

Within a few hours Pat knew the truth. The word flashed from one "passer" to another that two men had been arrested by the Germans at the Line—and thrown into jail. Bit by bit Pat pieced together the story, and in one sense it was a very dangerous story. Hurt by Debaume's words, afraid that he would kill the German at any cost, Bortolia had determined to strike out on his own, and against all orders had chosen a new point for crossing the Line, a highly experimental point where little was known of the guards' behaviour. They were seen, shot at and arrested. Matters could scarcely be worse. It meant that the developing cell in the Calais area was in great danger. The German would certainly talk and give everyone away in the hope of saving his own skin.

Instantly Pat warned Jean. Messages were flashed to the northern network and everyone was alerted. Once again it proved futile. Rooted for centuries in their farms, homes and jobs, one agent after another shrugged his shoulders when warned and decided to accept whatever fate had in store for him. It was disastrous. Within twenty-four hours the German revealed everything he knew and six agents were arrested.

Regret, fear, sympathy . . . once again they had to be suppressed. A whole cell in the Pas de Calais area had collapsed, men were even now being dragged off to every kind of horrible fate. It was an inevitable part of the underground life. It had to be accepted, dealt with, and if possible, overcome quickly. Once feeling got the better of one everything was liable to slacken in confusion.

Arrests of one kind or another were made daily in the streets of Paris. Walking the streets the threats were constant. There was always the moment when two S.S. troopers appeared to be walking directly towards one with the worst possible intentions, only to hurry past and allow one to breathe again. There were the moments when an unmistakable Gestapo agent sat opposite one in the Café Aux deux Magots and talked in perfect French about the inevitability of a German victory in six months. Or that time when the front door bell of Levêque's flat rang at the hour when arrests were often made; they slid the curtain aside, saw the postman and breathed again. Once the Gestapo came asking for a mysterious M. Raon and they were able to plead complete ignorance. Once arrests were made two doors away while everyone at Levêque's slept blissfully on. Every ring on the bell different from the special ring, every ring not part of the normal routine of living, stirred fear somewhere at the back of the mind. Every day men were shot or deported to Germany, and the walls of Paris carried fresh warnings; and once with the moon on the Sacre Cœur and the interminable steps pouring down into Paris, a fusillade was fired at the flitting figure of an agent who leapt into an alley and appeared to fade into a solid brick wall.

There remained long intervals when life moved normally; one ate under the noses of German troops, travelled, laughed, made an elaborate irony of politeness to the conquerors or received their presence in organized silence. Extreme irony could be protective. When they cordoned off the Invalides station on the Metro and searched everyone, an agent, carrying a forbidden wireless set sewn in a canvas wrapper was asked what it contained. He smiled: "Oh—a wireless transmitter of course." The Gestapo, pleased to understand French irony, returned the smile and said, "Yes, of course," tapped it and passed on.

The story of the two Belgians became legendary in the Organization. Jean told Pat one day that two Belgians on the run from the Gestapo had arrived at Madame le Prêtre's in Lille. Pat went to meet them and at once established that they were Belgian terrorists who had set out to murder a Belgian Rexist, found him protected by two Gestapo agents and quietly eliminated all three. Both tall, thin, blond men, very nervous, but clearly capable of anything, Pat reckoned them worthy of the best that the Line could offer. Escorting them to Paris proved to be straightforward, but entering the Paris Metro at St. Lazare one day *en route* for Nevers, a startling thing happened. Pat had bought the tickets, pushed through the iron gate and walked to one end of the platform. A train drawn up on the opposite platform obscured the advertisements on the wall, but as it drew out there were suddenly revealed two huge photographs of a very desperate looking pair with an announcement that 100,000 francs would be paid to anyone giving information which led to their arrest. The Belgian terrorists found themselves looking at life-size pictures of their own faces. Hastily turning away, they pulled down their hats and remained in a closed group talking quietly with Pat, subduing their voices to conceal the Belgian accent. Entering the train, they preserved the group, still presenting to the outer world as little as possible. The train was fairly empty. At the next station Pat anxiously scanned the walls as the train drew in. Sufficient repetition of these pictures would make things very difficult. There was no sign of the glaring notices on the walls of Madeleine. In the carriage people seemed supremely unaware that the Germans ever wanted to arrest anyone. The little party reached Nevers without so much as a suspicious glance and Pat hurried the two men into hiding. Ten days later Debaume escorted them south.

Not even the classic occasion when Pat was forced to

settle an R.A.F. pilot opposite two Germans in a railway restaurant car had the kind of consequence which seemed inevitable. Convoying two airmen from Lille to Paris, neither he nor they had eaten for twenty-four hours, and the smell of food from the restaurant became overpowering. Taking an appalling risk, Pat led the airmen down the corridor and spoke to the attendant, who seemed very doubtful whether he could find three places together. A swift glance round the car and he beckoned them in, indicating one seat at a single table occupied by a Frenchman and two seats opposite two German soldiers. Pat's heart suddenly stopped. To withdraw at that point might arouse suspicion. There was nothing for it but to settle his two men in the seats offered. Conceivably it was the morose atmosphere generated by war-time travel which prevented spontaneous talk between the single airman and his Frenchman. For the next five minutes all six sat in silence while the train flashed along and the waiters began serving. Pat ordered three beers for himself and the pilots and at last they arrived. Disaster quickly followed. In his nervousness the R.A.F. pilot sitting next to Pat upset his glass and the beer flowed across the table straight into the laps of the Germans. They leapt up cursing. For a second the scene was paralysed. Pat had stopped breathing, the pilot half-stood, his hand arrested in mid-air, and the Germans were immobilized, half-risen from their seats. A moment later, red-faced and furious, the Germans sank into their seats again, mopping their trousers, and it was then that the workings of unpredictable impulse brought a second, far worse crisis. The pilot burst into uncontrollable laughter. . . . Spirit the R.A.F. men off before the Germans can recover from their astonishment, Pat thought swiftly. Fear went through him, his hands were suddenly cold and he burst into profuse apologies. His words were lost in a roar of laughter from the Germans. Something in the completely uninhibited laughter from the pilot had proved irresistible and now the Germans released one guffaw after another. It was funny—outrageously, idiotically, insanely funny. Since they spoke not a word of French and the R.A.F. pilot spoke not a word of German, the universal language of laughter permitted them to communicate uproariously in perfect anonymity. Pat joined in the laughter. The carriage tittered, Pat offered his napkin, the pilot continued to laugh, the waiter mopping with his napkin laughed too, the Germans, drying themselves, laughed, and when Pat apologized for his friend's lack of German, the Germans brushed it aside as a quite understandable shortcoming. For the rest of the sandwich meal there were occasional exchanges between Pat and the Germans, a knowing grin or two between the pilot and the Germans, and at last they were walking down the corridor, back to their seats.

"Phew!" said Pat in perfect English as he sat down. "Never tell me the Germans haven't got a sense of humour."

And the slight, elegant Frenchwoman sitting opposite looked up. "*Pardon, m'sieu?*" she said.

6

THE horizon was aglow, the sky serene as the dawn came up over Marseille and the relentless sunlight poured into the streets. It moved down the broad boulevards, was checked by the labyrinth at the Old Port, and never reached the teeming life of black alleys where children already played, shouting in the dawn. A dirty train pulled into the station, hardly identifiable as the once crack express from Paris.

Behind the frosted-glass doors of the Petit Poucet, M. Dijon stood fingering his black moustache, and wondered whether any "parcels" would be delivered that morning. It was a neat, small café, with the regulation sawdust on the floor and the rows of tables stretching either side of a narrow gangway. Outside paraded a plain-clothes police inspector.

Ten minutes later, with no preliminary, two men came tramping through the door and sat down, attempting a casual air. As the waiter walked over to take their orders, one whispered: "From Uncle Victor," words which produced some alarm on the waiter's face and sent him scuttling back through the frosted-glass door. Outside the police inspector passed the café, paused, came back, and began walking to and fro before the door. Inside, the French workers, sipping *pastis*, stared stonily at these new arrivals who were clearly not locals, clearly from a strange part of France and had about them something markedly alien for any part of France.

A moment later the waiter swung back into the café, invited the newcomers to follow him and took them into the back room, where Dijon stood, his long face showing every sign of annoyance, his highly strung nerves evident in the movement of his hands. He asked abruptly for the password. Both Englishmen gave it. He then asked for the

71

second password. Again they repeated it in unison. At last Dijon burst out: "Why the hell did you come in like that! You should have been more discreet." Suddenly, as if materializing out of the wall, the police inspector was there. Everyone except the proprietor and the waiter froze. One Englishman started towards the door and Dijon said: "It's all right, it's all right. This is Monsieur Boulard. He's one of us." Boulard was a police inspector long in the pay of Organization Pat. Bensi the Greek now appeared from the café, and Dijon said: "Bensi will fetch someone. We still have to confirm your identity." Tall and swarthy, always elegantly dressed, Bensi nodded, smiled, and disappeared into the street again. From his air he might have been the receptionist of a big hotel in search of accommodation for harassed guests.

Half an hour later Louis Nouveau, in Savile Row grey, slid through the door, nodded a greeting and ran his eyes over the two tired, unshaven Englishmen in the party. They repeated the password once more and looked in wonderment at this apparition which might have stepped into the Mall from one of the more exclusive London clubs. Today he wore the red bow-tie with white spots, today his suède shoes and creased trousers were, if anything, rather too immaculate, today his choice of English came echoing straight out of the languid 1920s.

"You chaps had better call me Maurice. It's not my real name, of course. But we must have our little joke. . . ." His smile was overwhelming, the grace of every movement courtly, his ease a deliberate contradiction of his job. They sat for a time and drank. Suspicion disappeared as Nouveau's talk dispersed the tension, but the Englishmen wondered at this long interval as the wine flowed and an atmosphere almost convivial pushed the clumsy business of escape aside.

"Pierre Laval . . ." Louis said, and repeated again the name which had just broken into the conversation. "Pierre Laval. . . ." He used the words with that distaste which accompanied the very essence of bad smells. "There must be something false about a man who always affects a long white silk tie," he said. It was delivered with complete

English understatement. It charmed his English hearers.

Then abruptly he came to his feet, gave instructions to be followed at twenty yards and set out through the tangle of streets towards the Quai Rive Neuve and his flat on the fifth floor. They arrived without incident.

Airey Neave, D.S.O., O.B.E., M.C., had made a spectacular escape from the notorious German castle, Colditz, and overcome every kind of hazard to make his way into the hands of the Organization. Captain Hugh Woollatt, M.C., of the Lancashire Fusiliers, had duped the guards of Biberach Oflag with no less skill and joined Neave in Switzerland. From the moment they left Switzerland, every tortured attempt to outwit guards and defences was done with, and they found themselves carried along by the smooth machinery of Organization Pat, each difficulty anticipated before it was reached.

At Annemasse on the Swiss border they had met the man wearing a blue smock and sabots who introduced himself with the words, "I am Louis, formerly of the Ritz, London." They had entered the no-man's-land between Switzerland and France, passed into the hands of Mademoiselle Jeanne, travelled on again in the care of Cécile and finally set out for Marseille under the wing of yet another agent.

Now, in this extraordinary flat on the Quai Rive Neuve, the first astonishment at meeting Louis Nouveau grew. The furnishings were in the best possible taste, the books extensive, the pictures rare, but Nouveau swept aside these impressions as he emerged with two pairs of slippers and asked his guests to don them.

"The chaps downstairs," he said, by way of explanation, and his hands went up with the palms turned outwards, a characteristic gesture of distaste. "They may be Vichy-ites."

Within the next few days, Neave and Woollatt became familiar with many small precautions. On the second day they heard a series of quick knocks on the door. Louis smiled: "Friends," he said. "Our special knock."

Mario Prassinos came in, his mahogany stick over his

arm, his gloves carried flat in his hand, an air of sophisticated ease pervading his whole person. "Charmed—charmed," he said, shaking hands with both. "I am so sorry the chief is abrrroad." This was a reference with rolling r's to Pat's absence on urgent business. Leoni Savinos called next, tougher, not given to gallantry but none the less charming, and with him his flaxen-haired wife. There was much talk far into the night. The atmosphere grew thick, the wine flowed, and with no thought of danger it was as if a civilized soirée had run on rather late.

There followed the familiar routine of near prison-life in the flat, with agents coming and going for almost a week until one day Nouveau announced that everything was ready for the next move, and would they please shave the night before and be ready when he called them at four in the morning. Breakfast followed at five, a limited breakfast of bread, margarine and ersatz coffee, and they left for the station escorted by an agent called Francis Blanchain. Dark, vivid, audacious, Blanchain knew every trick of the trade. He went to the *guichet* and bought the tickets while they waited in the background. Suddenly Neave was aware of two other people hovering near by observing them much too closely. Francis, returning with the tickets, turned and said: "This is Monsieur Coubert and his son. They are going with you to Spain."

M. Coubert, an elderly man once employed by a tourist agency in Brussels, did not at first glance seem the ideal person to scale the Pyrenees. He was frail and had a certain querulous air. He carried two suitcases, one of which turned out to hold nothing but travel books. The nineteen-year-old son was all blushing eagerness to get to England in order to join the Free French and fight the Germans. Their joint journey to Toulouse was uneventful but crowded. Passengers so jammed the carriages and corridors that the full glory of the Mediterranean coast in midsummer passed as glimpses between heads and shoulders. It was very hot, with sweat pouring down many faces, the varnish of the wooden carriages blistering and the impossibility of reaching the lavatory without trampling over many bodies adding to their discomfort.

The fixed rendezvous at Toulouse was the Hotel de Paris. For the first time Neave set eyes on this extraordinary edifice and its still more remarkable proprietress. Madame Mongelard was of tough peasant extraction and sat hour after hour in the glass case of the cash desk, looking out on the world with an expressionless face and all-seeing eyes. She had been like that the first day Pat met her and invited her to join the Organization, wearing the same white scarf over her grey hair, the same clothes of unrelieved black from head to foot, buttoned closely at the chin.

Now, when she asked for the password her face was not so much ferocious as stonily unaccommodating, and one felt that even the Gestapo might have quailed under her cold stare. But Madame Mongelard was a deep-feeling woman who eventually paid an appalling price for her courage and audacity. Papers, passwords and security regulations had to be correct in every detail before she made the slightest response, and even then she retained the air of a female dragon and drew from her greatest admirers the word, *"Formidable!"*

In her hotel a glass-roofed courtyard, gloomy as a cavern and surrounded by a rockery, gave upon an even gloomier lounge with stairs climbing to an interior gallery off which ran a honeycomb of aged and decaying rooms. To be absorbed by this honeycomb was to enter a presence which drew one on into unfathomable depths, from whence, without a guide, there was little hope of return. Every night the gendarmes solemnly examined the register and asked a few questions from normal visitors while double the number of guests were hidden away in remote rooms. The Hotel de Paris became famous in Resistance Movement annals and all Frenchmen honoured Madame Mongelard and her hardly less brave husband.

It was in this hotel that Captain Woollatt and Airey Neave spent a week in a moth-eaten double bedroom full of faded splendour. It seemed to them a long-drawn-out and altogether irritating delay. Other, Polish "parcels" in the convoy went into hiding at Gaston Nègre's great rambling wholesale grocery store in Nîmes, where he entertained them royally, producing champagne and caviare from the hidden depths. When they finally joined the convoy at Toulouse they were in high fettle and ready to face anything.

At last, one night, all twelve members of the party were equipped with fresh papers by Francis Blanchain and ready for the next steps. Interlocking with forged Czech identity papers they now had forged instructions to report to the *centre d'accueil* at Banyuls-sur-Mer. This brought them, as genuine Czech refugees, close to Port Vendres and the Spanish border. Their arrival at Port Vendres had its moments. Re-assembling some distance from the station they suddenly sighted a number of gendarmes tearing down the hill on bicycles. Francis shouted, "Meet at José's," and ran. They all scattered, Neave and Woollatt rushing towards the foothills, finding cover in brushwood and remaining there until sundown. In total darkness they fumbled their way back towards the town, came upon a house resembling the description given, took a risk and made the prearranged three knocks on the door. A tall female shape opened it, glanced at them and at once stood aside. *"Entrez, messieurs."*

Inside, the room was lit with candles and by their light they could see nine of the twelve escapees gathered round a green baize table drinking rum and eating sandwiches. They were given bowls of soup, joined the group and took their tot of rum. Immediately, a short, wiry Spaniard with a face like lined mahogany came into the room, asked for the fees, and as everyone took out bundles of notes, carefully counted them. He licked his finger and thumb and mouthed as he counted. His face made little wry gestures as if the taste of money disagreed with him, but he was as business-like as a bank clerk. There followed a brief surveillance of everyone's baggage and he stepped amongst it saying in bad French: "You must leave that behind— and that—and that." Cherished possessions were abandoned and M. Coubert fought to save his travel books, but

José overruled him. With great reluctance the second case containing clothes was allowed to pass.

A distant clock struck midnight. José called for complete silence, opened the back door and one by one shepherded the men out into a cold starlit night. With everyone moving down the path in single file at intervals of four yards, José took the lead and they saw that he was wearing white boots which seemed in the darkness almost to glow.

The early slopes were comparatively easy, but behind them the Mediterranean sky looked threatening, big storm clouds gathering at sea. No one spoke. Everyone tried to conserve breath and strength as the chalk and scrub gave place to stone, the inclines steepened and the black mass of the mountains rose steadily until presently it seemed they must blot out the whole sky.

One hour went by and already M. Coubert was panting. His case, manhandled from one person to another, had become a senseless burden infuriating everyone. Two hours, and Neave and Woollatt were breathing deeply, two Poles were making comic complaints in several languages and a Canadian priest was white and silent. At three in the morning they had to stop, and the tireless José looked around at the prostrate forms with amusement. The groans of M. Coubert drew his attention and he muttered: "So you wanted to bring your travel books, did you?" Sympathy was not an emotion he understood. Fifteen minutes and they started again. Heather and chalk gave place to shale and rocks. The path no longer seemed to exist, but José's white boots mysteriously held the invisible track, and when his figure was flat against the black mountains the boots gave the extraordinary impression of being empty boots, moving ghostlike of their own accord.

Four o'clock brought another rest, and now everyone's energy had drained away; feet were sore and swollen and limbs exhausted. Even the young and healthy Airey Neave felt as if his heart would burst. His breath was coming in gasps, and his legs were full of shooting pains. Coubert dropped down into a groaning heap; he was suddenly very afraid. His energy gone, his thoughts wandering, his body in pain, there was a danger that he might be left alone in that utterly desolate spot to die slowly of exposure and exhaustion.

When they started again, Coubert, with his arm around someone's shoulder, was half-carried along, each man taking it in turn to help him. The case had become a nightmare. It was kicked, buffeted, dragged, and threatening to burst at any moment it was destined to certain destruction. At times it was difficult to know how Coubert himself was not quietly forgotten and dropped in his tracks.

As the sky began to lighten before the dawn, the character of the country again changed, the shale and rocks, the bleak ridges and jutting flint blackened, and a certain brooding majesty invested the landscape. Soon, magnificent peaks came rearing out of the darkness, glowering above their heads, only to vanish again as the clouds closed in. These was something breathtaking about their quick materialization. Presently mile upon mile of desolate mountains stretched away in every direction and then, on the icy wind, came the first hint of rain.

They swallowed a hurried breakfast of hard-boiled eggs and brandy. The clouds darkened, the rain beat down and the wind rose. Steadily mounting in force it made standing upright hazardous, and any attempt at walking a feat of strength. They struggled on, Coubert almost dragged by force in their wake. Suddenly his suitcase was flung crashing amongst the rocks and the old man groaned afresh.

The rain became a whip in their faces, the paths filled with water, and icy torrents rushed down the mountainside. Coubert slipped and fell, and lay on the path. His son pulled him up, slung him on his back and staggered on. Presently he too could go no further. Neave relieved him of the old man, dragged him on his back and plunged forward. Woollatt took him the next few hundred yards, and there he slithered to the ground again.

Afraid that he would be left, Coubert set up a protesting wail. The son pulled him on his back. The rain had soaked through all clothing, no one had breath left to speak and the wet, miserable bundle of human beings floundered automatically on. It could not go on much longer, but the indomitable José kept them moving.

Half an hour later the gradient levelled and began to move downwards. The rain ceased, fog settled on everything and somewhere behind the fog was a hint of sunshine. Another hour's stumbling crawl with the backs of heels brought to agony by the downward slopes, and then with the border in sight they almost ran into a patrol of light-green uniforms and black cocked hats. Turning aside they struggled on. When everything seemed over there was still hours of tramping along soaking tracks and fields and as the afternoon deepened, Coubert again showed signs of collapse.

Various methods of reception were open to anyone arriving at the Spanish border. One could straightforwardly pass into the hands of the remarkable José II, who tended to concentrate on important people, or perhaps Manuel, dark and languid, with broad black eyebrows, an immaculately fitting suit, gold-set teeth and beringed fingers. He owned a villa near the border which took in refugees and in the dawn roused them with fastidious fingers and escorted them to the Barcelona train. Or there was Pedro and his "shed", a contrivance of wooden planks where refugees spent the night before facing the public glare of the station.

José handed Neave, Woollatt, and the rest of his party over to Pedro. Another perfumed sophisticate from Madrid, Pedro had powdered white cheeks, even more rings than Manuel and the most seductive of voices. They spent an uneasy night in his shed, and he roused them in the dawn to catch the train.

"What time does it go?" someone asked.

"Six o'clock."

"Shouldn't we clean up?"

Pedro shrugged his fashionable shoulders and gestured with infinite subtlety. "There is no longer need to worry. My friends will see to everything. But perhaps . . ." a fluttering and quite different gesture. Was it a hint that

79

his own exquisite self could hardly be expected to exist alongside so many mud-stained, dirty, stinking bodies?

They left shortly afterwards, reaching the Barcelona train without trouble. Pedro nodded and smiled to the clerks, the merchants and the lawyers who crowded silently into their seats on the glistening express. The group of dirty men proclaiming to all the world their origin might not have existed . . . until the tall, hawk-like policeman with his five-pointed badge came striding down the corridor. Neave held his breath. The sudden thought that perhaps he had come all this way through Germany and France to be arrested by a fancy policeman barely over the border of Spain was too much. The train had already crashed forty miles nearer Barcelona at breakneck speed but the policeman was coldly examining the papers of the most plainly Spanish citizens. Neave glanced at Pedro. Suddenly rising to his full height, switching on a smile of electric radiance, Pedro advanced to meet the policeman, whose face at once relaxed. They greeted one another effusively. They came back to the seats and Pedro said with an expansive sweep of his glittering hand: "My friends!" whereupon the policeman gave a half bow, nodded and murmured: "So—so. . . ." Then he pursed his lips, cocked an eye at Pedro, nodded and passed on, his face instantly freezing into official ice again.

Pedro sat down, took a perfumed silk handkerchief from his pocket and dabbed his brow, murmuring in Spanish— "But *so* expensive."

Many distinguished "parcels" passed through the Organization between 1941 and 1942, including Brigadier-General Roupell, high-ranking officers who became members of the House of Commons and the American-born Whitney Straight. Pieced together from many sources Whitney Straight's story began when he set out one day on a special mission which his A.O.C. laconically described as "having no future". The words were all too prophetic. Shot down, he crash-landed in France at tremendous speed alongside an astonished farmer. Dragging himself from the wreck he zig-zagged into the countryside and kept going for hours until he was fifteen miles from the plane. Already equipped with a leather jacket to disguise his R.A.F. uniform in case of just such an emergency, he felt he needed to top the jacket with a French hat of some kind. Curfew time was approaching and he had to get under cover somewhere. Boldly he went into a farmhouse. The farmer sold him a hat but told him to leave at once because the farmhouse was requisitioned by the Germans. The soldiers were billeted in the very barn where Straight wanted to sleep, but it was too late to move anywhere else, and he decided to reconnoitre. There was nowhere but the barn and in desperation he approached it, found to his delight that it was empty, and tunnelled into a great mound of hay. Presently he heard the Germans returning. Their boots trampled within a few yards of him, and he could hear everything they said, but no one suspected his presence. Gradually tension subsided and he dozed off. Before the dawn he awoke, heard the Germans snoring all round him, peered out, and slipped silently away into the dawn.

Boarding a train for Paris the inescapable Germans were there again, but the French cap and the leather jacket seemed to mask his identity effectively. At Rouen he had to change trains, and while waiting for his connexion he wandered through the streets for an hour carefully slipping British pennies into the letter boxes of German-requisitioned houses.

In Paris he made for the American Embassy and was ringing the bell without response when he saw a notice which sent shivers down his spine: "This Embassy is closed and enquiries should be addressed to the United States Embassy, Berlin. . . ." Suddenly a frightened official opened the door a few inches. Straight gave his name and the man whispered: "I heard you had been shot down on the radio —but you must go immediately—there are German guards across the street. . . ."

Straight hurried away again, went into a café and telephoned the embassy. Presently a man slipped into the café, gave him 10,000 francs and vanished again. Hurrying to the hotel at which he normally stayed in Paris, Straight was warmly welcomed by the concierge, but was told at once that the hotel was full of senior German officers. Montmartre seemed the obvious alternative and he hurried through the streets full of German soldiers to the obscure Hotel de Moscou, where no one thought of asking questions.

Next morning he bought a map and decided to move south, intending to cross the demarcation line at Chenonceaux, where the Cher marked the boundary. The train journey proved uneventful and presently, on a glorious July afternoon, he sat near the bank of the Cher, timing, with his stop watch, the German guards marching to and fro. When the nearest guard was at the furthest extremity of his beat, he slipped into the water before the astonished eyes of the Sunday fishermen. A considerable underwater swimmer, he remained beneath the surface until nearly half-way across. Then bursting lungs drove him to break water for two seconds while he gulped fresh air and slid down and forward again. His appearance out of the water on to the opposite bank was achieved with great stealth and passed undetected.

Drying out in the sun, he determined to try to cross the Pyrenees. Presently he took the branch-line train between Loches and Châteauroux. He met the inevitable check on the train with immense skill and in fluent French began a long story of how his bad memory had made him forget his papers; he was sorry; it was crassly stupid and another time he would certainly see . . . . The gendarme passed on down the train. But the questioning had shaken him a little. He decided to get out at the next station and walk to Châteauroux. Clearly he must eat before starting the long journey, and he went into a small café, ordered a meal and pretended to read a newspaper. The woman who brought the food eyed him curiously and an odd feeling that she was distinctly unsympathetic drove Straight to begin eating rapidly. Two minutes later three gendarmes entered the café. Straight dashed towards the door, a revolver was levelled, a scuffle followed and he was arrested.

At first he gave his name as Squadron-Leader Smyth and was quickly transferred south to St. Hippolyte du Fort.

With another R.A.F. pilot, Gibbs, he at once began planning to escape. One day they launched a simultaneous attack on a guard and Gibbs slipped away, but Straight found himself looking at the muzzle of a pistol and had to surrender once more. His second "escape" was a straightforward case of repatriation skilfully encouraged by the duplicity of Dr. Rodocanachi. As the American representative on the Repatriation Medical Board, Rodocanachi had considerable influence with his German colleagues and Straight himself encouraged some old wounds received in Norway—a hole in his back, damaged eardrums and a fractured skull. Unaware that they were dealing with one of the most distinguished American-born R.A.F. pilots, known throughout the world, the German doctors, under subtle pressure from Rodocanachi, agreed to pass Straight as unfit for further service. The Organization had many concealed victories of this kind. Their true extent is difficult to determine because Rodocanachi eventually paid the extreme penalty for his work, but at this period he reaped a rich harvest, with no less than eight of these faked repatriations.

Things went wrong for Straight. Escorted to Perpignan under special surveillance, eight repatriates—among them Straight—found the station bristling with fully armed soldiers and there, while the train idled for hours and steadily became more uncomfortable, a rumour spread that Paris had been bombed the previous night. It proved to be true and left such bitterness in the minds of the Vichy officials that they decided to make life more difficult for British prisoners-of-war, and sent the eight repatriates to the Pasteur prison hospital at Nice. If the British could violate international law, so could they.

It was now clear that something special had to be done to extricate the person of Whitney Straight, already emphasized by London as important, and the Organization went to work. Pat sent news to Francis Blanchain in Toulouse that Whitney Straight was in the Pasteur Hospital. This man's escape must be given priority over everything else, he said. Blanchain began his investigations at once. Blanchain was already established in Madame

Mongelard's Hotel de Paris and had spent some weeks convoying parcels on the Nice-Toulouse sector of the Line. Many mysterious people had been introduced to him in Nice, among them a man called Albert Cohen, who first put him in touch with the woman who became the key to Whitney Straight's escape. Nicole Brugère was the daughter of a one-time French Ambassador to Belgrade, a pretty girl violently opposed to Vichy and devoted to the British. She had taken a course in nursing purposely to qualify for the Pasteur Hospital at Nice, in one section of which British prisoners were treated. Blanchain discovered from her the routine and layout of the hospital, and established that two armed guards were permanently on watch inside the British section. Escape was only possible if they could be dealt with first of all. Moreover, any attempt to subdue them must coincide with that period of convalescence when patients were allowed to walk for half an hour on the flat roof of the British section. Blanchain reported back to Pat and developed his plan in detail.

With the help of a certain Dr. Levy, Nicole was given a packet of powerful sleeping tablets to be placed in the hands of Whitney Straight. In the lunch break the guards sometimes played cards with the sick prisoners and 1.45 was the ideal time for any attempt at escape. At 1.10 on the appointed day, two other patients playing cards suddenly burst into hysterical laughter, drawing the attention of the guards. Whitney Straight slipped the tablets into their glasses. Everything ran smoothly, except for the effect of the sleeping tablets. First their reaction was slower than anyone expected and instead of slumping back unconscious the guards merely fell into a heavy doze. No one could guarantee that they would not start up at the sound of a patient opening a door. But the risk had to be taken. As swiftly and silently as possible Straight and another man climbed into singlets and trousers which Nicole had hidden away under the bed. In stockinged feet they moved towards the door. A guard grunted and stirred. Suddenly he stuck out one leg grotesquely. But they were at the door and a moment later slipped through.

The lock of a gate at the end of the roof had been suitably doctored and they walked casually through. There on the side of the hill which ran up behind the roof Francis Blanchain sat waiting. He rapidly passed over papers covering Czech agricultural workers and they strolled towards the bus stop and joined the queue. Even for foreign workers their clothes seemed odd, and Francis Blanchain kept the group exclusively to itself, talking to Straight in French while the British soldier looked suitably bovine. Everyone was tense. Back in the hospital the drugged guards must by now have been discovered. Already in the queue there were curious stares. The whole impossible business could not hold out very long . . . and if the bus were late . . .! One minute afterwards it came bouncing and swaying down the road.

There remained the ordeal of boarding the bus under the driver-conductor's eye. He scanned their faces and clothes expressionlessly. An imperceptible shrug of the shoulders and he clicked out three tickets for Juan les Pins and set the bus roaring away. It was a tremendous relief to leave the vicinity of the hospital, but now began the old familiar business of stopping anyone talking to the British soldier, who spoke no French. Blanchain sat next to him on the outside. Straight occasionally talked his perfect French from behind. The journey to Juan les Pins was very long. Two of the three men felt nervously exhausted by the time they arrived. Immediately they slipped away towards the villa of Dr. Levy, and the two "parcels" went into hiding.

Blanchain at once set out for Marseille to report to Pat. Before he left he instructed Levy's daughter to take the two men next day to a photographer who could be trusted to provide the snapshots necessary for new and more convincing papers. Blanchain returned the following evening with fresh clothes and papers. Newly disguised and carrying papers correct in every detail, the three men set out at once, back along the coast to Marseille. A whole intricate shuttle service, first one way and then the other, had to precede the normal process of going underground.

In the fifth-floor flat at the Quai Rive Neuve, Louis

Nouveau and Pat were waiting when they arrived. They were very interested to meet the famous Whitney Straight. Thick-set, dark, dynamic, he talked far into the night. He spoke of England, the R.A.F., the crazy old prison at St. Hippolyte, the tactics of the Germans and the way the war was going. The news he brought was reasonably optimistic. Inspired by the four-square courage of Winston Churchill, Britain was steadily preparing one of the most powerful and effective war machines the world had ever known. Retribution for the Germans might not be so far away.

A great hue and cry ran through Marseille and along the south coast when the Englishmen's escape was discovered. The German overlords threatened terrible reprisals and many people were falsely arrested. But Whitney Straight and the British soldier remained snugly in hiding at Quai Rive Neuve for two weeks, becoming very familiar with the old bridge of the Port, the teeming life outside, and the strict routine of living virtually imprisoned amidst the luxury of Louis' flat.

Then one evening came the warning to be ready to move, and in September 1942 Whitney Straight left France by boat with Leoni Savinos. Another operation had gone through flawlessly.

7

It was early in 1942 that a message came from Donald Darling, then M.I.9's agent in Gibraltar, saying: "Want to see you as soon as possible. Speak to no one." M.I.5 was restricted to resistance and espionage work; M.I.9 dealt with escapes. The message had come across the Pyrenees by one of Vidal's Spanish guides. Addressed to Pat, it was written on a small scrap of paper and signed Cheri, the pen-name of the man known only to three members of the Organization as Donald Darling. It had passed from the Spanish guide to Mario Prassinos, from Mario to Leoni Savinos, Leoni had given it to Debaume, who was about to return to Paris after successfully completing another convoy south, and Debaume conveyed it to Pat, who was at that time in Paris.

There were two possible explanations of the summons. The Organization had achieved such complexity that M.I.9 in London wanted to discuss its future, or the sudden change in the reports on Paul Cole called for explanation. Until his arrest Ian Garrow had constantly sent to Gibraltar favourable reports on Cole and now, suddenly, when a man they knew to be of Belgian extraction had taken over, Cole was described as a blackguard, womanizer and traitor. The abrupt transition must have sounded odd. Leaving Jean de la Olla in charge in the north, Pat hurried south, passed over command there to Mario Prassinos, and set out at once to see Vidal at Toulouse.

Vidal always greeted Pat like a brother. A man who never said he could do anything without promptly carrying it out, he did not particularly like the English, the Germans, or the French, regarding them all as so many pawns in his own game of undermining the Franco régime and replacing it with anarchy. He had one complaint against life. It did not yield him enough arms. He needed, he continually said to Pat, more revolvers, more rifles, and perhaps if it could be managed, an occasional machine-gun. Pat quietly bought a few revolvers in Marseille and passed them over to Vidal as products flown direct from England for his especial benefit. It was the one small deception between them, and sometimes the shadow of a smile in Vidal's dark eyes hinted that perhaps he understood the nature of the trick.

Every meeting was a great occasion. In Vidal's dark, old-fashioned house Pat was escorted into the not too clean kitchen where a log fire seemed to burn eternally. The table was heavy with food and expensive wines, one underground chief never failing to entertain another royally. They ate and drank, Pat explained his mission and Vidal at once said: "You shall have José II himself."

"José II?" Pat said.

"A wonderful man. None other. A very distinguished servant of the Generalissimo—and, oh, so clever. . . ." José II, it seemed, not only performed the acrobatic feat of serving Franco, Germany and Vidal simultaneously, but gave considerable satisfaction to each of his employers. His income was astronomical. The Germans paid him more than the Spanish and Vidal less than either, but what Vidal lacked in money he remedied with information. No small part of Vidal's leisure appeared to be employed in the production of information for José II, who duly sold it to the Spanish Government, its secret archives groaning not so much with international secrets as the fantasies of Vidal.

"Perhaps, Pat," Vidal said, towards the end of a sumptuous meal, "perhaps you could spare time to invent a little information for me. It gets a little trying sometimes. . . . I must keep José II well supplied with secrets."

Vidal thought it unwise to allow José II to know that the man under his wing was anything more than just another escapee and Pat's identity was temporarily submerged in that of Captain Rogers. He travelled swiftly to Perpignan, from Perpignan to Banyuls and there made his way to one of the small houses under the hills where another party waited to cross the Pyrenees at midnight.

The crossing was exhausting but without major incident. Tired, dirty and hungry, they stumbled into the small Spanish station at Villajuiga at three in the morning and there, by the light of a single lamp, José II was waiting. Swiftly escorting them to a broken-down wooden hut, he produced some pieces of black bread and a sinister mess of sardines. Then he shook hands and vanished. Ten minutes before the train was due he reappeared, and soft, cat-like, saying very little, he selected Pat from the group and escorted him alone to the train.

He had an oily smile, his hands were manicured and he fingered the pocket in which lay his miracle-working police badge as though continuously afraid it might be stolen. Twice the police came to check passengers on the train, twice the small badge was casually shown and produced immediate deference. Each time José II turned a little towards Pat and permitted himself a half-smile as if to say, "It is not so difficult." They hardly talked at all. Pat had been warned by Vidal to give nothing away. Sometimes sitting alone in the reserved compartment, mysterious tensions developed. The fair-haired man beside him would suddenly become sinister, and Pat began to wonder whether it might have been better to travel in a less exclusive way. The journey to Barcelona seemed very long. Twice Pat felt the large eyes watching him, trying to pierce the precise nature of this rather unusual escapee who looked so French and did not seem inclined to talk. Once José II began asking questions in Spanish and finding the answers halting and evasive shrugged his shoulders and lit another black cheroot. At Barcelona he vanished for twenty minutes and Pat knew that he had slipped away to the German Consulate where his false documents would be carefully photographed and recorded. He came back full of apologies. Together, quite openly, they then took the underground train towards the British Consulate. José II slipped away before they reached it and Pat rang the bell, asked for Mr. Farquhar and gave his real identity.

"I've been waiting for you," Farquhar said. A drink

followed, they talked at length and Farquhar began asking about the Organization. Pat remembered the explicit instructions from Donald Darling to speak to no one and as his enquiries produced nothing but evasive answers, Farquhar first seemed put out and then almost angry.

"Every pilot coming over mentions your Organization," Farquhar said. "We want to know more about it."

Pat explained the order for total secrecy.

"It doesn't apply to me, surely," Farquhar said.

"I don't know," Pat answered. "The instruction made no exceptions."

He spent the night at the flat of the Press attaché. Two days later he was on his way to the British Embassy in Madrid, and from there the First Secretary drove him by car towards the border. In a small bungalow close to the border, Pat was briefed for the final crossing. A big car with a large boot would be driven over the border by an agent, and securely locked in the boot would be Pat. "I shall talk with the guards, show them everything and hope they will not ask for the boot to be opened. If they do ask I shall search for my keys, pretend to have forgotten them and turn the car back."

Five minutes later they set out. It was cramped in the boot, the air was stale and the smell of petrol strong. As the car swayed on the bad Spanish road, Pat braced himself against the shocks. At the border the car came to a stop and Pat heard voices speaking in rapid Spanish. There followed a ripple of laughter, the self-starter buzzed, the engine burst into life and then came the sound of tyres echoing on a bridge. They were moving across. Once over the bridge the car accelerated, and shot towards the centre of Gibraltar and the Admiralty offices. Five minutes later the car jerked to a standstill and a voice said in a loud whisper: "Quick as hell when you get out. Into the door on your left."

So it was that an English representative of M.I.9 first saw the chief of an escape organization already known in London amongst Secret Service men, stumbling out of the boot of a car. Donald Darling greeted Pat enthusiastically. He swept him from one office to another introducing him to people until he reached Lieutenant-Colonel Codrington, chief of his department, and fondly known amongst his intimates as Fishpaste.

Over the next few days, safely closeted in Darling's flat, Pat compiled his report on the activities of the Organization and the double-dealing of Paul Cole. When Darling read it he at once asked for the Abbé Carpentier's letter. Rapidly scanning the letter he said: "Well, that's that. No doubt about it, is there? We knew Carpentier well. A remarkable man."

Darling said that a call would go out to all French Resistance workers known to M.I.9 within the next few weeks, informing them that Cole was a traitor. If discovered he should be killed.

"Now what about yourself?" he went on. "Do you want to go on with this work?"

"If you think I'm more useful that way, certainly," Pat said.

"We think you're very useful indeed."

Pat at once plunged into a prearranged statement. Nothing would please him more than continuing to run and develop the Organization, but they needed more support from England, they needed money, a wireless transmitting set, a wireless operator, arms; they foresaw combined sea and air operations carrying "parcels" away *en masse,* but this could not be done without direct contact with London or Gibraltar. The picture Pat drew grew to dazzling proportions and Darling responded enthusiastically.

Three weeks later Jimmy Langley arrived by air from England. Langley, who had lost his left forearm in 1940 and entered Military Intelligence, was very interested to know more about the mysterious Patrick O'Leary. They plunged into talk and discussion. Presently Langley read Pat's report and it was clear to him that Paul Cole bore all the signs of a particularly nasty traitor.

"I gather," Langley said later, "that you want a wireless operator."

"We certainly do."

"I think I have one for you."

So it came about that Pat first met the tall, thin, contradictory Belgian who will be referred to as Feriere. He was something of a shock. Combining characteristics unmistakably bourgeois with a certain nervousness of manner, he didn't seem at all the man to become the wireless operator of an underground organization. When he spoke his voice so perfectly fitted his type that Pat found himself visualizing the suburban family background from which he sprang. At least he opened their conversation with a show of enthusiasm.

"I'm pleased I'm going to work for you. I gather you are doing very interesting work."

"It's very dangerous work."

"You operate in the south?"

"We operate all over France."

There was a moment's hesitation. "In Paris too?"

"Yes."

The change in Feriere's countenance was striking. Struggling to conceal his fear, he only succeeded in making it more evident.

Later Pat said to Langley: "You don't seriously expect me to take that chap over to France, do you?"

"Remember radio operators are scarce," Langley said. "He's been trained, and you haven't tried him yet."

"But his whole character's out of keeping with the job."

Later Pat took Feriere drinking one night and deliberately set out to discover what motives had driven him to volunteer for this job. He found that Feriere, very much in love with his wife, had been parted from her by the war and was hopelessly at a loss. A conventionally sentimental picture representing all the values for which Feriere stood, there was nothing unexpected about it until Pat suddenly said—"And where is she now?"

At this Feriere broke down and disclosed that she was in the south of France, and a long story of guile, courage and ingenuity became clear. Pat felt very angry. The efficiency and security of the Organization was to be jeopardized by a love-sick husband and his ill-conceived plot to rejoin his wife.

92

He went straight to Langley: "This just will not do," he said. "I cannot take him now."

Still Langley reasoned with him. "You must realize that radio operators are scarce and not easily replaced."

"But this man is———"

"He can work a radio set—that's what matters. We'll get him to dinner with Fishpaste and have him thoroughly briefed."

Pat was unconvinced.

"After all, I was very happy even to find you a radio operator," Langley said. "And we have a trawler all ready to take you back to the south coast."

The dinner with Codrington was reasonably successful. Outlining the disciplines which must be followed, Codrington said to Feriere, "You must take orders from O'Leary here, as you would from Whitehall. As for your wife—I'm afraid we cannot allow you to get in touch with her." White-faced, unhappy, poor Feriere listened as his long-matured plan to recover domestic happiness was quietly demolished in its entirety. With a great effort he tried to face up to the situation.

Pat and Feriere left Gibraltar some days later in a disguised trawler. They approached the coast towards Le Canet-Plage without incident. At two in the morning a small boat edged its way inshore from the trawler. This strip of coast, well known to Pat, was probably deserted at that hour. With hardly any sea running and in pitch blackness they slipped ashore and waited. It was a still, warm, starlit night, a night where violence had no place, a beautiful night with only the sound of the sea and an occasional cry from a bird deeper inland. They waited, listening and peering into the darkness, but nothing stirred. A whispered farewell and Pat led the way soundlessly into the sand dunes. He stopped again, listened and reconnoitred. Black shapes were a continual delusion in the dunes. Through the darkness he could feel the fear which radiated from Feriere. He moved on again.

When they were well away from the sea he said: "We'll dig here." With their hands they dug a hole big enough to take the canvas-wrapped transmitter. Then they sought around for a sheltered spot to sleep. Entering the town at that hour was hazardous. Pat lay in the sand beside Feriere and felt the balmy Mediterranean air moving gently over his face. He was back again. The old familiar sights and sounds would merge out of the darkness, the old tensions return, the task of picking up the threads begin with the dawn. What had happened? How many more men had gone over the Pyrenees? What new threats had come to harass their lives? Slowly something more personal dominated everything. Why had he come back to all this? What was it in him which insisted that this was now the only possible way of life . . .? Surface motives were easy enough to find—a dislike of a bully with a gun telling him precisely what to do—but was there some other hidden compulsion . . .? He fell asleep.

Before dawn they woke and moved off towards Canet-Plage. At the first sight of a human being fear came flooding across from Feriere once more, but Pat pressed on. They reached the Hotel du Tennis without incident.

Madame Chouquette—her real name was Lebreton—always had a smile for Pat in her soft brown eyes. Devoted to Pat, her hotel had become a centre of escape activity. She was astonished to see him suddenly emerge from the sea.

"I thought you were in Gibraltar?"

"We came in on the night service."

They spent two days in the Hotel du Tennis. On the third morning, before dawn, they dug out the wireless set and caught the train for Perpignan and Marseille. In the train they held whispered conference standing in the corridor. How were they to get the set past the controls at Marseille? The thought of smuggling a wireless set through a dangerous area reduced Feriere to sudden silence. Quite clearly if anyone was to get it through successfully, it would not be Feriere.

Suddenly a loud voice speaking in a broad Marseille accent said· "Why, Pat! You here! I thought you were in. . . . Pat gestured for silence. The irrepressible Gaston Nègre could never quite believe that the sphere of his influence did not extend from his home in Nîmes to the remotest corner of Marseille. He seemed, if anything, a little fatter, his cheeks were pinker and the inevitable cigarette remained screwed into the corner of his mouth. Lounging in the corridor he smiled comfortably as Pat explained in a quiet voice, lost in the noise of the train, his trouble with the canvas parcel.

Big, booming, without any regard for the elementary laws of secrecy Gaston laughed. "Don't worry, Pat, don't worry! I'll fix that!"

"I'll fix that!" With extraordinary consistency, Gaston always did. Whether it involved spiriting away secret documents from a gendarmerie, forging passes, smuggling prisoners into his house or providing food for half a battalion of escaped British soldiers, he always did what he undertook to do. The comedy was constantly renewed. "The Germans have this new pass for crossing the Line," Pat would say, handing it to Gaston. "Who can forge it best?" "There's the Italian engraver," Gaston would answer, "but he's expensive and I don't think this is his kind of job." Or "There's François, he's better at this kind of design—or should we have the little Jew . . .?" Clearly the mere matter of getting a large transmitter weighing twenty pounds through the controls in a huge station was to him child's play. Precisely how it was done, no one ever asked. Obviously he had some secret method of egress from the station which not even the stationmaster seemed to know. He met Pat two hundred yards from the station, swinging the canvas parcel ostentatiously in his hand and said: "When are you coming to see us? We don't see enough of you."

Everyone was delighted to have Pat back. There was much embracing, hand-shaking and kissing and then they told him the news. Shortly after Pat had left for Gibraltar, another summons had come from Barcelona asking for the second-in-command to report to Geneva at once, Mario Prassinos had set out, run into trouble, and returned. Louis Nouveau then took over, reached Geneva and reported to a very British-looking gentleman who refused to have anything whatever to do with him . . . until he mentioned the name Paul Cole. He then sent a long cipher telegram to London. London immediately wanted to know what Louis thought of the Paul Cole episode and of Patrick O'Leary. Louis had told them in no uncertain terms.

Jean de la Olla and his wife

Robert Leycuras, known as Albert

Celebrating the safe arrival of an R.A.F. pilot (seated, in dark shirt) are Mario Prassinos on the left, and next to him stands the inimitable Gaston Nègre

A street-photographer in Marseille took this photograph of Pat a few days after he had assumed control of the Organization

★ 8 ★

CALLING on Gaston Nègre was always something of an adventure. One never knew who would be there, what kind of party might be going forward, how many local dignitaries were being fed on black-market food. Even amongst the splendours of Gaston's life this evening was somewhat distinctive, for it combined power, spectacle, luxury and danger, in the right proportions to satisfy an Al Capone. Gaston escorted Pat from one end to the other of his huge, rambling, fourteen-roomed "flat". In the first room, gathered about a table heavy with food were a local *juge*, a police official and two other men, drinking champagne. At the other end of the flat, separated by a long corridor, were three Allied pilots, two French Resistance workers and an escaped British prisoner-of-war, eating caviare, drinking expensive wine and combining in a confused rendering of "Roll Out the Barrel". And in Gaston's own rooms Marie the cook and Thérèse the maid had prepared a sumptuous meal for Pat and Gaston. Grinning, Gaston took Pat from one party to the other and as they settled down to a meal which would have done credit to the best Parisian restaurant in the forgotten days of peace and plenty, Gaston said: "It's nice to see my little circus working so well—eh?"

If there was a certain vulgarity in the English eating caviare to the accompaniment of "Roll Out the Barrel", that was in keeping with Gaston's big, bluff self. If Marie the cook had to hurry down to the English and ask them to restrain their song, which threatened to penetrate several thicknesses of wall, that disturbed no one. If the German agent pricked up his ears at the sound of muffled cries and the policeman stopped in mid-career of a champagne gulp, the local *juge* at once said, "The birthday party of Monsieur Nègre's cook. He warned me . . ."

For Gaston, enormously happy with life, the only experience which matched these feasts was to sit far into the night sipping *pastis* with underworld characters who regarded him as a magnificent recruit lost to their cause.

Tonight he said to Pat: "I have the little bit of information you wanted. . . ."

When it came to secret information, the stocks of food in the wholesale warehouse beneath his flat worked wonders. The local official for receiving and distributing food, Gaston had an imaginative interpretation of his responsibilities. "Just take ten tins of beans round to Monsieur —— with my compliments, Marie," he would say, "and tell him I'll call to see him on Wednesday." When Wednesday came Gaston lounged in with the cigarette screwed in the corner of his mouth and said: *"Bonjour . . . bonjour. . . .* Did you get my little present?"

Ten minutes later a reasonably circuitous route led naturally into: "Now I was wondering if you could tell me what time the prison guards are changed up at the fort . . .?"

One such piece of information Gaston now passed over to Pat. The dinner lasted until two the next morning. When Pat left, the sounds of revelry from the English end of the corridor were unabated.

The test rendezvous with London through the new wireless operator Feriere was arranged for six o'clock one March evening. Moving between the flats of Gaston Nègre and Rodocanachi, Feriere was warned that Pat would return to Rodocanachi's at five on the appointed day. Slipping quietly in with his own key, Pat could not at first see any sign of Feriere, but found himself trapped by a tangle of wires which seemed to climb up and round the walls like an elaborate festoon. The trail of wires eventually led him to the bathroom and there sat Feriere, his set precariously balanced on the bath, manipulating the dials as if they were electrically charged. Pat's eye ran enquiringly down the wires covering the sitting-room and Feriere at once explained that this was the very latest method of disposing an aerial for maximum efficiency.

Pat said dryly: "So," and sat down to wait, watching an obviously ill-at-ease Feriere.

The clock crept round and Pat rehearsed the message he wanted to send. At five-to-six he noticed that Feriere had gone very pale and was perspiring. At three minutes to six Feriere's hands were trembling and at six Pat had to urge him into action. Suddenly he burst out: "Now we can be heard!" This so plainly referred to the Germans and not to London, that Pat was furious. "Get on! Get on!" he said. Feriere pressed a number of buttons, but nothing seemed to happen. "Oh, for God's sake," said Pat. "Go away and leave it to me." He snatched up the headset. He could hear London sending their call sign. He began tapping a reply. Two minutes past six, three minutes, four minutes. Suddenly he heard London again and furiously answered. London stopped and there was silence. Pat threw off the headset in a rage. He knew now that Feriere's placing of the aerial had made it impossible for London to pick up the signals. "You bastard!" he said to Feriere and stalked out of the room.

The second test was even worse. Arranged once more for six, Feriere simply did not turn up. At a quarter past, Pat still sat fuming in the small room glaring at the dead set. At seven he was busy with other work, reading a letter from Jean de la Olla, thinking of the various beaches from which they could make the mass embarkations they were planning, wondering where he should next meet the Greeks Mario Prassinos and Leoni Savinos. At eight Feriere arrived, white and panting. He had missed his train from Nîmes, caught the next one and run all the way from the station. Clearly fear had made him miss the train and Pat now knew that no amount of experience or training would ever convert him into the kind of radio operator they required. Ignoring Feriere, Pat walked out into the night. Fear, he reflected, was no new phenomenon, but it was a luxury they could not afford when it paralysed a wireless operator.

Some days later he decided to meet Feriere's wife. She turned out to be a very pleasant middle-class Belgian woman who was astounded to hear that her husband had volunteered for such a job. "The trouble is," she said, "he loves me. I'm sure that's why he did it."

"Well, look," Pat said. "I'm going to arrange for you to meet one another—but you must not say a word to anyone. We cannot have so much as a whisper going around. Then I'll have you both sent back to England as soon as possible. I'm afraid your husband is no good to me."

It was Paula who arranged the rendezvous. The daughter of a German M.P. who had left Germany when Hitler came to power, she had volunteered to work as Pat's secretary and now took over much of his paper and some liaison work. She carried messages along the coast from one agent to another, acted as liaison between Madame Mongelard, Gaston Nègre and Pat, and once, when Pat fell ill, nursed him through it devotedly, quite unaware that her sensible, down-to-earth cures were inflicted on a doctor.

Once more without a radio operator, Pat turned to the infallible Gaston Nègre and was greeted with the same cheerfully assured answer.

"A wireless man—but of course, Pat—you shall have one tomorrow."

Miraculously, Pat was introduced to Roger, a French radio operator who once worked for a French aerodrome on the outskirts of Nîmes and was now jobless. In the small Nîmes bar Gaston ordered *pastis*, and as his geniality expanded, more *pastis* followed, the talk flowed freely, and Roger came to understand the nature of the work he was asked to undertake. Two hours later, he accepted the job. So, at last one night, the first message came in from far-distant London, and Pat knew that he now had the whole brains of M.I.9 at his back ready for any emergency call. It was a reassuring thought.

There presently arrived from London a familiar figure —Jean Nitelet—the dashing young Belgian pilot who had fought with the R.A.F. and passed through the Organization's hands when his plane was shot down. With his one blind eye, the R.A.F. could no longer accept him for flying duties when he returned to England, and he had at once volunteered for special duties with Organization Pat. He was to be wireless operator, air evacuation officer, and attempt to set up an escape route by sea through Brittany. Flying back to France one dark night in a Lysander, he at once ran into trouble again. The plane came down in a field, the pilot tried to take off and failed, and no amount of jettisoning spares and equipment seemed to do any good. The engine roared, the frame of the plane shook and vibrated, but it remained immutably still. Brushwood was thrown beneath the wheels, the engine throttled to its lowest pitch, the gentlest acceleration tried, and the Maquis reception party heaved and pushed, all without avail. By now the Germans were approaching the area and the Maquis were not anxious to shoot it out. There was only one thing left to do—burn the plane and disappear. Petrol was sprinkled over the wings, tail and undercarriage, and as everyone scattered, the plane burst into flames. Nitelet arrived safely at Louis Nouveau's flat one night but the pilot was captured, taken south under armed guard and imprisoned in La Turbie.

Nitelet became a great asset. Enormously vital, active and self-reliant, he could fulfil many difficult roles and Pat was rapidly approaching the time when he needed all-round men. Installed in a flat next to the Italian Consulate half a mile from the Rodocanachis', he received and transmitted messages through an intermediary to Pat. All lines leading to Pat were now broken at a certain stage as a double precaution. Nitelet also brought to bear all the technical devices of the fully trained wireless operator.

More than three messages were never sent from any one flat, and Nitelet kept constantly on the move from flat to flat with a wide variety of disguises for transporting the set. The German detectors were so sensitive that they could identify a given "touch" within a few broadcasts. Nitelet set out to confuse this by tapping first with the left and then the right hand, alternatively using finger and thumb. All messages were in code and nothing could be understood without the code. Far more subtle, whenever a radio operator transmitted freely and not at the command of someone who might have arrested him, he always made deliberate and prearranged mistakes in certain key letters. When these mistakes did not occur they knew in London that the operator was being forced to transmit. How vital such measures were became very clear within a few months.

Nitelet brought from London instructions for three special missions, one of which Pat now passed over to Louis Nouveau. It is impossible to convey the extent and intricacy of Nouveau's work in the following months but as a veteran agent he had more success to his credit than anyone, revealed immense audacity and, at this stage, knew more about the Organization than any other member.

Pat's encounter with the French double agent occurred about this time. A young man giving his name as François Dulais had come into the Petit Poucet one day and let it be known that he could feed the Organization with details of German counter-activities in the north.

Pat said he did not deal in counter-espionage, but would think it over. He saw Vidal some days later and mentioned the young Frenchman and his odd proposition. Vidal was at once alert. "What's he like?" he asked. Pat described him. "Wait a bit . . ." Vidal said, and after rummaging in a back room produced a photograph. "Yes, that's him," said Pat.

"That man tried to pierce my Organization two months ago," Vidal said. "We have proof that he's a German agent. He must not get away."

It was arranged that Pat should invite Dulais to Port Vendres on one pretext or another and two of Vidal's men would be waiting. Pat met the young Frenchman in the Petit Poucet again.

"I think there may be something in this after all," he said. "I want you to come and talk to two other members of my Organization in Port Vendres."

It was an uneasy journey along the coast. Arriving at Port Vendres Pat explained that it wasn't safe to meet in the town and they must go some distance into the mountains where his men would be waiting. Confronted by two swarthy, tough-looking Spaniards, the Frenchman suddenly became suspicious, but it was too late. They surrounded him and began to question him. Ruthlessly, the Spaniards pressed home one question after another, revealing such an intimate knowledge of his movements for the past three months that the Frenchman at last broke down. Hoping for mercy he then admitted that he had worked for the Gestapo in Paris where he was employed solely to trace the British escape organization, but this meant that he could in turn dupe the Germans, and pass on to Pat. . . . He spoke eagerly and urgently, and there was fear in his eyes. The shorter of the two Spaniards broke in mournfully: "We must kill you." The Frenchman caught Pat by the coat, pleading for protection. Then he fell on his knees, burst into tears and begged for mercy. The Spaniards looked at Pat, clearly asking for his decision.

Pat saw the boy, swaying from side to side, tears streaming down his face and pity stirred. Then he remembered the last time he had permitted pity to intervene with Paul Cole and the appalling consequences. The place where they stood was isolated. The early slopes of the mountains gave upon great peaks rising sharply against a serene sky, the air was still and crisp, the sea in the distance a great glittering disc. It was not an evening for violence but Pat made no move to defend the boy, and at last, while the hard eyes of the Spaniards remained fixed on him, the Frenchman screamed and tried to run. They caught him and one held his arms while the other jabbed powerfully at his throat with the edge of his hand. Slowly, systematically, they strangled him. When his face was blue and distorted and consciousness almost gone they carried him to a spot above a ravine. There they shot him through the head. The shot echoed dangerously round the hillsides. Immediately they removed all papers and identity marks and sent the body crashing fifty feet down into the ravine. Then they separated and carefully made their way back to Port Vendres. It was dark as Pat entered the outskirts.

A second stranger came among them claiming to be in touch with the Germans. Tall, blond and boyish looking, he said he had in his possession a copy of one of the key German Naval codes which he was prepared to sell for a million francs. He elaborated the events which brought this priceless document into his hands until it sounded like the perfect confidence trick. Pat met him several times in the Petit Poucet. Negotiations drifted on. Presently Pat decided that it was too dangerous to continue their meetings. He could not really believe this man's fantastic story and the stranger, who called himself Pierre, refused to hand over the code for examination before receiving payment. Six months later, in the hands of the Gestapo, Pat learned that the blond young man did indeed have a copy of a Naval code worth considerably more than a million francs. The Gestapo had spent weeks combing France for him.

★ 9 ★

THE arrest of Leoni Savinos came in April 1942. Pat pieced together one version of the story some time afterwards. A Greek of immense drive and intelligence, with marked resemblances to a younger Tito, Savinos had played the part of interpreter between General Plastiras, then living in the south of France, and Nosek, a high-ranking S.S. officer suspected of belonging to the Gestapo. The Germans were very anxious to win the Greek general over to their side and found Savinos' fluent German indispensable to the subtle blandishments they employed. Granted an official pass between Marseille and Paris, Savinos had carried out a number of daring missons for Pat under its guise. But suddenly one day things went wrong. He had arranged to meet one of the agents of another Organization at a kiosk in the Gare Montparnasse. It was a very hot day, trains were delayed and the meeting was thrown into some confusion. Leoni at last encountered his assistant, Pierrot Lanvers, and they went together into the buffet to wait for the unknown agent. Against all instructions, the agent, when he came in, went up and spoke to them, saying that he would be with his wife in the waiting-room. A few minutes later the Gestapo descended. They cornered Leoni and Pierrot at pistol point, and demanded the identity and business of the man who had spoken to them. Neither knew his identity and had no intention of giving away his business.

Savinos, always sure of himself and contemptuous of Gestapo thugs, threw at them in perfect German again and again: "I do not know his name. I have never met him in my life before." Truth gave this enormous force, but he and Pierrot were rushed off to Fresnes prison near Paris. Pierrot Lanvers was savagely beaten up and the same fate would have awaited Savinos but for the pass they found in his pocket. There were many things in his pockets—the key of Prassinos' flat, the plan of a factory making vital accessories for German fighter planes, a photograph of a Belgian officer wanted by the Germans, £1,500 in francs and the official pass. One by one Savinos explained away each object. The key was just the key of a flat; the plan carried the actual name of the German fighter plane but it was a name resembling a commercial product, and Savinos claimed that he was trading between the two zones. When they came to the pass he said: "If you want to know how I got that—ask Nosek."

This bold reference to a revered German name known to his inquisitors made them hesitate. They decided to check back on his story. Parts they found to be true, parts uncheckable, but Nosek himself not only knew this man; he said he was coming to Paris and would interrogate him personally. For weeks Savinos lived in a damp, dirty cell with a straw palliasse and little food. They continued to beat up Lanvers in the hope of squeezing out of him what he did not in fact know. Savinos lost weight rapidly but was busy, very busy, inventing conversations between Nosek and himself, exploring every possible avenue with a variety of answers. Granted a mind as subtle as it was powerful he foresaw one possibility after another and steadily moved towards a plan of action.

Nosek smiled when he met him. "Well, you have got yourself in a mess, haven't you?" he said. Then came the stream of questions, cold, deliberate, probing every detail. For a long time Nosek clearly did not know whether Savinos had abused the protection of his pass or not, but slowly, deftly, with hardly a false move, the conversation came round in the direction which pleased Savinos. Here was a man who spoke French and German fluently, who was in touch with an underground Organization and prepared, it seemed, to sell his services to the highest bidder. An ideal man to act as a German agent. At last, by whose will it was difficult to say, Nosek put the proposition that Leoni should act for the Germans, find out everything about Organization Pat and report back. Allowing just the right interval for reflection, Savinos at last agreed. It would have been interesting enough as an interview if it had stopped there, but the real subtleties arose when Nosek sought to establish the inevitable safeguards.

"As you know," he said, "we cannot afford to trust anyone, and it will be necessary to hold a hostage in the interests of your loyalty."

"Who will that be?"

"Your wife."

Savinos fell silent. It was said that somewhere in the Gestapo records his wife figured as a passionate anti-Nazi. It might be fatal if they arrested her.

"Doesn't it make sense to you that I could never operate without suspicion in the south if you release me and arrest my wife?" he said.

Nosek considered this. Savinos had come to the conclusion that Nosek was a man who regarded his own mind as subtle and was quite prepared to examine any subtlety presented to him. Savinos elaborated the point. Slowly he convinced Nosek that he could not operate freely as an agent if his wife were arrested.

"Very well then," said Nosek at last. "We'll hold Pierrot Lanvers instead."

This was much more formidable. There seemed no valid reason why they should not do their worst to Pierrot, imprison him, torture him, transfer him to the usual concentration camp in Germany. With Teutonic patience and logic, Savinos now tried to question the expediency of this too. He started from the assumption that a stool-pigeon must return to its nest without arousing any kind of suspicion whatever. He must be quite without blemish. He pointed out that Pierrot was his assistant. There was something very odd about releasing the leader and holding the assistant of two arrested agents. It might easily seem sufficiently curious to the people in the south to arouse their suspicion and—he could not repeat it enough —it was impossible to penetrate their inner councils without having their complete confidence.

Unless he returned to a situation exactly resembling that which he had left he could not guarantee to work efficiently. They wrangled for some time. Nosek sought fresh guarantees. Nothing seemed to offer itself. Perhaps he knew that other agents would keep careful check on Leoni whatever happened, and hostages didn't gravely matter; perhaps, if he suspected double bluff, he felt that he could cover that too in the end, but quite clearly he did not want to lose the opportunity of creating a perfect counter-agent.

In the end he agreed to release Pierrot. Superficially it was a remarkable feat. A German agent had slowly given every point to a man lately arrested on suspicion of espionage. Savinos was himself free and had won the freedom of his assistant. Clearly there must be some double cunning within all this. Pierrot could not believe it when they came to his cell in Fresnes prison and told him he was free to go. Still in great pain from his beating up, his face swollen, his teeth broken, his body covered in bruises, immediately he found himself outside Fresnes he ran for it. He had been told to collect his papers, but driven by an appalling fear that he might be arrested and beaten up again he set off for the south without papers of any kind. The inevitable check on the train quickly brought him under suspicion and arrest once more. If his story had elements of originality, it remained to the police nothing more than an ingenious fabrication. Pierrot was thrown into prison again, suffered fresh and appalling nightmares, and as one week grew into another, began to think that he was doomed. Six weeks elapsed before confirmation of his story came through, his papers were returned and a haggard Pierrot once more staggered out to freedom and made his way back to Marseille.

Immediately Pat arranged to transfer Leoni and Pierrot to London. Two more valuable agents were lost to the Organization and a deceptive subtlety marked their going.

Roger was arrested next. In the very act of receiving a message from London, the French wireless operator felt a pistol at his back and was dragged off to jail. Pat did not hear of his arrest for two days. In that time he could not understand why no messages were coming from London. Nitelet was away on a special mission. Who could he send to find out what had happened? He thought of Paula, remembered her German nationality and fell back on a woman called Rambaud who volunteered to act as go-between. She, in turn, simply disappeared into the void and sent no message back; but within twenty-four hours Pat knew the truth.

Like every other minor arrest Roger's was quickly overwhelmed by the pressure of events. Pat never knew exactly what happened to him. Anxiety, feeling were once more stifled at their source, but two arrests like this . . . Pat had lately been sleeping only four or five hours a night. Now he slept with his gun under his pillow. Everyone was warned to move with the utmost caution. Mario Prassinos —who never quite overcame his nerves—was very upset by the news. Many others were suddenly tense.

Before his arrest Roger had tapped out a message in code to London: "Everything ready for first shipment—can you send ship?" And in due course the reply had come: *"Les carottes sont cuites."* Translated into slang it meant: "It's all up." Translated into code it meant: "All arrangements have been made."

They were now in touch with several groups of English prisoners in Nîmes, Montpellier and at Fort de la Revère. A Polish priest, the Abbé Myrda, took communion in the prisons and kept lines of communication open. More important Pat was also in touch with Tony Friend, a police officer, in turn in touch with Val Boroushkine, a physical training instructor at Fort de la Revère.

Pat knew that London badly wanted Squadron-Leader Higginson (alias Bennett), a prisoner in la Revère, back in the R.A.F. One cryptic message after another had been smuggled to and fro between Boroushkine, Nitelet and Pat until a date—August 6 at nine in the evening—was fixed for Higginson and four others to make a break.

Detail by detail, each step was planned, one step dovetailing with the next until a long chain reached from Fort de la Revère to Marseille, from Marseille to a beach near Canet-Plage and from there to Gibraltar. Agents were alerted all along the coast and security tightened. Only three key members were told the precise night on which embarkation would take place.

It was arranged to co-ordinate the escape of the men from the fort with the arrival of fresh R.A.F. pilots sent down by Jean de la Olla from Paris. The whole party was expected to total forty persons and every kind of hazard threatened quite such a wholesale attempt to outwit the Germans at a single stroke.

Among the men coming from the north would be Postel Vinet. A very cultured man, tall, thin, bespectacled, he had worked for Garrow and Pat in Paris over many months and then one morning he went to a rendezvous at the Café Aux deux Magots. Two Gestapo agents came strolling in, suddenly changed the direction of their walk, went swiftly to his table and arrested him at the pistol point. There are at least three versions of what followed. As Pat remembers the story, Vinet paced his cell in Fresnes for many hours, waiting for the torture to begin, and quickly found himself in a state of appalling stress.

Somewhere among the papers they had taken from him was a small notebook which contained, among other things, the code names of certain agents. There were no addresses, no detailed information, but he knew that when the torture began he might easily break down and disclose enough to endanger the lives of many people. Vinet was an intellectual scrupulously following principles distilled from years of thought, reading and experience, and now, pacing his minute cell, he decided that suicide was better than betrayal. In great mental anguish he tried to determine how he would kill himself. All the cells of Fresnes opened on a balcony with a courtyard thirty feet below. He could easily throw himself down.

There followed a long and terrible interval. At last he steeled himself to the act, jumped from the balcony and crashed to the stone floor of the courtyard. He was horribly injured, his spine fractured, his pelvis and one thigh broken, but as he lay moaning the guards came rushing into the courtyard, handcuffed him and bundled him back into another cell without troubling to find out why he screamed as they lifted him. Then pain was swallowed in unconsciousness and he lay on the concrete floor without medical attention for two days.

No one will know just what it meant. He had attempted annihilation to escape a pain he could not face and only succeeded in inflicting worse injuries upon himself; he had tried to make betrayal finally impossible and now was incapable of bearing any further torture at all. The weeks that followed became blurred. He knew that he was in hospital, he knew many things were happening, and dreadful pain alternated with complete blackouts.

Six months later, under the care of a German doctor in the Val de Grace Infirmary, he showed signs of recovery. The doctor spoke a little French, was fascinated by the great French writers and talked of novels, poetry and criticism with considerable insight. At length when Vinet could just walk he said one day: "Come down to my office. We can talk better there."

There was a guard outside the door of his office, but Vinet noticed that the main doors to the street were not far away. Their talk ran its course for half an hour with the doctor continuing to treat Vinet's back, when suddenly he said, "Excuse me. I'll be back in a minute." He went away and time slipped by. Vinet became absorbed by the furnishings of the office and then suddenly he thought of the street just beyond the corridor, and the Paris he had not seen all these months.

It happened again on his next visit. The doctor talking, treating him, and excusing himself for one minute to stay away for ten. Vinet could hardly walk, he was very weak and he needed the help of sticks wherever he went. Could it possibly be that the doctor was encouraging him to try to escape, or did he believe it impossible for a physical wreck to carry out any such plan? Vinet determined that if he was granted another visit with the doctor once more absent, he would see what lay outside the door.

It did happen again. The doctor smiled and excused himself. Abandoning his sticks, Vinet walked carefully towards the door expecting to find a guard outside. There was no one. He waited a moment, watching every door, and in that moment he saw some workmen who had just completed repairs, coming down the corridor. They were walking slowly and he slipped out and followed them. Keeping his face averted as he passed the inquiry clerk, he remained close enough to the workmen to be mistaken for one of them.

Hobbling along he knew he had no time to spare and no energy to hurry. A terrible feeling of weakness and strangeness assailed him in the open air. A crowd of small boys came down the street, inclined to jeer at the old man. Rapidly explaining that he had just escaped from the Germans and needed money to travel on the Metro, Vinet saw the boys excitedly put together a few francs, took them, and certain that the doctor had returned to his office by now, felt his way down the steps, clinging to the rail, trying desperately to control his wavering feet. He took the first train and sank back exhausted. He was nearly asleep when it arrived at the terminus. Struggling up from his seat he made his way into the station, and accosted an old lady. Once more he explained his plight and asked for money to telephone. She gave him just enough. In the café with the telephone, his reserves of strength were almost gone. A fit of nerves made him dial the wrong number. Presently it seemed impossible to get the right one, objects were beginning to waver before his eyes and a terrible faintness assailed him. Staggering back to the Metro he found the stationmaster and once again explained his situation. The stationmaster helped him to hide in a closet in the station while he went off to telephone Vinet's sister. Later that night she came and took him away. Six weeks later he arrived on the Line in Marseille and met Pat. Then began the wait for the ship which would carry him away to safety with forty others.

There were to be six of these mass sea embarkations. One from Port Miou, one from St. Pierre Plage, another from Canet-Plage. As yet, the precise hazards involved were unknown.

★ IO ★

SQUADRON LEADER HIGGINSON chose two officers, Barnet and
and Hawkins, and two sergeants, Nabarro and the New
Zealander Hicky—to accompany him on the break from
Fort de la Revère at nine one evening, an hour when the
guards, safely through the day, relaxed, and Pat's men
could take up positions near the fort. The five men would
fiddle the lock of the cookhouse, slide down the coal chute
leading to the kitchen, lever back the iron bars which
gave on to the moat, drop into it and crawl through a
sewer. The usual diversion would be created simultaneously in the prison itself. One difficulty remained. The
bars of the kitchen did not look as if they would yield
easily. To meet any emergency, Nabarro devised a bar-
bending instrument from a strong piece of wood and an
iron magnet, once the heart of a camp loudspeaker.

At a quarter to nine on the appointed day a guard
accosted Nabarro in the sergeants' quarters and began
bargaining over a length of French bread. It was very
beautiful bread, he said, the best bread baked in France;
it was a brand of bread considered a luxury in the camp,
it had near whiteness, the taste . . . his fingers snapped
expressively—and it was going dirt cheap. As the minutes
slipped away the terrible fear that this man would still
be there at nine o'clock suddenly assailed Nabarro. One
of the group listening to the Frenchman's sales talk suddenly bellowed: "I said too bloody dear at any bloody
price!" and the guard, nonplussed, said: "Temper—
temper." Then he looked at Nabarro more closely:

"All dressed up—where do you think you're going
tonight?"

In a flash of comedy, Nabarro told the truth: "We're
off to Nice for the night," and the guard threw back his
head and roared with laughter.

A party had been organized to divert attention, and at nine precisely a skeleton key unlocked the door of the cookhouse; they heaved a mass of barbed wire from the mouth of the coal chute, swiftly knotted a bed sheet round an iron bar and began the descent into the kitchen. Nabarro slipped and crashed to the floor. Everyone froze as the crash seemed to send echoes back into the fort. A whispered "Are you hurt?"—a blasphemous reassurance and the next one went down. Already Nabarro was busy with the bars of the window and found the gap between the stonework and the top of the bars dangerously narrow. He could not get his bending instrument to work. By sheer brute force he bent one bar slightly, slipped in his instrument and levered with all his strength. The bar gave, but the space left was still too small to crawl through. Higginson suggested bending the instrument itself backwards and forwards. In silence they watched Nabarro bend first one bar and then another. In silence they saw his instrument show signs of strain and then, as the third bar was dealt with, the iron magnet groaned ominously. Sweating, he tackled the fourth bar and the instrument sent out a cracking noise. He stopped. The wooden lever was working loose. On the fifth bar the lever broke, but by now there was room enough to crawl through.

They paused. The voice of a prisoner observing the moat near the drawbridge sang out his favourite ditty— a signal that the moat could safely be crossed. It was a considerable drop from the window to the dry bed of the moat, and the arc lamps converted it into a white river in which the slightest shadow would stand out sharply. Worse still they had no more than thin cords wound together for the second rope. Nabarro, the first man down, felt the cords sear his hands, then his feet touched ground. He gave a flick on the "rope", crouched for a moment against the fort wall and darted across, a silver flash gone in a second. Four other flashes followed in quick succession. Panting, they entered the mouth of the tunnel. At once a gust of stinking vapour rose with suffocating force. Ignoring it Nabarro pressed on to reconnoitre the full length of the tunnel, able at first to walk upright, then crouching and at last on hands and knees slithering through the foul accumulation which generated gases of lethal power. Rats scampered out of his way. The smell became overwhelming. Then the gleam of light at the end was broken by something. There was an iron grating over the mouth of the sewer. It looked like disaster. The bending instrument was broken, the tunnel very narrow and the fumes asphyxiating. One hope remained. They carried with them an old hacksaw blade provided by Father Myrda and Organization Pat.

In the next twenty minutes each man took his turn at the mouth of the tunnel, sawing furiously. It could not be long to roll call now. Possibly a faked voice would deceive the guards for a time, but it was unlikely.

The hacksaw broke. They looked at one another. Was this the end again? Higginson suggested levering their feet against the grating in an attempt to break the half-cut bars and burst through into the open. A tremendous heave and the rotten stonework collapsed, the bars split outwards and they staggered through, swallowing the fresh air in great gulps.

What happened in the next few hours has been recorded in Nabarro's fascinating book *Wait for the Dawn*.* The rush through the terraced vineyards and jagged boulders; torches flashing to life on the hill as the alarm was given; dogs baying and the sudden stretch of thorn bushes which tore at their clothing and skin and momentarily brought them to a standstill. There was a road which was really a track winding steeply down, and then a tunnel which might have police waiting inside; there were motor-cycle patrols and police cars beginning to race through the night; the whole countryside was stirring out of the beginnings of sleep. They came across a number of cultivated gardens, and once they dived into bushes as a car raced by, and then they were searching for the rendezvous with Pat.

It was still unidentified twenty minutes later. Endlessly the search went on until the shapes became less familiar, the countryside more hazy, the repetition of gardens and

* Cassell, 1952.

vines steadily more confusing in the near darkness of a moonless night. What had familiarity in daylight was hopelessly different after dark. Thirty minutes later, exhausted, they held quick conference. . . . Try to hide up for the rest of the night and send off the best-dressed man in the dawn equipped with their single set of forged papers in search of Pat—that was the best thing to do, Higginson said. They found cover behind some bushes over the mouth of one of the tunnels, and crouched there, watching the lights flashing on the hills. All four smelt appallingly and no amount of brushing relieved the stink. They were filthy, depressed and badly in need of a drink.

The night dragged on. The lights, the police cars and the sound of the dogs subsided; peace came warm and close on the scented hillsides of Provence; the shrilling cicadas dwindled, the glimmering plain blackened, the remnants of a medieval castle vanished, and at last an uneasy likeness of sleep overtook Hawkins, Nabarro, Hicky and Barnet, while Higginson took the first watch.

Crouched in the shadow of some bushes, Tony Friend and Jean Nitelet waited for the signal of the prisoners remaining in the fort singing "Tipperary". From where they were hidden they should just be able to pick up the strains. Suddenly there were footsteps. There had been no singing, no preliminary signal, and now footsteps might mean anything. They were uncertain footsteps which could belong to a man trying to escape in unfamiliar country, or . . . "C'est toi Bennett?" Nitelet whispered. There was the suspicion of a hiccup quickly stifled, the footsteps paused and then wandered off as a very French voice muttered something unintelligible in a Marseille accent. A guard. . . . A guard returning to the fort after an evening's drinking. It seemed disastrous. But the man passed on.

Presently the strains of "Tipperary" came distantly from the fort. More footsteps and voices exclaiming—the unmistakable voices of guards probably sent out by the returning reveller. Friend and Nitelet rushed away. They cut straight down across open country, over the winding path which led to the fort, rejoining it again at another point and—there were the guards waiting for them. There was a short struggle and they were handcuffed and hurried through the night. When the guards saw that Friend carried police papers from Monaco police station they were astonished. He brusquely stated that he and Nitelet were on police business and this arrest was an outrage. The guards hurriedly released them.

Pat met Nitelet very early the following morning and heard the news. He had himself been challenged in his hotel room by gendarmes searching for Jews and asked to show evidence of circumcision or otherwise.

Before the dawn Higginson made the first dismaying discovery. They were not where they should be; they were not on the outskirts of Monte Carlo at all. The nearest station, clearly visible as the sun came up, was Cap d'Ail. Hawkins swiftly put his clothes and shoes into whatever order was possible, and full of a confidence no longer shared by the others set off with the words: "Expect help some time this afternoon." He left a tired, evil-smelling group of men who shifted uncomfortably in the filth that covered them, and now referred to escape organizations in lurid terms.

The tea-shop rendezvous given in Monte Carlo was owned by the Misses Trenchard—Grace and Susie—two angular, grey-haired Scots ladies thrilled to be involved in underground work and regarding Pat as a Resistance God. They saw Hawkins walking towards the shop early next morning with considerable relief. Waiting inside the shop were Pat, Nitelet, and Wattebled—a seasoned agent. The three at once hurried back to Cap d'Ail with Hawkins, found the bushes above the tunnel and Higginson emerged stinking of human excrement as he stood in a bed of the most beautiful Mediterranean flowers.

In the bushes Pat opened two suitcases and handed round trousers, jackets, ties and shoes. Next they split into pairs and Pat moved off with Nabarro—asking the usual routine questions as he went—place shot down—circumstances—type of plane, name, number and rank, as he headed straight along the beach to a villa specially hired by Tony Friend.

By nightfall the escapees had been gathered at the villa. Pat left explicit instructions. They must keep the blinds drawn, never answer the door, make as little noise as possible and never go out. Once more the hue and cry must subside before the final steps were taken. In the following week meals were delivered by the Misses Trenchard, and the five men played cards, smoked, lazed, steadily reaching a stage of almost hysterical boredom. There were times when they craved the activity of prison-camp life, when the long restless nights seemed unendurable. Accustomed to physical danger in quite different circumstances, this small, private world with its alien tensions extended different defences.

Ten, eleven, twelve, the days crept towards the time limit Pat had given, and at last one day they were ready for the next step. In twos, once more, with intervals of a day, they set off for Marseille, Pat escorting Nabarro. Police were still checking the trains and they had to proceed with the utmost caution. Once a ticket inspector eyed them curiously, examined their tickets and seemed on the point of engaging Nabarro in conversation. Then he passed on.

Reaching the platform at Marseille, Nabarro was suddenly aware of a short, olive-skinned man hurrying towards them, but Pat showed no alarm. A brief signal and the man talked volubly in subdued French to Pat, whose face looked suddenly grave. The man went as swiftly as he had come and Pat seemed less inclined to talk afterwards. He had just received news from a very disturbed Mario Prassinos of the arrest of Nitelet and Gaston Nègre. Gaston, the big, bluff, grinning Gaston, miraculously protected against all those ills which overtook lesser men— arrested! It was impossible. But Mario had the story in detail. . . . The plane from London arriving at two in the morning to parachute the special supplies to the triangle of men waiting below; Nitelet and Gaston rushing furiously from the moonlit fields to the woods with one heavy container after another; all running smoothly just as Pat had arranged until the guards burst out of the woods, and arrested both at the pistol point. Mario dashing half-clothed into the darkness as the police arrived to investigate the rambling mystery of Gaston's grocery store; and a sleepless, dishevelled Mario appearing at Marseille station next morning to inform Pat.

Pat mentioned the arrests to Nabarro. "We'll get over it," he said, feeling less optimistic than he sounded. It was bad; very bad; but nothing must deflect his attention from the detailed workings of the mass shipments. Once more Nabarro, Hawkins and Higginson went into hiding, divided between the flats of Rodocanachi and Louis Nouveau. Once more the half-imprisonment in surroundings comparatively luxurious revived the boredom, the desire for any kind of action.

Presently the lines between Tony Friend in Monaco and Val Boroushkine in la Revère were tapping again. Encouraged by their first success, Pat now sent messages arranging a second and even bigger break-out. It did not work quite according to plan.

Within forty-eight hours of Higginson's escape the remaining officers had been transferred to a prison camp in Italy where conditions were far worse. Deprived of normal leadership a group of aircrew sergeants automatically took over, and if the plans were not altogether subtle, they achieved a wholesale character which none but the boldest mind could have envisaged with any hope of success. They managed to chip away one of the stones from the wall dividing the occupied from the unoccupied part of the fort, and within a week of the sewer escape, sixty men burst through the hole, rushed into the empty rooms and went over the wall, some slithering down ropes to the moat, some using sheets, some, confronted with the drop, simply falling down in the rush of excitement and others deliberately jumping. A cascade of human beings flowed down the wall, to land in a struggling heap in the moat before making off in all directions, leaving behind two men screaming from the pain of broken limbs. Sixty men made the first jump. Only thirty-four reached the prearranged hideouts. It was a wasteful method but the news of thirty-four escapes at a single stroke gave Pat great pleasure.

Yet now the flow of escaping men threatened to choke every hideout and block the escape routes simultaneously, with a maddened commandant browbeating the guards into a frenzy of activity. The whole countryside was suddenly alive with guards, gendarmes, and dogs.

Clearly the interval between going into hiding and crossing the frontier had to be extended. All the men crowding hideouts along the coast heard the news with a certain indifference. What did another two weeks matter? But as the days slipped away, one week grew into two and the third week of hidden life in the strict confines of a flat began, restlessness broke through. Complexions became wax-like, eyes clouded, and a once superficial acquaintance with one another deepened as enforced community took its toll.

Twenty-one days after Higginson, Nabarro and Hawkins made their breakaway, Pat arrived at Louis Nouveau's flat and said all was ready for the final step. His mind was crowded with fresh worries, but nothing must stop the sea-convoy from going through smoothly. What incriminating papers the police had found on Nitelet or Nègre he did not know. What was happening to them he dare not, at this stage, think. Precautions were intensified, every agent freshly alert. The despatch of the prisoners dominated everything.

Once more in pairs the escapees left to catch the train to Perpignan, and Higginson found it wonderful to be walking freely in the streets again, hearing people talk, his eyes full of fresh sights, colours and faces. All carried the usual forged papers. All were carefully disguised in true French fashion and the journey to Perpignan began. Three weeks instead of the usual ten days had sufficed to dampen the ardours of the search. From the train they watched the vines, the trees golden in the sun, the land burnished to the colour of brass, and the rich, slow Mediterranean at its most brilliant blue.

At Perpignan, Higginson found some difficulty in keeping a straight face as they left the train, for there were no less than twenty other passengers all clothed in quite convincing French fashion and all completely familiar. Leaving hideouts scattered along half the length of the south coast they had come together and now—dangerously —were concentrating on the same day in Perpignan. Widely distributed down the queue they passed through the barrier at Perpignan and began to make their way according to plan towards a villa on the beach at Canet-Plage. At long intervals, in dribs and drabs, they continued arriving at the villa until thirty men were crowded into a space intended for four or five. There were many English, Free French, Poles, Belgians, a nondescript person or two whose national origins were vague, and the sick, pale, crippled Postel Vinet. Food was shuttled to the villa in stealthy relays from Madame Chouquette's Hotel du Tennis, and everyone waited for zero hour.

Due to leave France at the same time, Paula, Pat's German-born secretary, was staying at the Hotel du Tennis, and as she saw the men coming in she grew steadily more troubled. A sudden horror of being German and of going to a Britain dedicated to fighting the German nation to the death overtook her. Pat reassured her. M.I.5 knew her story, her heroism in the Organization, her anti-Nazi record. But doubt, nostalgia, and a sudden desire to remain in the world she seemed to have known half a lifetime, brought her to the verge of tears. At first Pat reasoned with her and then, as her tears flowed, he became annoyed. Presently they were eating a magnificent dinner at the Hotel du Tennis, and Pat continually refilled Paula's glass with nothing less than champagne. By the time she left to go to the villa she was feeling so much better that she almost sang.

Shortly after midnight Pat made his way by a circuitous route towards the villa. At 12.30 he briefly explained the operation to the thirty men and one woman overflowing the four small rooms.

"First of all, absolute quiet is essential. When we leave here, we will move singly in file at intervals of twelve feet.

If there is any trouble, or any sign of a stranger, dive flat on the sand and stay there until we clear things up. But there shouldn't be any trouble—that is, if our information and calculations are correct."

They left at a quarter-past one. A silent trek along the sea in the shadow of the sand dunes. Paula was almost comatose. She felt herself sleep-walking, but at the back of her mind was the knowledge that the break was about to come, and an overpowering sense of what lay unknown beyond set her tears flowing again. By the time they reached the rendezvous she was crying to herself.

Absolute quiet now became imperative. Somewhere higher up the beach the night was full of danger; no one knew what guards might suddenly appear, and even the casual customs officer spelt every kind of peril. It did not need massed guards suddenly ambushing the whole caval-cade to bring disaster; it needed only one man detecting the shadows almost hidden between the dunes.

A pause. A careful scrutiny of the sea and the coast. Then three blue flashes sent out to sea by Pat in quick succession. Another pause when no one breathed and only the sound of the sea against the sand broke the silence. A single answering flash came back. A whisper ran through the group huddled in the sand. After fifteen agonized minutes of waiting and listening an ordinary rowing-boat nosed gently shorewards. Twice the boat came and went and the silent group diminished. At last it was Paula's turn. Suddenly and vehemently she did not want to go. She simply stood there crying, and Pat picked her up and put her in the boat. As it disappeared into the night the three agents moved stealthily back along the beach. Thirty men had been shipped away to England with the smooth efficiency of a peace-time touring agency. It was a calm, beautiful night, the stars shone, the sea whispered, and a glittering phosphorescence ran along the crest of each small wave before it broke. On such a night the sense of security was reinforced by sheer beauty; but it was all too perfect to be true.

On board the trawler Paula slept as deeply as she had ever slept in her life. The boat kept steadily to its course, the sea began to rise, the huddle of figures muttered and talked. Twelve hours later Paula awoke to realize, with a rush of horror, that she was the only woman amongst eighty men—and what men. Poles who had fought their way out of prison, Resistance men who had come through every barbarity, criminals turned secret agents, Greek sailors, British airmen and one solitary man, more dirty than the rest, in ragged shorts, who mocked her isolation with very French irony and reached a climax of "concern" when her inevitable need arose and there was nowhere on the boat—just nowhere. The boat was Polish and the Polish captain finally summoned part of the crew up from the engine-room, offering her its dubious privacy. Two days later they were transferred to a British ship and reached Gibraltar. There, the tall, thin, dirty Frenchman was received with tremendous acclaim. He was, it appeared, none other than Colonel Fourcauld, the famous Resistance leader. Within two weeks they were all back in England.

"...ici Londres.... Les Français parlent aux Français...."

ONE at least amongst the men crowded round the wireless set experienced a sense of awe. Somewhere away in London a whole Organization had geared itself to send a single cryptic message. From free London it would come over hundreds of miles directed at this small flat in the heart of Marseille. The news droned on. No one spoke. The pause before the end, and then once again the miraculous words —heard by thousands but meaningless except to them. *"Les carottes sont cuites."* Everything was ready for the sixth embarkation.

Thirty-two escapees were scattered in hiding-places throughout the south, filling every crevice, with six in Nouveau's own flat, five at Nîmes, three lodged with the Martins at Endoume, five in Dr. Rodocanachi's flat, another seven at the Hotel de Paris, Toulouse, and more with the Duriez family at Antibes.

Presently Pat, Jacques Wattebled, Mario Prassinos, Renée and Louis Nouveau each took two or three men in charge, and buying tickets for Canet-Plage, they boarded the train. It took seven hours from Marseille to Canet-Plage, and there everyone moved off to the rendezvous. Chouquette had once more hired one of the more obscure holiday villas where everyone presently reassembled.

There followed the old problem of feeding thirty-odd men cramped into a villa consisting, on the ground floor, of a dining-room, kitchen and adjoining shed, and on the first floor, of three rooms with one bed in each. All shutters had to remain tightly closed and it was necessary to accept military discipline to prevent chaos. Jacques, Pat, Mario and Louis were busy buying rations eked out by supplies from the infallible Chouquette, while Flight-Lieutenant Amber took command in the villa and arranged distribution. A copper full of soup and a huge and mysterious dish provided by Chouquette was doled out, and the villa was packed by crouched, sprawled and doubled-up forms all eating from a variety of earthenware, on the floor, at tables, in chairs and on the beds.

To ease the situation Pat, Jacques, Mario and Nouveau dined with Chouquette at the hotel. With some elaboration they went to their respective rooms at 11.30 and pretended to go to bed. At 11.45 they slipped away separately in the direction of the villa. There Pat found the men sweltering behind closed shutters and the rooms thick with cigarette smoke, but everyone was alert and ready for the next step. Briefly he repeated his instructions.

At a quarter-past one precisely they slipped, one by one, from the back door into the garden and on to the beach. The first to leave were Pat O'Leary and Dumais, a French-Canadian commando captured at Dieppe, who carried an iron bar capable of silencing anyone at a single blow. It was a warm, still, moonlit night, and their black shapes merged into the blacker shadows of the sand dunes. Thirty men walked in single file at wide intervals, their footsteps muffled by the sand, their rear covered by Louis Nouveau.

At the outset it was discovered that one of the French civilians had brought two heavy suitcases which he could not manage single-handed. A few curses and two English airmen took over the cases. Shoes were quickly full of sand, the tiny grains bit into the feet and the shuffling shapes seemed to lose touch with one another too easily. Once a seabird startled them with its call, once a grey hump materialized in the distance and threatened to become human, but Pat pressed steadily on.

1.25 a.m. The mouth of the River Tet within easy reach. Some trick of reflection seemed to make the river mouth dangerously clear, as though it drained whatever light remained from the sky. A hundred and fifty yards of shallow water had to be forded with quicksands threatening at every other step. Creeping close beside the edge of the sea gave firmer foothold but everyone had been instructed to test the sand before releasing his full weight. The cavalcade hesitated, lost its pattern, spread in odd pairs into the river. Some took off their trousers, some rolled up trouser legs, all knew that a few false steps in the wrong direction might find a man trapped by the feet, the sand slowly sucking him down to the waist, the whole group thrown into confusion.

Silently they tested their footholds, moved a few paces, tested again and crept forward. The gurgling water absorbed the splash of their feet but occasionally a foot sank too far and a man stumbled as the yielding softness dragged suddenly at his ankles.

At last, one by one, they came out on the other side, where they silently re-formed and moved forward again as Pat began pacing an exact distance from the river mouth. At seven hundred yards he stopped.

It was almost 1.45 a.m. Groups of men huddled down in the sand to wait. No one could talk, no one smoke. The rendezvous with the ship was set for two o'clock. Once again it seemed suddenly fantastic that a ship could travel hundreds of miles from Gibraltar to this minute and forgotten corner of the Mediterranean coast to keep a rendezvous made to within fifteen minutes with a pinpoint of light. At two o'clock Pat sent the signal with his torch —three red flashes, the third fast on the heels of the second —and everyone stared out at the dark sea. The blackness remained unbroken. Pat repeated the signal. Still no reply.

Whispered conversation was quickly silenced, eyes began to turn in the darkness towards the village. Five minutes later the three vivid flashes and again the empty sea with no reply.

2.30 a.m. Three attempts at communication had failed. By now the whole operation should have been over. His mind disciplined to emergencies, Pat brushed aside a sudden uneasiness and sat on the sand. There had been a small delay. The ocean was big, incalculable, not prepared to serve the petty punctualities of man.

Suddenly, far away to the north-east, a red light flashed and Pat raced off instantly. Plunging through the sand he ploughed on, straining every nerve to speed. Panting, exhausted, he reached a point a mile from Canet-Plage and there, blandly winking away with rhythmic certainty, was the light of a buoy. To reach that point and return occupied an hour. He came back to the groups of men, his feet sore from the sand, his muscles aching, a carefully concealed discouragement fighting with anger that Gibraltar had not sent the ship exactly to time. But there was still hope. A wind had blown up and the men huddled deeper into the sand for shelter. Fine, stinging sand came in gusts and a continual small movement filtered sand into clothing, ears and nostrils.

At intervals the signals were released again as another hour dragged by. Cramped, cold, unable to disperse their growing depression in talk, the men moved restlessly, staring into the sea, constantly checking the five minutes which seemed to take an hour to pass.

At four o'clock Pat decided to give up. Slowly, the cavalcade unwound itself, the cases were humped along, the river forded, the creeping edge of the sea traversed. The sky was lightening as they reached the back gate of the villa, stumbled in and settled down to try to sleep.

At the Hotel du Tennis Chouquette came down in her dressing-gown to open the door to Pat. She heard with relief the news that nothing worse than a missing ship had brought them back so late. It was clearly understood by radio from London that the ship might call on the 5th *or* 6th of October. Heavily disguised to resemble trawlers and flying Spanish or Portuguese flags, the rescue ships often found it expedient to make wide and time-consuming detours.

In the villa everyone did their best to sleep until midday. It wasn't easy. The rooms were so jammed with bodies that only half could lie down to sleep. The other half stood, crouched, or lounged half-asleep on their feet. Presently they took it in turns to lie down.

As the morning slipped away, Canet-Plage came to life in the blazing sunshine, the fishermen sold their catch, the cafés filled and two gendarmes lounged under a striped umbrella sipping red wine with bored indifference. The hot, still afternoon wore away, and as the cool of the evening began, the fishermen came to the cafés to drink, and a restrained gaiety gave Canet-Plage a semblance of its peace-time self. By ten o'clock they were returning to their cottages, by eleven the tables were deserted, the streets emptying, and the few street lamps remained unlit.

From the Hotel du Tennis five men moved swiftly through the dusk carrying a heavy container full of rations. In the villa, airmen sprawled everywhere, mattresses had been pulled to the floor, carpets rolled for pillows, cushions distributed in every corner. No one complained, and everyone stood in line to receive his share of the food. Fresh supplies of cigarettes were smoked, the already thick air of the villa became worse, and everyone was relieved when at a quarter-past one they set out for the dunes once more.

Five minutes later Jacques Wattebled heard the murmur of voices and suddenly froze, pushing his group down into the sand. Two shapes appeared, talking Spanish. It seemed impossible that they should not see him. As the voices grew louder, Jacques could pick out a word or two and his breathing stopped. Someone laughed, and the words were very clear . . . then they passed on and began to fade again. A moment later the figures vanished in the blackness. Jacques rose and moved on once more.

Again the straggling column forded the river, and then Louis Nouveau noticed a boat lying just offshore. Could it conceivably be that the trawler had mistaken the rendezvous by more than a mile? Was this launch a boat from the parent ship? Moving cautiously down to the water's edge he called the password softly: "Where are the strawberries?" and getting no answer repeated it. Suddenly a French fisherman let out a vigorous expletive and wanted to know what the hell he meant. Nouveau faded back into the sand dunes as quickly as he could, watched for a moment and rejoined the column, invisible to the fishermen among the dunes.

Seven hundred yards from the river mouth they gathered silently around Pat. At 2 a.m. Pat once more signalled out to sea and everyone stared into the blackness. Again Pat's torch flashed, but the darkness of the empty ocean was unrelieved by any answering light. A small movement running amongst the men made evident their uneasiness. Pat wondered whether discipline might suffer, but no one said very much, no one questioned his authority.

After a quarter of an hour Pat signalled once more, and then again at 2.30 and 2.35. There was still no reply. The cool wind began to move again, the sand whispered and filtered from one dune to another and the black line of the hills seemed less black tonight. From the roadway, two hundred yards distant, they might be visible unless they remained lying in the sand.

3.0 a.m. The signal again repeated and absorbed into nothingness. 3.15. Some of the men were asleep, while others crouched low in the shadow of the dunes, their tired eyes staring out over the comfortless sea. They heard the faintest whisper of conversation from Pat, and a Frenchman trying to say something which was cut short. A sense of heaviness was apparent in their attitudes. Would this ever work, or were they doomed to retrace their steps back to the villa, to Marseille, and the suffocating life of the prison camp? Fear of the hasty guard shooting to kill in the night, anxiety from a sense of isolation, from weeks of being hunted, and now this—a second night of waiting hour after hour—and no one there—no ship, nothing.

At four o'clock Pat gave the order to return to base. Wearily the column re-formed and moved towards the village. Back at the villa Pat explained that this had never happened before in his experience and the men, with red-rimmed eyes, heard his words with a certain indifference. Some were obviously doubtful. He had felt it out there on the sand as he sent the message for the fifth time. Was this fellow really a secret agent, had he some means of tele-graphing London, did the boat which everyone talked about so much even exist? Pat said he would hurry to Marseille, make contact with England at once, clear up the confusion and be back with fresh plans within twenty-four hours. Twenty-four hours! Their faces fell. Another twenty-four hours in this villa. Suddenly Flight-Lieutenant Amber twisted his moustache and said, "Tell 'em Flight-Lieutenant Amber hasn't tasted bitter for ten weeks," and there was a half laugh from the English.

In the morning Pat and Louis Nouveau left for Marseille by the first train and their talk continuously came back to the missing boat and half a dozen possible reasons why it had not come. Pat was angry and uneasy. It was the worst moment of strain for weeks. Months of shadow-living, of moving from flat to flat, of never knowing what lay hidden behind innocent faces; months of irregular sleep, and considerable feats of sheer physical endurance; months of growing responsibility as the tentacles of the Organization reached into fresh fields; months of tension in case the Gestapo detected the inevitable indiscretion, had culminated in two sleepless nights, thirty-two men cooped up under intolerable conditions, fresh "parcels" beginning to arrive and choke the system, and a threat that paralysis would inevitably give the game away if the ship could not be summoned at once. Within the major crises many lesser ones already required attention. Pat had not forgotten Nitelet and Gaston Nègre. The complexity of a staff officer's work had to be carried out under hopeless conditions and nerves threatened to become raw.

At Marseille they plunged into work. Drafting and coding a lengthy telegram to England was a laborious business. First the grid of paper on which to spell the ordinary phrases, preceded by some key phrase known to M.I.5 in London, *"Tout le long de la Riviera ou murmure une brise enbaumée."* (All along the Riviera there blows a fragant breeze.) From each following phrase a letter would emerge and fall into place as quite different sentences were unwrapped from their camouflage. The process became dismayingly complex. First the letters were written from left to right in the columns of the grid according to a preordained order; then the same letters were rewritten vertically in another order; next from right to left, and finally from the bottom to the top; a series of Chinese boxes which, if one knew the key to the labyrinth, would eventually yield up a message beginning: "Waited nights 5 to 6 and 6 to 7 seven hundred yards from River Tet. No sign of boat."

When Louis Noveau re-read the completed message he was suddenly overtaken with the conviction that it was altogether too restrained. They sought around for some phrase to give anxiety, anger, urgency to the message. They were furious to have been let down at a peak moment of danger. Already an hour had gone by, and the accumulated strain and tiredness was beginning to tell, but Pat and Louis drove on heedlessly. Inspiration came to Nouveau, who suggested sending, *"Pas plus de bateau que de beurre au cul"*, an Army slang phrase meaning "No more sign of a boat than of butter on your backside". It contained the force of all things vulgar. Pat agreed and the message was completed. Passed at once to Philippe Valat, a stand-in operator for Nitelet, the message went off to London immediately. The appalling thing was that no reply could come before the following afternoon. Overcrowded channels of communication were severely rationed and two periods of transmission and reception alone permitted to Organization Pat.

The picture of the men cooped up in Canet-Plage kept coming to Pat's mind. The danger of discovery multiplied in proportion to the delay in shifting men from one point to another, and the possibility of thirty-two men remaining choked at one centre for over a week presented nasty problems. Worse still, there was no certainty that the radio message would be clearly understood in London. Reception could be very bad, words sometimes called for repetition and the cost of expressing colloquial indignation might turn out to be unfathomable obscurity. As it happened Jimmy Langley received and deciphered the message at once, and when he checked the slang phrasing with a French colleague, he at once burst out laughing. He did indeed understand what it meant.

At 7.30 the following evening Pat hurried to Nouveau's flat with the coded reply, and at once began the long and complicated process of decoding. Again the grid was applied, the sentences manipulated this way and that, and slowly certain letters stood out. At first there were long intervals between them and both men, hunched over the table, guessed and reguessed what the words might be, filling in missing letters long before the skeleton justified it. An S appeared, followed five minutes later by an H, and both guessed at "ship", but it was wrong. One S followed at an interval by another at last spelt "vessel".

With the words "vessel proceeded" the next letters didn't make sense and tension became unbearable. Then HAL leaped into completion with "half", and at last the words began to run together. "Vessel proceeded half mile N. River Tet nights 5 to 6 and 6 to 7. No one there. Must carry out instructions to the letter." References to the impossibility of tolerating inefficiency followed and then, "Return of vessel dependent on fuel supply. Already 140 miles towards Gibraltar. Instructing vessel return if possible. Next message will confirm or otherwise". If possible. . . . Confirm or otherwise. That meant another twenty-four hours.

Pat flashed back a message explaining the threat to the whole Organization, acidly remarking that the rendezvous had been kept and that conceivably someone else might be at fault. There was nothing for it, after that, but to wait.

Several telephone messages to Canet-Plage followed. There, an atmosphere described with British understatement as unpleasant was fast becoming impossible. Smuggling in sufficient food invited disaster at a seaside resort where any mass movement did not go unobserved; worse still, the lavatories had seized up.

Somehow the twenty-four hours dragged away. The next evening a message came back from England. Tearing it from Philippe's hand Pat strode round to Louis Nouveau's and without a word they plunged into the jungle of ciphers. It was the first law of decoding that rush meant delay and they now justified the principle completely. The first three-quarters of an hour produced an entirely incomprehensible jumble of letters. They began again.

Both faces were white and drawn under the desk lamp and the cough which Nouveau had picked up in the first World War was becoming very troublesome. Neither said an unnecessary word. Renée Nouveau moved silently about the flat providing coffee. Often, in the past, her part had been very active and very brave. All the scores of airmen hidden in the Nouveau's flat came under her direct care; she had faithfully carried out many dangerous missions, once convoying a wireless set under cover of a nurse's uniform from Marseille station. For the moment she merely plied them with coffee.

Pat watched some preliminary words spring to life. Another and another word came up. At last came the letters "SHIP". Whatever followed sealed their fate. . . . They strained at the letters: ". . . RETUR . . ." They knew the rest but spelt on fiercely. "Ship returning 11 or 12. . . ."

The two men jumped up and embraced one another. Pat telephoned Jacques at Canet-Plage immediately. *"Mon père étant maintenant en bonne voie de guérison—je te rejoins pour terminer mes vacances avec toi,"* he said. (My father is better again—I am returning for the rest of my holiday.) Pat hardly waited to hear how things were at the villa. In any case it was never easy to get depressing news from Jacques, who went rolling cheerfully through every experience that came his way, talking volubly about it in three languages.

Mario Prassinos took over in Marseille. Pat and Louis left by train for Perpignan. The journey seemed interminable but they were light-hearted. When they arrived at Canet-Plage the news was bad. The continual traffic between the village and the villa had aroused comment, imprisonment in a stifling box had undermined morale, the lavatories were still out of order and two men were ill. Pat's news revived spirits at a dangerously low ebb, the two sick men brightened, and even the stench of the lavatories seemed to lessen. "Anyway, you get used to it after a bit," said Amber.

Pat issued a careful warning: there were two alternative nights on which the ship should arrive and even now it might be necessary to repeat the grim pantomime of men sallying forth and returning at dawn. They must be prepared for one more disappointment.

Optimism would brook no such depressing possibility and once more at 1.15 a.m. the men slipped away by the back door and moved along the edge of the sea to the river mouth. The river seemed higher, the current fiercer, the threat of the quicksands multiple, but they forded the river with comparative ease and took up the old position. Three times Pat sent out a signal. Silence. The sea was beautiful, vacant and unanswering.

At 2.30 he repeated his signal. A curious afterlight seemed to have remained in the sky from a sun reluctant to leave a land so blessed with warmth and beauty.

Still no answer. In every man's mind was the knowledge that this could not go on. Every fresh delay increased the danger. Ten minutes later the man on watch near the village saw a shadow move and as it lengthened, knew it was a man. Seeing the man he felt that he must himself be seen; in which case any stranger should be met with casual confidence. . . . That was the instruction . . . confidence at any cost, as though the beauty of such a night on such a coast would keep any poetically minded person from his bed and demand mutual respect for that solitude which alone could savour its full loveliness. . . . The hat over the face, the casual gait, the muttered *"Bonsoir"* and a guttural voice replying with equal restraint *"Bonsoir"*. The shadow faded into the night. Perhaps another agent for another network equally eager for the anonymity of night; or perhaps a spy on his way back to report mysterious movements.

2.45 a.m. Pat received news of the incident. He continued to send the three red flashes on their journey, but no one seemed to notice—friend or foe. By 3.30 everyone was quite still. Listlessness expressed the growing sense of despair of men brought precariously near to exhausting their reserves. By four they were shuffing gloomily back and yet again the Frenchman's heavy cases were man-handled with rage.

In the villa, under the electric light, eyes were red-rimmed, faces haggard. "Where's that bloody ship?" was the catch-phrase delivered without hope and yet without anger. But some looked at Pat in an unmistakable way. They had lost faith in him. The ship would never come. Huddled groups settled down to try to sleep as Pat went off with Louis Nouveau to Madame Chouquette's once more, two casual figures dressed like locals, silent as anyone might be before the dawn.

Another day. The foul stench increased; the longing to throw wide the shutters, to burst out into the street, to sit at the café tables, to talk at the top of one's voice almost unbearable. This was the tenth day of living virtually imprisoned in a stinking match box, trying to believe all would be well.

Somehow it was evening of the next day. No one ate very much; there were bags under eyes, throats were dry, nerves raw. At 1.15 a.m., for the fourth time, Pat, calm, driving, full of the ruthless purpose which had continuously sustained him, led the column off once more, Dumais swinging his iron bar with deliberation.

There was the sea again and the river. There was the dreary repetition of quicksands and the crossing, only this time the routine was changed. Pat reasoned that a boat missing the rendezvous and still professing navigational accuracy could repeat the mistake with some conviction, and he spread the men in groups over a length of a mile of the coastline, with instructions that anyone sighting the boat or a signal should send a message down the line at once.

2.0 a.m. and the signals sent out. 2.15 . . . 2.30 . . . 2.45 . . . Uncertainty multiplied because of the scattered groups. Together news was instantaneous.

3 a.m. A clock chimed distantly. Jacques Wattebled left his two Englishmen to make contact with the next group. "*Pas de nouvelles, les gas?*" he whispered (No news, boys?). And they answered "*Pas de nouvelles, Jacques*" (No news, Jacques). Jacques moved on towards the third post and suddenly a black mass seemed to materialize in the sea. A moment of stupefaction was followed by a fierce whisper: "It's a boat—a boat—without lights."

The small creaking of muffled oars, and then a shadow rose from the boat. "*Où sont les fraises?*" it said, softly.

"*Dans le jus!*" Jacques replied, completing the password.

Away at his own post Pat was about to light a cigarette under his raincoat when footsteps rushed through the dark and a voice broken with relief whispered, "The ship! It's here! The ship!" It was hopelessly wrong in its reckoning.

It had touched the south-western extremity of the chain of men. *But it was there.*

One minute later a gigantic seaman held the boat steady and men began to get aboard. One man amongst the huddled group was crying openly, but the usual reaction was to demand of the huge Pole, "Where the bloody hell have you been?"

The first boatload disappeared into the darkness, then another and another. Four trips in all, the last carrying the heaviest load and bringing the boat's gunwales level with the sea, only the dead calm avoiding disaster.

As the last load went away the four agents watched silently. They sat a moment in the dark. Weariness, held in check by excitement night after night, now rose in waves and a sudden heaviness came down like a blanket. They were alone again. The others had gone off to a world of comparative freedom where there was no need to watch one's own shadow. They were left in the old familiar web, and raw nerves were at last permitted to ache. The great plains of Provence glimmered in the half light as they had done down the centuries; the sea was almost silent; the earth distilled the same beautiful scents; the contours of the sand dunes shifted and changed.

When they arrived back at Marseille four new and completely strange airmen were waiting. They had just come in from Jean de la Olla in the north.

12

AT THE height of its success the Organization was very wide
and complex. In Paris Jean de la Olla moved from flat to
flat among a network of agents; in Normandy Jacques
Wattebled had established a new system alert for anyone
needing help; in the Pas de Calais area the Fillerin family
had their own very active cell; in the Rouen area Louis
Nouveau's work extended and deepened another network.
Until his arrest Gaston Nègre had performed little
wonders with anyone who came his way at Nîmes, and
Madame Arnaud had reduced the hazards of crossing the
line of demarcation to a minimum. Madame Mongelard at
Toulouse ran a prisoners' rabbit warren and the American
Consul at Lyon, George Whittinghill, could be relied on
to help in any emergency.

Along the south coast Nouveau and his wife Renée,
Mario Prassinos, Robert Leycuras, Francis Blanchain and
Françoise Dissart continued to operate, while Vidal and
his guides crossed and re-crossed the Pyrenees. There remained dozens of ordinary householders throughout
France, men and women unaccustomed to bravery who
risked everything to shelter an occasional airman.

Led by Pat, the Organization reached the borders of
Belgium, Italy and Spain. Agents were continually
shuttling to and fro and something like two hundred and
fifty men and women were involved. In Marseille itself the
Organization had at its disposal forged papers, identity
cards, clothing and ration cards, money, black-market
food, engravers who could copy every fresh French or
German pass within three days, and Paul Ulmann, a
Jewish tailor, who could produce perfect imitations of any
given uniform within forty-eight hours. It had its own
post-boxes throughout France—empty flats and the like—

where letters to and from agents were delivered without disclosing addresses.

Everywhere eyes and ears reported to Pat. From prison camps, military forts, police stations and even some Gestapo headquarters; from Paris, Lille, Lyon, Madrid, Barcelona and Gibraltar information filtered through continuously. Dominating every move for big or small escapes was the radio transmitter at Montauban, the sixth sense by which Pat kept in touch with far-away London.

Remarkable feats were now within the Organization's power. A man crashing in northern France could be picked up on the same night, sheltered, dressed in civilian clothes, equipped with forged papers, escorted to Paris and openly conducted through streets teeming with Germans.

A few days in hiding and if he did not go straight through on the normal route to Lyon by train, risking the controls, he might be convoyed via Châlons, across the Sâone at night, sometimes swimming, sometimes on drifting logs. From there he proceeded to Lyon and Marseille. At Marseille a brief period of lying low in Louis' flat and then he was moved along the coast from Marseille to Perpignan, over the Spanish border and away to England. The whole journey for one pilot from the moment of crashing sixty miles north of Paris, to returning to England, occupied twelve days. Some peace-time travel agencies did little better. Over three hundred soldiers and airmen had now found their way back through Organization Pat.

But it was not so much their own virtuosity which held Pat's close attention in the later months of 1942. It was the growing unwieldiness of the Organization. New recruits were still being accepted and not merely an element of risk was inevitable in the employment of any new man, but grave risk. Counter-agents in the pay of the Germans always had infallible alibis and usually it came down to personal judgment, to long and penetrating talks in which the "feel" of the person decided the issue. There were now so many people employed in Paris, Lille and the Calais area that Pat no longer knew the names of some men accepted locally. An unpleasant feeling that detailed control was slipping from his grasp began to trouble him in the latter months of 1942, and the threat of someone he had never known carelessly dropping a fatal word made him determine to restrict recruitment.

Money troubles had once more become acute. Gosling's last million was exhausted, the funds passed down the line by M.I.9 were insufficient to sustain the enlarged Organization, and private contributions—on a generous scale—still did not meet the deficit.

Over the months M. Fiocca had contributed £6,000, while his wife Nancy, an Australian woman who became a daring agent, had sold her jewels and given the money to Pat.* Louis Nouveau had added another £5,000 from private sources. There were many other benefactors but the Organization was still running into serious debt. Pat decided to leave on a special money-raising mission to Farrell, a British representative in Geneva. Passing over control in the south once more to Louis Nouveau, he deliberately booked a seat on the German plane from Marseille to Lyon. Travelling cheek by jowl with the men who were now hunting for him over a large part of France, men who had put a price on his head, he regarded as the best security measure. Certainly the German officer sitting beside him in the plane showed no sign of suspicion.

In Lyon, Pat called on George Whittinghill, the American Consul. They exchanged news, and Whittinghill suggested a new method of crossing the Swiss border.

Reaching the border Pat sought out a French priest at the little frontier village of St. Julien, and gave the password, as instructed, "I am from Uncle Vic." He was warmly welcomed at once. The priest then took him to the top of the tower of his church where the landmarks of Geneva rose into view, and explained the precise route across the border. He isolated a certain light visible from the tower. "Once you reach that light you are all right," he said. Between the light and St. Julien were woods, fields, a railway, a road and a dense, heavily patrolled barbed-wire entanglement. They made a formidable combination. But by counting twelve paces along the barbed wire from

* Nancy's story has been told by Russell Braddon in *Nancy Wake*, Cassell, 1956.

a certain point there should be a place where the wire was cut. Descending from the tower the priest next introduced Pat to an old shopkeeper who escorted him at night through the fields to within sight of the railway. "Be very careful crossing the railway," he said. "Put your ear to the ground, listen for footsteps and then jump!"

It was now very late, the roads deserted and the night black. Crossing forbidden borders had become so familiar that Pat came to this one with a certain *panache* which carried him easily across the fields, but in the pitch darkness he must have lost his sense of direction. Approaching the railway line he turned and walked casually beside it taking exactly twelve paces. A moment later he dropped down and pressed his ear to the ground. For a moment he wasn't sure whether he heard footsteps or not. Then everything seemed muffled and silent. Bent double, he swept across the line and entered the wire. Simultaneously a voice shouted "Halt!" a torch flashed and he heard footsteps running towards him.

There was no cut in the wire. It did not yield to his touch. He plunged in and the wire tore at his clothes. It seemed deeper than he expected, one coil entwined murderously with another. A bullet whistled past his thigh, and two more came in rapid succession. Another torch was flashing somewhere. The temptation to run, to burst through the coils dragging them after him was overpowering, but years of discipline came to his aid. With enormous effort he moved deliberately, pushing the spiked snakes from his path, slipping carefully through loops, ducking and straightening. The whistle of another bullet and his breathing stopped. The wire seemed endless, but one false rush and he would be imprisoned, a sitting target.

Then he was out the other side and running as he had never run before, swerving and ducking at every other yard. The bullets spattered each last step he left. Suddenly they stopped. Silence came down. His lungs heaving, his legs painful, Pat saw that he had reached the light.

An hour later he approached the British Consulate in Geneva and knocked on the door. It was by now one o'clock in the morning and the building shut up for the night. He knocked again. At last the door was opened by a grumbling figure clad in a dressing-gown.

"I come from Uncle Vic," said Pat.

"What?" said the concierge, and glared stonily at him.

Pat repeated the password.

"You can't expect Mr. Farrell to be up at this time of night," said the concierge.

"I must see him," Pat said. "I've come all the way from Marseille."

"He's not in."

Pat burst into a torrent of explanation. When this had no effect he said, "I'm bloody well going to see him whether you like it or not!"

The concierge breathed heavily. "Wait outside and I'll phone."

"I can't stay out here," retorted Pat. "I've just broken over the border."

The concierge relented. "All right then, come inside—you can sit over in that corner. I'll phone Mr. Farrell."

A moment later he was back, full of apologies. "Mr. Farrell is driving over at once. Come this way, sir." Farrell had jumped out of bed, dressed hastily, and ten minutes later reached the Consulate. He greeted Pat warmly and told the concierge to put up a bed in one of the offices. While they were waiting, Farrell handed Pat a drink: "You must be very tired—have this and go to bed. We'll talk again in the morning."

They met at ten and Pat passed over the latest news. "Our greatest trouble is money," he said at last. "We've simply got to have more money."

Farrell smiled. "As a matter of fact I've just received a million francs for you."

It was wonderful news. They talked on for some time and presently Farrell said, "I think it would be unwise to take the money back yourself. If you were caught with it on you. . . ." He thought for a moment. "I'll have it taken down to Lyon by an agent I know."

It was two weeks later that Pat sent a special envoy to Lyon to collect the money. It was not there. Somehow it had vanished *en route*. They were accustomed to these

141

accidents. Many millions of francs had evaporated over the years. But this was a most unfortunate moment.

Back in Marseille Pat found that a new recruit had arrived direct from England. Tom Groome was dark, young, good-looking and full of a quiet zeal. He had been dropped by parachute to take the place of Nitelet. Pat liked him from the start but neither then dreamt of the experiences they would be forced to share.

Far more urgent matters were toward. As the Allies swept back Rommel in North Africa and British troops appeared across the Mediterranean, the numbers of hidden German agents, Gestapo men and special French police all multiplied, until at last the tide burst and the Germans ran over in full strength into the south. New German passes were quickly stolen and copied, passwords revised, precautions redoubled. Dramatically Paul Cole, the English traitor, reappeared, overjoyed at the news that the Germans were pouring into the south. Since that far-distant day when he had escaped from Pat at Rodocanachi's flat and carried out his wholesale denunciations, he had led a wild and varied life until the French arrested him on some charge or other, and there then seemed every likelihood that he might be shot.

Determined that he should not escape the firing-squad, Pat set moving an underground intelligence intended to reinforce the charges against him. For a time it looked as if he were succeeding. Then the French lawyers began to hedge, the delays became long-drawn-out, the Germans arrived and Cole was released and acclaimed as their long-lost collaborator. But this was still only the beginning of a career later to become spectacular.

Cole for the moment was forgotten, overwhelmed by the news of Louis Nouveau. Towards the end of 1942 two agents indicated that Louis Nouveau's name might be known to the Gestapo headquarters in Marseille. Suspicion of any kind demanded immediate action and Pat at once suggested to Louis that he should close the beautiful flat in the Quai Rive Neuve and travel north to take charge of the Organization in Paris, while his wife Renée went to live with Françoise Dissart in Toulouse. For the Nouveaus it was an appalling break. Marseille and the flat had been their home for years; their friends, memories, a whole way of life was concentrated there; but they knew too well the disastrous results of refusing to move at the first whiff of suspicion, and at last agreed to go. Louis was to become a quite different person. His papers eventually identified him as Hector Ludovic Nadier, a member of the Rouen Football Club and Public Library, tickets for both of which were carefully forged.

The farewell dinner to the Nouveaus took place at 28 Quai Rive Neuve. It was one of those rare, gay evenings full of reminiscence from the far-off days when the Organization first began. Three bottles of Château d'Yquem of three different and distinguished years were served. Always the connoisseur, bringing the subtlest palate to all forms of living, Louis pronounced the 1921 vintage the finest year of the century and they drank his health in the third and last bottle. The party lasted well into the night. Everyone was very happy when they at last broke up.

Some days later Louis stood on the platform at Toulouse with his wife. They knew that they would not meet again until—the Victory; and none knew when that might be. The last moment was deeply troubled. As the train rattled away Louis felt drained of thought and life. Pat travelled with him to Montauban. On the platform at Montauban Tom Groome was waiting; Pat left the train and at last Louis was saying farewell to him too: "*A bientôt!*" Pat said. "*A bientôt,*" Louis answered as the train moved away, and somehow there was a terrible finality about the words.

13

SUDDENLY Ian Garrow came back into the picture. News from Meauzac, the prison camp where he was serving a ten-year sentence, said that he would be transferred to Germany in the next few weeks, and something had to be done rapidly to save him from certain death in Dachau.

Pat radioed London: "Shall I take risks involved to save Garrow?" The answer was non-committal. Left to make his own decision, Pat sent Francis Blanchain to the Meauzac area to assess the precise difficulties and make all possible contacts. What followed was too long and complicated to record in detail. Suffice it to say that Blanchain rode out a number of difficulties with great courage and audacity only to be trapped by a document found in his case. Gendarmes twice cross-examined him at Limoges, and on the second occasion, opened his case, read the document and at once handed him over to the "political section" of the French police. Blanchain made a spectacular escape but not before his usefulness as an agent was hopelessly compromised.

Presently a second agent made contact with a jailer in Meauzac who was not altogether in sympathy with the Germans and their methods. Meauzac was one of the harshest and most bleak prisons in France, taking only two classes of prisoner at the request of the German overlords; those sentenced to death and those sentenced to imprisonment for life. Getting anyone alive out of Meauzac was regarded as one of the eighth wonders of the world.

"Pierre", the jailer selected, lived in a small house at Sarlat, some distance from the prison, and when finally they knew that he could be trusted and asked for his advice, he simply said: "Give it up—it won't work!"

Pat and Nancy Fiocca talked at length one evening to Pierre in the kitchen of his small home. "In any case,"

Pierre said, "if I get mixed up in this and anything happened to me, what would my wife and children do?"

Pat reflected. "Tell me," he said at length. "How much do you earn a month?"

"Three thousand francs."

"And how long do you think the war will last?"

"Oh—at least another three years."

"Supposing we double your salary for three years—how much would that make?"

They estimated 216,000 francs and Pat at once said, "I'll pay your wife here 100,000 francs if you help us now—and the rest when Garrow has escaped."

Pierre was astonished. "That's wonderful!" was all he could say.

But insurances against the future were useless without a plan capable of breaking open Meauzac. How on earth could a key prisoner, jealously guarded and specifically earmarked for deportation, be taken from the prison through three lanes of barbed wire under the eyes of heavily armed guards, and safely hidden away in a countryside alive with military, gendarmes and special French police? One by one plans were examined and rejected. Traditional techniques were inadequate to special cases, and it seemed at first as if something very clever and very audacious was required. In the event they fell back on the simple principle of disguise. If Garrow wore the uniform of a prison guard, his chances of escape increased tenfold, but Pierre knew no method of getting a spare uniform. At last Pat said: "If I can find a uniform will you try to get it to Garrow?" They talked at considerable length and Pierre finally said he would try. Pat and Nancy now rushed back to Toulouse and sought out Paul Ulmann. "We must have a French N.C.O.'s uniform within forty-eight hours," Pat said. Ulmann nodded. "All right," he said.

Just forty-eight hours later Pat was on his way back to Sarlat with a uniform which would have done credit to the state suppliers. Pat arrived at Pierre's house full of enthusiasm, only to be told that the uniform was now useless. Vichy had decided to demobilize all remnants of the

French Army at the request of the Germans, and before the Germans themselves took over, gendarmes from scattered parts of the countryside would guard Meauzac.

"But that's wonderful," Pat said. "It means they won't know one another. And if we can get a gendarme's uniform in place of this one . . ."

Pierre agreed, but found it difficult to believe that a second and quite different uniform could be conjured out of the air as easily and rapidly as the first. By now he had analysed the duties and routine of Meauzac in detail and selected, as the most promising period, seven in the evening, when the day shift of guards went off and the night shift came on. Many guards left simultaneously, some on foot, some by bicycle, jostling past the gate and if, in winter, it meant facing the glare of the searchlights continuously trained on the barbed-wire defences, the sheer intensity of the glare tended to blur exact outlines. Garrow, given a certain amount of luck, clad in the right uniform, might be able to slip out.

Again Pat dashed back to Toulouse, but this time Ulmann was in despair. "It simply cannot be done in forty-eight hours," he said.

"Try," said Pat. "It's terribly important."

"But I haven't even got the right material."

"Can it be bought anywhere?"

"I doubt it, at such short notice," Ulmann answered.

In the end it was his former employer, who took no direct part in Resistance work but seemed mysteriously aware of Ulmann's activities, who hinted that perhaps the resources of his large shop were rather better than they imagined. Ulmann had the cloth by that evening and with his wife, set to work at top speed. It was necessary not merely to produce the cavalry trousers, cape, cap and braid, but many other minute details which, with the N.C.O.'s uniform, had been added later by Pierre. There were no surplus gendarmes' uniforms in Meauzac from which fragments could be stolen. This time everything must be complete. Right through that night Ulmann worked, and far into the next day, cutting, stitching, pressing heroically. Then came the delicate business of faking the Francisque insignia worn by Pétain's gendarmes alone. Pat had already substituted Garrow's photograph on false papers, bought a small knife and pistol, and carefully added all those incidentals any one of which might arouse suspicion by its absence. Remaining awake with great difficulty, Ulmann put the finishing touches to the uniform that night, and Pat pushed it into a suitcase and caught the fast train to Souillac *en route* for Meauzac.

With him went three agents, Guy Berthet, Fabien, an agent recommended to Pat by Farrell in Switzerland, and Tom Groome the wireless operator. So vital had this operation become that Pat took the wireless transmitting set with him to keep in direct touch with London. Berthet and Fabien were both remarkable characters in their own right, specially selected for this operation because they knew how to handle guns and had shown great determination and ingenuity in dangerous situations. Together, Fabien (who later excited the admiration of the Gestapo itself), slim, dark and energetic, and Berthet, tall, drooping and mercurial, made an odd pair.

Coming and going between Toulouse and Meauzac was full of hazard, but the four men arrived without trouble, went straight to Pierre's house and held immediate conference. Step by step they made their plans. Every detail of the events which would take place from the moment when the gendarme's uniform was smuggled into Garrow's cell by Pierre, until he reached the hideout away in the country one hour later, was carefully rehearsed. Present at the conference was Philip Brégi, a plump, forty-year-old Gaullist farmer who owned a big and very isolated farm in the district, where Garrow was going to hide up.

Two days later, at half-past six, on a crisp winter evening, everyone moved into prearranged positions. The camp was dominated by two machine-gun towers, one at either end, and Guy Berthet lay concealed near the northern tower covering it with his gun, while Fabien covered the southern tower. Clearly, revolvers were futile against machine-guns but they did not intend launching any kind of attack. Pat himself lay amongst the foothills of the mountains which rose directly above the main entrance of the camp, watching the guards, his own gun ready.

The searchlights already held the barbed wire and the entrance in a blinding glare. Nothing could escape their scrutiny and Pat noticed with dismay that the face of the occasional person coming through the gates was thrown into a green relief which did not disguise its features.

At a quarter to seven a stirring began within the prison, the guards prepared to open the gates, and Pat felt his heart beat faster. If Garrow was recognized as he came through he had instructions to run for it, and if the machine-guns opened up, Guy and Fabien would draw their fire by shooting back, while Pat drew the fire of the guards on the main gate. The impression would be of an attack coming from three directions and in the confusion Garrow might reach Philip Brégi's car waiting near by in the woods. Death by machine-gunning was one of several possibilities.

6.50. Inside the prison something unforeseen happened. Successfully reaching the lavatory with the uniform, Garrow locked the door, swiftly climbed into the cape and trousers, and then heard footsteps. A man turned the handle, knocked, shouted and waited. Who was it? Had someone suspected him, or was it just another prisoner? Garrow stood frozen, expecting the knocking to come again. When it did not, he completed his disguise. Five minutes later the man was still standing outside the door. One more minute and everything might be wrecked, but then Garrow heard a disgusted grunt, and the man moved away. Swiftly Garrow slipped through the door, his mind repeating the details. . . . Gun, holster, cape, cap—everything exactly in position. Footsteps were moving everywhere, doors clanged, keys were being turned in locks, and presently Garrow saw the gendarmes beginning to enter the first corridor of wire on the way to the main exit. Casually, with an air of tiredness, he followed a few feet behind a carefully selected man, and was himself at once followed by Pierre, in wait for just this moment.

Suddenly Pat could see Garrow. His face looked ghoulish in the glare, his gait painfully English. . . . Pat's gun levelled, his heart racing, the swift conviction that no one but a fool would be deceived by Garrow's walk—and then his heart seemed to cease beating. Two gendarmes ahead of Garrow had stopped to talk.

Garrow's face went tight, his steps became uncertain and suddenly it seemed there was nothing for it but to run, to risk the shooting. His French was bad, more than a year in jail had seriously weakened him, and it would be more than difficult . . . the two guards had moved on again.

Garrow followed, reached the gate, smartly saluted the guards, and looking tense as a statue, marched through as the guard on the gate eyed him curiously. Once outside, Pierre overtook him, wheeling his bicycle, and talked quietly as they moved up the road. Ten yards, fifteen, twenty. . . . The temptation to run must have been over-powering. At fifty yards Pat relaxed his gun-hand for the first time as he saw the two men take the right-hand turn according to plan.

Once in the shelter of the wood they were running, and Pat wriggled rapidly away in the same direction, Berthet and Fabien withdrawing independently. Once out of view of the prison Pat ran straight to the car hidden in the woods, where a white-faced Garrow was already struggling into civilian clothes. A breathless greeting and Garrow explained the lavatory trouble as they fell into their seats beside Philip Brégi. The starter was pressed and did not respond. Brégi pressed it again. The growling went on and on. Everyone tensed afresh as it became quite clear that the car showed no sign of starting.

It could not be more than five minutes before Garrow's absence was discovered. Phut—phut—phut—phut—went the starter, the noise sounding thunderous in the silent woods. Supposing a gendarme decided to be helpful and turned off his track . . . or could the noise be heard by the prison guards on the gate . . . ? Probably it could. Brégi leapt out, cranked up the car and immediately there came a blessed roar. With a back-breaking jerk they swept away, the car holding the road miraculously as they took the corners with screaming tyres.

It was twenty miles to Brégi's farm and they shot down the narrow French roads at a disastrous speed, hurtling over cross-roads without a pause. For half an hour the car bumped and bucketed along, sometimes skimming the surfaces at seventy. Waiting at the farm with food and wine were Brégi's wife and Tom Groome. A swift meal and the two agents and Garrow retired to the attic where presently Groome sat tapping out a message to London: "First stage successful."

In the early morning Brégi heard the sound of dogs and went out to reconnoitre. Not more than two hundred yards from the farm he came upon two gendarmes.

"Bonjour! Bonjour!" he said. "What are you looking for?"

"A British prisoner escaped last night," one said. "You heard nothing, I suppose?"

"Nothing," said Brégi.

"We have reason to believe he may be in this area. You've seen nothing suspicious?"

"No," Brégi replied.

"All roads are blocked—he won't get very far."

There was a moment when it looked as though the gendarmes would accompany Brégi back to the farm, but at last he slipped away and warned Pat to go immediately. The wireless set was hidden in the attic and they left carefully by the back door. Across the fields, flattening themselves in ditches at the sound of a voice, carefully following hedges, crawling through tall grasses—it was rough going, and Garrow, weak from imprisonment, found it hard to maintain the pace.

Soon they were mud-stained, dirty and very tired. It would take a whole day to reach the second hideout at Bergerac and it now became necessary to slacken the pace. Time and again at the sight of a distant figure they slipped into a ditch and waited: every footstep, the slightest sound of a voice meant another period of hiding. Towards sundown they reached M. Belin's small, red-brick house at Bergerac, where everything was ready to take them in.

German fury when Garrow slipped through their fingers set the whole countryside afire, and everywhere passes were checked, cases opened, and innocent people rushed off for cross-examination. Patrols of dogs, soldiers and gendarmes systematically combed every inch of the Meauzac area. All surrounding areas were alerted, road barriers erected, armed patrols sent panting across country, and houses ruthlessly searched. There was talk of taking hostages, there was talk of retribution amongst the civilian population. Death threatened anyone sheltering escaped prisoners.

It made all the more remarkable the reception given by Françoise Dissart whose strange dark flat in the heart of Toulouse became their third refuge. A grey-haired, middle-aged woman, she lived an isolated life with a cat no less remarkable than herself. Mifouf arched its back and spat as the dusty group trampled into the flat, and Françoise threw her arms round Pat's neck and kissed him on both cheeks. At a word from her the cat retired sulkily and Françoise swiftly settled her guests in the back room.

As she prepared a meal Pat could not help marvelling afresh. Her age was indeterminate. She might have been forty-five or sixty, but she strode about with immense vigour, a cigarette in a long black holder never absent from her mouth. He knew that she lived largely on coffee, adored her cat, had a nephew who was a prisoner in Germany and hated the Nazis with a white fury, but what other forces sustained her spirit he could not fathom. Her devotion to Pat was unqualified. When he agreed that she should join the Organization she had said, "You are my saviour, Pat." Now a dedicated woman driving a frail body to do her bidding, an order from Pat was absolute. She would say, "If you say so, Pat—I'll do it," to propositions of a kind before which other women might have quailed.

They became very familiar with her guttural voice, the endless cigarettes, the powerful jaw which jutted at the mention of the Germans. They came to know the psychic powers of Mifouf, who understood the moods of its mistress, comforting her when she was tired, entering into her activities with half-human comprehension. Coal black and a little dowdy, Mifouf seemed to share Françoise's indomitable spirit and eventually lived to the extraordinary age of eighteen. Françoise survived the debacle which carried away almost everyone else because the

151

Germans saw her as just an eccentric old lady incapable of carrying on any part of the Organization. This was a very odd oversight. She might be eccentric but the power of her personality was unmistakable.

Three weeks passed between Garrow's escape and his crossing the Pyrenees. Pat went with him almost to the Spanish border. Then he made his way back alone, sleeping one night in a shepherd's hut. Lying there, high in the mountains, smoking a cigarette, looking out on the desolate slopes rising to magnificent starlit peaks, for the first time in months the thought occurred: "Can this go on much longer . . . ?" They had been duping the French and Germans for eighteen months now.

A new agent went to the town of Castres, took a room and began investigating the plight of Gaston Nègre, who was still held in the local jail. Once more the power of the Organization must concentrate on rescuing its own kind from the threat of deportation to Germany. Once a French Air Force pilot, the new agent, Bernard Gohon, had thrown in his lot with Pat some months before, and now, day after day, he moved amongst the people of Castres searching for information. Nobody wanted to talk. Gaullists were arrested in increasing numbers and treated ruthlessly; anyone hinting that he was an agent for a foreign power met with extreme hostility among ordinary people; few dared to be implicated. Two weeks went by and Bernard Gohon had drawn a blank. He reported back to Pat.

At this point Françoise Dissart said that she knew the sister of one of the jailers in the prison who was discontented with his lot. He could be met at a small bar near the centre of the town where the jailers often gathered. Gohon spent several days drinking in the bar and at last negotiations began with a thin, blond young man named Robert, who had secretly desired to escape to England for months. If Organization Pat would guarantee to smuggle him to England—whatever happened to Nègre—he would certainly try to help.

The plan this time was changed entirely. Train travel

had steadily grown more difficult as the Germans increased check-points, and to take advantage of the weakest moment in the prison routine meant escape in the early hours of the morning into a town where no hideouts were readily available. Something very different was required. First they hired an old furniture-van of four or five tons and forged a German pass which permitted lorries to travel by night on the road to Toulouse. Three-quarters packed with junk furniture, the van had an empty space between the furniture and the panel behind the driver's seat in which seven or eight men could, with difficulty, be crushed. Parked a mile from the prison the van might drive away in the middle of the night without attracting too much attention. Inevitably checks on the road would follow but with luck, convincing talk and the pass, all should be well.

At Pat's suggestion Bernard Gohon primed the young jailer Robert to invent a birthday, introduce a bottle of wine into the night shift and invite his fellow jailers to join him in a birthday drink. Dr. Rodocanachi had given Pat a number of prescription forms, and as a doctor himself, he now wrote out a powerful sleeping draught which Gohon bought and handed to Robert.

The lorry, the wine and sleeping draught were all co-ordinated in a single plan. One cold February night in 1943, an odd little party began in the mess-room of the jailers' quarters in the ancient prison of Castres. It was a gloomy building with massive walls, stone-flagged corridors and a single huge key which turned the lock of the main gate. A bright moon threw sharp shadows in the courtyard, the air was frosty and everything promised perfect driving weather as Robert brought out his bottle of doctored wine and filled four glasses. Sitting relaxed at a trestle table before a stove which gave little heat, there was no marked enthusiasm in the beginning. The warders were tired, the limited fuel made the night shift depressing, and the deadly monotony of prison life had eaten into their souls. They toasted Robert and drank quickly. Robert kept the glass, which he had filled before entering the room, and pressed the others to finish up the bottle. They drank again, rather more warmly, toasting peace, freedom and a number of other magnificent abstractions. They sighed and sank back to desultory talk and a game of cards. A yawn, an exclamation, a moan from a prisoner in the grip of nightmare, and slowly one jailer's head sank down on his chest. A moment later he started up again and shook his colleague: "Wake up! Wake up!" The man muttered drowsily, opened his eyes and shut them again.

Fifteen minutes later two men were sound asleep and the third in a very somnolent state. Taking off his boots Robert crept quietly to the wall where the cell keys hung, slipped out of the room and went along the cold stone corridor. Gaston Nègre, far too excited to sleep, was beside himself with joy as the key turned silently in the lock. Robert motioned him to take off his shoes and moved on to the next cell, and the next. Two American and one British airmen, a French sailor and two friends of Gaston Nègre, gathered silently in their stockinged feet and at a signal from Robert followed him down the main corridor. They moved stealthily into the courtyard, keeping in the shadow of the wall. Opposite the prison was a *gendarmerie* where another dozen gendarmes slept. Robert inserted the gigantic key in the main gate with extreme caution. It groaned aloud. He stopped and listened. Distantly there was the sound of snores; nothing else. As the door moved open the hinges groaned again and the noise seemed enormous in the moonlit, deserted night. A careful examination of both sides of the street; no guards in the cavernous door of the *gendarmerie*; no late-night window still lit; and eight shapes merged into the dark shadow thrown by the prison wall as Robert tried to bring the heavy gates noiselessly together. The groaning came once more and it seemed impossible that someone should not hear. Then Robert padded quickly after the prisoners, took the lead, donned his boots in a side street, and in pairs, with intervals of ten yards, they set out towards the lorry a mile away. The cavalcade flitted in the shadows of shops and buildings hoping against hope that they would meet no one.

They reached the lorry. The canvas hood was rolled

back and then began the acrobatic feat of climbing on top of the roof and sliding down ten feet into the hidden compartment. One after another they went in. Feet crushed on shoulders, curses were muffled, bodies struggled for standing space. Eight men were hopelessly jammed against each other bolt upright like toy soldiers in a box as the lorry lurched off into the night. It was fifty miles to Toulouse, the road was in a bad state of repair, and travelling in the stuffy compartment threatened asphyxiation to eight men fighting a continuous action to prevent a cataract of furniture from overwhelming them.

The first hour went by, the smell of petrol mixed with that of old furniture, the dust from the road seeped through the floorboards and the swaying figures rocked to and fro. Suddenly two lamps signalled in the middle of the road, a voice shouted "Halt!" and the lorry jarred to a standstill.

"Your papers, please."

Inside the compartment they could hear the muffled conversation.

"This is a fine time of night to be carrying furniture."

"The roads are clearer."

"Let's see what you've got in the back."

As the doors were opened the eight men crouched in absolute silence, afraid that someone might cough. The gendarmes pulled at a stick or two of furniture.

The driver said: "You're very fussy."

"We have to be," a gendarme retorted. One minute later they stepped back satisfied.

The doors were shut, the eight men breathed again and the lorry drew away.

. . .

Françoise Dissart owned a small dress shop near her flat. At four in the morning the lorry drew up outside the shop and Pat appeared in the doorway. A swift survey of the empty street and the men staggered out of the van, dirty and dishevelled. Gaston embraced Pat and began kissing him, *"Mon Pat! Mon cher Pat! Pat! Pat! Pat!"* It went on and on, Gaston changing his embrace to hand-shaking and immediately embracing and kissing Pat again. Pat broke in at last. This was dangerous. They must move at once.

He had taken a small two-roomed flat in an old house in the middle of Toulouse and now the eight men slipped away one by one towards the flat. Ten minutes later they had all successfully reached it. Some ghost of the old Gaston Nègre appeared behind the thin, pale person who sank wearily into a chair and said: "Let's eat." Presently a cigarette was screwed into the corner of his mouth, *pastis* appeared and the unshaven jowls broke into something resembling the old grin. It was a saddened grin. Something unforgettable had shaken the big frame of Gaston Nègre. But as he puffed and drank, the dull eyes lit up occasionally with the old raffish joy in living.

Chosen because they were part of a labyrinthine old house where dozens of people could legitimately come and go at all hours of the day, the two rooms were hopeless for ten men, and presently they were lining up to wash and shave in the one bowl. Pat talked with the American pilot, Waine, a slow-speaking Southerner, who said, "Gee—you move fast. I was only in that jail twenty-four hours. And it's only a couple of days since I crashed!" Presently Gaston was grumbling that he did not want to cross the border. French to the core, longing to breathe the rich air of Marseille, he would dearly have loved to return to his old haunts, but that was clearly impossible. Remaining in France at all, such a distinctive figure invited disaster.

In the next three weeks the party split up. Through Pat, Gaston set moving that highly personal network which step by step brought him into touch with the underworld of Paris, and presently he travelled north, heavily disguised, to become just another *bistro* character in the confusion of Montmartre. Growing fat once more, adding a little grease to the appearance, recovering the old grin, Gaston nodded slowly to the passing German soldiers and spat at a safe distance, mysteriously earning a living in the darker places and shaking with laughter at night to think how blind the Paris Gestapo could be.

Meanwhile Pat arranged yet another crossing of the border to include the British and American airmen, the

French jailer and sailor, and Nancy **Fiocca**. The French Government, under pressure from the Germans, had decided that any foreigner who had married a Frenchman after 1938 no longer held French nationality and Nancy Fiocca had to be hurried away before she was declared an alien, subject to quite different laws.

One February day another convoy caught the train from Perpignan to Banyuls. The party, twenty-five in all, dispersed in twos and threes down the train. It was a slow train but when at last it shunted into Argeles Pat had an unpleasant shock. Under the dim station lights he could see many grey-green uniforms pouring into the train, and he suddenly realized that German soldiers were travelling with them to Banyuls. When the train resumed the journey a French railway worker slipped into his compartment and warned him that a check was to be made. He left Nancy Fiocca, swiftly signalled to Guy Berthet, who was convoying two Englishmen in the next carriage, and held a quick consultation in the corridor. "Warn everyone," he said, "to leave the train before it enters Banyuls station. Jump as it slows. Meet in the mountains near the shepherd's hut." It was no easy matter to make one's way down a German-ridden train, signalling to each group, delivering the message and moving on again without arousing suspicion; particularly for a tall, stooping man like Berthet. Half an hour later his face appeared at the corridor window of Pat's compartment, and he indicated that he had completed the job.

Everyone waited tensely. The first application of brakes would be the "ready" signal, the train speed dropping marked the signal to open doors or windows. The grinding of brakes duly came, the train shuddered, the speed dropped and Pat jumped up, flung open the door, and leapt out into the night. He ran alongside the train, and as Nancy jumped, he grasped her hand and tried to break her fall. All down the train, doors were opening, forms were hurtling into the darkness and almost at once came the crackle of rifle fire. Because they had fallen the first volley went over Pat and Nancy's heads. Stumbling up they zig-zagged towards the foothills, crouching low, while all along the train other figures rushed off into the darkness. Hoarse cries and the sound of bullets whistling past in the darkness pursued them; straining every nerve to run faster, they flung themselves down again three hundred yards from the train and looked back at the scene. Flashes came from scores of rifles and revolvers, bullets hissed on the air like hail, and nearby someone was sobbing hysterically. The sound of someone running in heavy boots grew louder. For a moment they seemed to be heading directly towards Pat and Nancy; then they passed and Pat whispered, "Stay here. I must try to see what's happened."

He began crawling back. Black shapes moved in confusion around the train. Bullets still whipped on the air. Suddenly a black form jumped up, heavy boots pounded the earth and there, not more than ten yards away, was a German soldier, his revolver already spitting as Pat whirled round, zig-zagged, crouched and raced back again. Miraculously he threw off the German, and, panting, he flung himself down beside Nancy once more.

Half an hour later all was quiet, but every black shape continued to threaten fresh attack, and no one knew how many Germans were still lying in wait. A huddled figure here and there would whistle softly, seeking contact. Gradually, much deeper in the hills, a central group began to attract other stray members, and slowly, over the next hour, the remainder of the convoy gathered together once more. When Pat counted, six were missing, and someone spoke of bodies lying beside the railway line.

Led by Pat they set off in single file towards the spot where the guide would be waiting. They moved with immense caution. It was possible that the Germans were lying in wait for just this move, ready to ambush them; certainly they would not easily give up. It was difficult in the dark to know the exact rendezvous, and when they arrived and found no one there, Pat wondered whether he had mistaken the place. An hour went by. Men reconnoitred in every direction, but the hills were silent and empty, the guide missing, and a fresh depression came down on everyone. Nobody could quite forget the bodies lying beside the railway line. Another hour and it was clear that something had gone wrong. The prospect of spending the night in the foothills with the constant threat of discovery by German patrols, and with no clear idea what the morning would bring, was not very pleasant. Pat told Guy Berthet to return to Perpignan and find a guide of some kind at any cost. He was to bring back a suitcase of food sufficient to last three full days, and to discover as much about the movement of German patrols as possible.

Towards midnight everyone huddled down, covered in coats and mackintoshes, trying to sleep. Cigarettes were smoked under mackintoshes, conversation died away, the stars seemed icily brilliant, the dark line of the mountains became immense.

Berthet set out on his mission in full confidence. He arrived safely at Perpignan—there were no checks on the journey back—and went straight to Madame Chouquette's Hotel du Tennis at Canet Plage. Unperturbed by the news she at once began preparing a suitcase full of sandwiches while Berthet went in search of fresh guides. He was offered the services of Jean Dalmau, the chief of a new guide system. Presently Berthet and Dalmau left together on the return journey to Banyuls. Both spoke perfect French, had flawlessly forged papers, and were men of considerable determination and ingenuity, but interrogation at Argeles was ruthlessly pressed home, and they were arrested. Unable to take Jean Dalmau in an overcrowded police van he was driven towards the police station in the sidecar of a motor-cycle. Waiting until they were shooting round a sharp bend in the road, he knocked the pistol from the hand of the man on the pillion and hurled himself clean out of the sidecar, rolling over and over into the bushes, where he leapt to his feet, oblivious of cuts and bruises, and ran headlong into the foothills. He escaped but did not reach the party waiting up in the hills. He knew it would be fatal if he led the Germans to them.

In the hills the escapees were now very restless. They had played cards, joked, slept, smoked, reconnoitred the harsh rocky country and endlessly questioned Pat about the journey across the Pyrenees. On the second night, in the starlit darkness, Pat lay and made a series of calculations.

Guy Berthet had left in the middle of the night and would take at least six hours to reach Canet-Plage. If no guide was available he might have to spend another twelve hours tracing one. Pat would need to start worrying when thirty hours had gone by and still there was no sign of his return. . . .

Forty-eight hours passed. They were tired, hungry, some very miserable, and the sheer boredom of waiting approached breaking point. Morale was at that level where Pat decided to try to return to Perpignan. Clearly something had happened to Guy Berthet, and everything, suddenly, seemed to be going wrong.

It was fifteen miles to Canet-Plage, and moving twenty people across country in broad daylight was a hazardous feat. Its accomplishment is dim in Pat's memory. They travelled in groups; they raised occasional supplies of food from friendly farms; they made wide detours to avoid villages where German soldiers were said to be waiting. Towards night on the second day the trudging groups presented an odd spectacle, and some had reached that state of hunger and exhaustion where they hardly cared what happened. It was pitch dark again when Pat, tireless, driving, led the first group to the back of Chouquette's Hotel du Tennis and knocked his special knock on the door. Quickly the dishevelled figures were absorbed into the hotel. They were back again exactly where they had started four days before.

Another week went by before fresh guides were found and a new method of avoiding Banyuls had been devised. The party set off one night all over again. It was a diminished party. Six members were still missing, among them the young French jailer Robert who had made Gaston's escape possible. No one knew the precise manner of his end later at the hands of the Gestapo. They only knew that he—like Guy Berthet—died an unpleasant death.

In the mountains the snow was very heavy. The French, the American and English airmen and the sailor struggled into a steadily increasing blizzard. Presently the snow

160

Two escapees are entertained at Louis Nouveau's flat on the Quai Rive Neuve. *Left to right:* Francis Blanchain, Mario Pressinos, Hugh Woollatt, Airey Neave and Louis Nouveau himself. (*Below*) Canet-Plage

Banyuls and the hills near the Spanish frontier

reached their waists and it was only possible to progress by gigantic goose-stepping, testing every foothold before it was finally made. The French sailor's feet became impacted blocks of snow. On the third day he dropped on his knees and began praying aloud to his God. Suddenly the prayer turned into a prayer to his mother. Then he fell semi-conscious in the snow. Somehow they managed to carry him. It took three times the normal period to cross the Pyrenees. When they at last staggered across the border down to the Spanish huts, they were in a state of collapse.

★ 14 ★

At two in the morning in a bedroom of Françoise Dissart's flat, with the rest of the household asleep, the street noises of Toulouse dwindled to an occasional murmur, and the last cigarette burning to its end, it was impossible sometimes to shut out the past, and the pale image of the Abbé Carpentier came up to bring Bruce Dowding, Paul Cole and many others in its train. Dowding and Carpentier. . . . Were they dead already . . . or were they now, at this very moment, broken men, lying somewhere in filthy cells . . . ?"

One scene recurred again and again. It would move to life with Mario protesting against killing Paul Cole, their voices raised in argument, and Paul Cole falling on his knees and pleading for his life. It was all a long way back, but it remained a vivid picture and, at two in the morning, ghosts sometimes walked with the power to rekindle feeling and the sound of a dead man's voice. . . .

Then the cigarette was stubbed out, Bruce's voice banished, the light switched off, and with it, all the past. Like a command to the senses rapidly obeyed, sleep came down with almost military precision. The ability to divide the mind up into watertight compartments wasn't easily acquired—one for death, one for fear, one feeling, one action, one sleep, the whole dominated by tomorrow's duty. Sleep was part of the apparatus of survival. One rose in the morning and began the day's duties irrespective of what the previous day had brought.

Early in January 1943, staying at Françoise's flat, Pat became worried by the lack of news from Tom Groome. A chain had been laid to dupe the Germans, running from whichever flat Tom Groome occupied to Madame Mongelard's Hotel de Paris in Toulouse. Groome had an assistant, Eddie Reddé, whose plain face and spectacles were remote from the glamorous world of female espionage. She picked up messages from Tom and brought them to Room 202 in the hotel, where Pat called regularly from Françoise's flat. Five messages was the maximum received in any one flat before Groome moved on again, and each time he moved Eddie continued to service Room 202.

January saw an unusually long interval between the messages, and Pat made his way to the Hotel de Paris one day, nodded to the white-shawled figure of Madame Mongelard, immobile in her glass cubicle, and passed upstairs to his room. It was two o'clock when he arrived and Eddie usually came at half-past. Pat remained for two hours and no one appeared. He waited another hour and still there was no sign of Eddie. Pacing the room he tried to tell himself that this was one of those accidental gaps which were uncontrollable, and then remembered the fate of Roger. Twenty-four hours later there was still no news. Pat, now very worried, entered the Hotel de Paris for the third time at two o'clock, and almost at once someone came stumbling along the corridor and knocked urgently on the door. A moment later there staggered into the room a woman crazy with fear, hardly identifiable as the plain, pleasant Eddie. Her clothes were disordered, there were tears in her eyes and her mouth was working as she stuttered out, "Tom's arrested—managed to escape—be careful. . . ."

Pat said, "We must leave at once. I will follow you. Make towards the Capitol . . . and Françoise's flat. . ."

He steered her through the door and watched her disappear down the corridor. The idea had struck him with tremendous force that she was acting for the Gestapo, that the Gestapo were already in the hotel and he must move with great speed and ingenuity if he wanted to avoid arrest. It seemed incredible that Eddie, a woman of not very powerful personality, intellect or physique could escape from the Gestapo while Groome remained under arrest. Every person now had a shadow. No one was quite free from suspicion. A network of intrigue and duplicity had forced an entirely new vision on Pat. Hardly anyone could be taken completely into his confidence, and the simple, blameless, so good-natured Eddie . . . was she a new kind of dupe?

His hand tucked into his coat against his revolver, Pat followed her at some distance, whispering to Madame Mongelard as he passed her desk, "Caution—the Gestapo. . . ."

At the door he paused, searching every visible foot of the street before he slipped out. He saw Eddie moving somewhat uncertainly down the street and followed fifty yards behind. At the Capitol there was still no sign of anyone following them. Ten minutes later Eddie entered Françoise's flat. Quickly Pat stepped in after her to find Renée Nouveau and Françoise trying to comfort the distraught Eddie. She was sobbing, and in between her sobs she said over and over again: "It's my fault. It's my fault."

"I don't know whether it's your fault. . ." Pat said brusquely. "Tell me what happened."

The story which followed was extraordinary. Eddie had sat next to Tom Groome absorbed in sending groups of five-letter ciphers over the transmitter. Half an hour had gone by and they were so deeply immersed in their work that they attributed a small disturbance downstairs to street noises. Tom sat, the earphones on his head, his revolver next to the set, tapping, while Eddie helped to disentangle the code, when suddenly something pressed into Tom's back and a voice said: "Keep on— finish your message—don't stop unless you want to be shot."

Eddie had stifled a scream and found herself covered by a second man. Tom went on with his message in the full knowledge that the next one would not contain the flaw always made in the key letters, and that away in London they would know he was transmitting under duress. Then he and Eddie were jerked to their feet, handcuffed and marched out to a waiting car. They were driven furiously to one of the most modern hotels in Toulouse, l'Ours Blanc, then the Gestapo headquarters.

Hurried up to the second floor they entered a large room

with a big window. Behind a desk sat a tall, thin Gestapo officer, his face expressionless.

"So—we meet at last," the man said ironically. "We have been listening to you for quite a time."

Every message to London in the past two months had been recorded by Gestapo detectors, but without the code they were meaningless. Now they had the man who knew the code, and Groome's blood froze as he realized that very soon the torture would begin and under torture he might talk, and when they knew the code and had broken open all the messages, if he was still alive, they would then shoot him, or find some slower and more painful death.

The questions began. Groome did not respond. Like Postel Vinet the thought was racing in his head that a quick and sudden death now was better than the ordeal which faced him. The idea grew with tremendous force and he suddenly leapt straight on to the desk, scattering papers everywhere, and with a second spring shattered the big window and dropped—down—down—into the street. It was the middle of the afternoon; the street was a busy one and the window on the second floor; miraculously Groome fell directly on his feet in a patch of pavement devoid of anyone, and driven by nervous energy of a horrifying power at once sped away. His body was scored by broken glass, his ankle twisted, but he felt nothing, and the strength of madness possessed him as he tore on down the street. Someone shouted "Stop thief!" stood in his path and was brushed aside with ease. Weaving between people, colliding, rushing on, he looked desperately for a side street, found one, dashed down it, crossed into another, saw a doorway and plunged inside. The Gestapo were there a moment later, combing the street, rushing back and forth down its length until suddenly a man said, "He's in there!" They found him two minutes later. Brutally he was dragged back to the hotel and up to the second floor, and then, suddenly, the Gestapo officer said: "Where's the girl?" Eddie had gone.

Eddie's story of her own escape was less spectacular. In the mad rush to recover Groome all four Gestapo men had left the room and she found herself, extraordinarily, alone. White and trembling, her limbs dragging from fear, she managed to reach the door and looked out into the corridor. A number of women secretaries were coming down the stairs. Waiting a moment, she followed in their wake, and with a jumping heart tried to walk naturally out of the main entrance. No one challenged her.

Increasing her pace she turned down the street, went along a few hundred yards and hurried into another hotel. She spoke to no one, stumbled up the stairs to the first floor, and choosing a room at random, entered it. Looking wildly round, she saw a wardrobe, plunged inside and drew the door behind her. There she tried to recover her composure but fear and the stuffy blackness of the wardrobe made it difficult to breathe at all.

She remained there for nearly half an hour. Slowly her heart ceased to pound, her breathing became easier and then footsteps approached and someone entered the room. Once again terror seized her. But the footsteps were quite casual, there were no guttural voices and presently she felt sure it was the owner of the room. More footsteps were followed by the door being shut and a key turning in the lock. It must be the owner of the room. Bursting from the wardrobe Eddie hammered on the door. The footsteps returned down the corridor, the door opened and there was a perfectly ordinary looking Frenchman. He belonged to the hotel staff and she poured out her story to him. . . .

In Françoise Dissart's flat Pat heard the remainder impatiently. Superficially it all made sense, but he still could not quite believe such a story, and asking Françoise to look after Eddie, set off at once for the Bar La Frégate, a centre of gossip and intelligence. If it were true such a story could not have passed unnoticed there. The bar was packed with people, and presently Pat picked out from the buzz of conversation the one dominant topic. "They didn't get them both," he heard. "One's a colonel in the Intelligence Service. . . . The girl got away."

Hurrying back to Françoise's flat Pat kissed Eddie on both cheeks, apologized for his suspicions and congratulated her on her bravery. By now the semblance of a smile had come into Eddie's pale face.*

But Pat felt grim and unhappy. He had come close to Tom Groome, and had learned to respect him. He dare not, must not think what might be happening to him now. Deliberately he shut down on feeling. The next mental compartment, action—counter-action—must work at once, but feeling struggled hard. He stayed awake the greater part of the night drinking coffee, smoking cigarettes, thinking and thinking. How much had Tom known? How much was he likely to give away? Who should be warned first thing in the morning? Whatever else he was forced to divulge Pat felt quite sure that Tom would never disclose the Toulouse headquarters in Françoise's flat, but there were other details which might be revealed under extreme pressure. As the sky was lightening, Pat fell into an uneasy sleep. For once the disciplined mind had not worked so well.

Many months later he learned the full story of the battle of wits which raged between the Gestapo and M.I.5 before Tom was taken away to a concentration camp. Under the illusion that their false messages could not be detected the Gestapo forced Tom to tap out a number of subtly constructed queries, all designed to give them further information about Organization Pat. Immediately the mistakes in the key letters of the message failed to occur, London knew that they must play out this game of double-bluff with Groome clearly under arrest. They answered the questions evasively and in their turn put a number of trap-questions designed to reveal German information. Presently every kind of snare and counter-snare was being set, and a whole long barrage of cunning and deception poured back and forth across Europe. Only when M.I.5 seemed to be gleaning more information than

* Here a word should be said about the Cheramy family. Tom Groome and Eddie Reddé were arrested at Montauban (thirty-five miles from Toulouse) in a house which had been provided for them by the Cheramys. Before that Tom had operated from the Cheramy's home.

The Cheramys were arrested and both sent to concentration camps. Cheramy's English wife, Patricia, who was in Ravensbrück, was particularly ill-treated by the Germans, but survived her ordeal.

they were giving did the Germans at last abandon Groome to the worst that the concentration camps could do.

If the arrest of Tom Groome marked the beginning of a wave of disasters in the south, strange things were already happening in the north. Moving between the flats of Madame Longaert, Paulette Goubert, and Legrand, Jean de la Olla returned one day to find German police seals on the door of Legrand's flat, and hurried away again.

Then one evening Louis Nouveau, staying at Paulette Goubert's, heard the special ring on the bell and there was Jean, unshaven, dishevelled, his trouser leg torn and mud reaching up to his knees. He poured out his story. Escorting five "parcels" south with Sebastien, one of his agents, a German customs officer had challenged them at pistol point. Jean had made a dash for it, heard one bullet whine over his head, knew that the next one would hit him and surrendered. Five minutes later, seeing a better chance, he had rushed away once more. The German fired again, blew his whistle and kept the remaining six men covered with his revolver. Dogs, police and soldiers poured over the countryside. Several times he had to throw himself into ditches full of water as the police rushed past. He reached Châlons in a bad state, but the hotel receptionist made no comment when he asked for a room. He remained there nearly an hour. Then he took the train to Paris, hurried to Paulette's flat, burst in on Louis Nouveau and told his story.

The bell of the flat rang again one November morning. Louis once more answered the door and this time it was a big, blond Frenchman in his middle twenties, asking for Paulette. She was out and later when Louis mentioned the caller to her she said—"That must have been Roger." Louis questioned her about Roger. Known as Roger Le Neveu he had spent three years in the Foreign Legion, and was engaged to Suzanne, the sister of a man called Barliet known to have been executed by the Germans. Louis thought he sounded a promising new recruit, but decided to consult Jean and Norbert Fillerin.

All three gathered one day at the Café Debas to meet Roger. Jean de la Olla approved of him, but at first, Norbert Fillerin did not. Louis pressed him to explain why, and when Norbert gave no very strong reasons he told the story of Roger's fiancée, now carrying on some of her brother's underground work. Clearly Roger seemed to sympathize with the right side, and there was no questioning his toughness and resource. Reluctantly Norbert Fillerin was at last persuaded that perhaps he was all right.

Presently Louis talked again to Roger and offered him a regular sum of money to escort rescued airmen from Paris to Marseille. Without any great show of enthusiasm Roger accepted. His first convoy to the south went off successfully. He returned early from the second in a disturbed state saying that he and the Australian airmen under his care had been arrested, but he himself had managed to escape by a trick. Something about the story seemed odd to Louis Nouveau. He made no comment. Small casualties of this kind were becoming more and more frequent.

From Rafarrin, the chef on the Marseille express, a long letter presently arrived for Louis from Pat. It brought the news of Tom Groome's arrest, explained the increasing difficulties in the south and said that Pat thought of going to Gibraltar to organize a new escape system by plane. The letter concluded, "I would like you to return south to take charge of all parcels in future. . . ."

Roger came back from his third convoy with his four airmen safely distributed to hideouts in the south and Louis' confidence in him revived.

Another letter followed from Pat. It concluded ". . . join me at once."

Louis arranged to leave Paris within a few days. Five American airmen, survivors from a Flying Fortress shot down in Brittany, had just come into Paris. Louis passed them over to Jean, who took them to Levêque's flat in the Avenue d'Orléans. They needed fresh identity cards, clothing, food, and above all a chance to shave and clean up. "Meet me," Louis said, "outside Austerlitz station at ten tomorrow. We shall catch the eleven o'clock train to Saint

Pierre des Corps." Roger and Norbert were to go with Jean and the airmen to the station.

Louis arrived at Austerlitz at ten o'clock, and stamped about the pavement outside. Restrictions were so severe that special admission cards were necessary even to enter the station. By half-past, nobody had arrived, and cold and angry, he was beginning to wonder what had happened. At ten-forty the convoy suddenly appeared and Louis asked where the devil they had been. Jean explained the time it took to eat and shave, change clothes and identities. "Anyway, there are still twenty minutes to go," he added.

When they tried to get admission cards to the station they were refused and the pressure of the crowds drove them away from the booking-office. With ten minutes left it looked as if they might have to take the airmen back into hiding again.

They held a hurried conference. Suddenly Roger said: "Leave it to me—I think I can get the cards."

He dashed off and the minutes slipped by. Five minutes before the train left he came hurrying back. He had the cards, and in the rush of relief, no one questioned how he had done it so swiftly. They had, after all, pulled off the same feat themselves before, if not with quite such alacrity.

Everything ran smoothly for the first stage of the journey south. As the train reached Saint Pierre des Corps, the American airmen were warned to be ready to change. Louis found an empty carriage on the little local train—they now avoided the expresses—and they filed in. A moment later the door opened and someone looked towards the two vacant seats. Louis turned his back on the door to block the newcomer's view. Something stabbed into his shoulder blades. "Put your hands up," said a voice with an unmistakable German accent. Louis felt as if he were in a lift, the cable had broken and he was falling, falling. . . .

The news reached Pat within twenty-four hours. It seemed unbelievable. Louis who had borne a charmed life all these months, Louis who had become indispensable to the Organization, Louis who had hardly ever known fear in his work, Louis who was close in everyone's affection. . . .

It was some time before Pat could bring himself to break the news to Louis' wife Renée in Françoise's flat. She did not say much. She went very white. She had some difficulty in speaking at all.

15

IT WAS a grey morning in Paris in March 1943. At the Café
Dupont in the Boulevard St. Michel, students sat behind
the huge glass windows sipping ersatz coffee, women stared
at empty glasses anxious not to return to unheated flats
and the grey-green uniform of German soldiers created
their own oases. The wind blustered against the windows,
the auto taxis plied for hire, and the hint of spring in the
air failed to enliven a city entering its fourth year of occupation with a new outcrop of German notices plastered on
every wall.

At a corner table Jacques Wattebled sat waiting for
Costa Dimpoglou, Norbert Fillerin and Jean de la Olla.
They were to collect another group of airmen to be
escorted to the south. Jacques had not only heard the
appalling news of Louis' arrest but something else which
he could scarcely credit. Pat, too, it was now rumoured,
had been taken. A traitor worse than Paul Cole was now in
their midst and Jacques thought he knew who it was. In a
tense, confused, anxious state, Jacques turned over every
detail of his association with Roger and steadily suspicions
deepened.

And then suddenly Roger himself was there, walking
boldly into the restaurant, coming straight over to his
table. They began talking. Jacques offered Roger a
cigarette and at last he said: "You are going to see Pat at
Toulouse?"

"Yes," Roger answered. "Tomorrow, with Jean. . . ."

If he knew of Pat's arrest this was a lie, but if the story of
the arrest was false or he did not know . . . Something in
Roger's face and manner convinced Jacques that he was
lying and he decided to play for time. He asked where the
English airmen were, which surprised Roger, who said:
"But surely you know."

"Henri knows but I don't," Jacques replied, inventing a quite new agent to confuse Roger.

"Henri? Henri? Who is Henri?" Roger said.

Through the window Jacques saw Jean and Norbert about to cross the road and enter the Café Dupont. He knew that they must be warned at once, and he turned suddenly to Roger. It was necessary to telephone the man who would provide the papers for their journey to the south. Would Roger do this immediately? Roger agreed.

The telephone was downstairs and as Roger disappeared below ground level Jacques leapt to the door, met Jean and Norbert, rapidly explained the situation, asked them to warn everyone known to Roger, and raced back to his place at the table in time for Roger's reappearance.

"Everything's fixed," Roger said.

At that moment the burly figure of Costa Dimpoglou came through the doors and walked straight towards their table. The sight of Jacques in intimate conversation with Roger made him hesitate—he too had reason to suspect Roger—but he came steadily on, greeted them, and sat down and joined in the talk.

As if the table was the centre of life in the café yet another man now appeared, making directly towards it, but this man was unmistakably different to the trained French eye.

"I'm going to telephone the Café Dupont Bastille to see if Jean is there," Jacques said quickly.

On a swift pretext Dimpoglou went with him. A Greek of powerful brain and personality, Costa had drifted step by step into the Organization. Temperamentally alien to espionage of any kind, first the pressure of so many friends in Resistance had made him feel that he should contribute, then he had carried a message as a token gesture, and at last convoyed an airman and suddenly realized that he was becoming involved willy nilly. But always at the back of his mind one phrase had repeated itself—"Whatever happens I will not be caught." He would kill himself rather than risk falling into the Gestapo's hands. Now, the appearance of this cool man in the glasses and raincoat, sitting at their table, made suddenly real what had until then seemed remote.

Downstairs in the telephone booth he talked swiftly to Jacques. Allowing as long an interval as possible they climbed the stairs again. As their eyes came level with the café floor they paused a moment, saw Roger deep in conversation with the Gestapo agent and felt at once that they were right. Roger was a traitor. As they reached the top of the stairs the Gestapo man drew his revolver and covered them. "It would be better . . ." he began to say, but "I will not be caught" raced through Dimpoglou's mind and he leapt towards the door.

The Gestapo man fired. The bullet seared past Dimpoglou through the plate-glass window. Seizing Jacques with his free hand the agent fired again, started after Dimpoglou and found Jacques dragging him back.

At that moment two gendarmes burst in, and affecting ignorance, grappled with the German instead of Jacques. Jacques, still held in an iron grip, shouted, *"Ce sont des types du milieu!"* The two gendarmes struggled with the hand holding the revolver as it veered from one to the other and the agent shouted something which was lost in the rising babble of voices, crashing glasses and a woman's scream.

The arrival of five German policemen now reduced the café to complete confusion. Tables crashed, the Germans shouted at the gendarmes, the Gestapo agent tried to issue orders and suddenly, seizing his chance, Jacques wrenched himself free and ran like the wind. As he reached the door bullets crashed through the glass again. He was out in the Boulevard St. Michel on wings of fear, racing breakneck towards l'Ecole de Médecine.

Well ahead Dimpoglou pedalled furiously up the Champs Elysées on a stolen bicycle. There followed a series of adventures which transformed the student of mathematics, profoundly aware of great philosophic issues, into a back-shop workman busy filling tubes with some mysterious cosmetic whose precise nature he never fathomed. Temporarily he found safety.

With Jacques it was different. As he raced towards the

Metro, the German police closed in on him, and diving into the rue Hautefeuille he flung himself into the nearest doorway. Just one woman saw him enter and he shouted: "If you are a patriot don't tell them. . . ."

Up the stairs to the first and second floors, and then a pause, crouched beneath a window, his heart pounding. The voice of the woman came up from the street: "He is in there!" Bitch! Bitch! The third and fourth floors reached and then he knocked desperately on one door after another. The knocks echoed in the corridor. Someone must have heard but the doors remained bland, silent, shut. In the lavatory he examined the narrow fanlight, stumbled out on to the roof, and realized suddenly that there was no way out; the block of buildings formed an island.

A new and paralysing rush of fear and sudden shivers at the thought of torture waiting a few hours away. Everyone knew it was better to die; better to die quickly than suffer a long-drawn-out agony which must end in the same way. A match struck, the lists of addresses burnt, the false identity card alone preserved and then a moment with all the senses frozen in horror and the last desperate burst over the edge as he leapt from the roof.

His senses recorded the glitter of broken glass, the flashes of pain and a crackling roar. What seemed like a court below was really a veranda, and the swift fall had ended with a great jolt, thrusting at every bone in his body, distorting in horrible pain the spinal column. Trying to rise, the dead bone unresponsive, the head seemingly split open, the fingers broken and useless, and somewhere a window thrust up and a woman shouting. "Help! Help! Police!"

Suddenly the veranda quivered, sighed and collapsed under him, throwing him down into the kitchen, a horrible confusion of injuries. Dust rose from the debris, bits of masonry continued to fall, and a babble of voices subsided into silence as the police walked towards him and picked him up and pain sent the world reeling back and back. . . .

A swift drive to the rue des Saussaies and the German counter-espionage officers at once began their questions, driving at the tangle they must unravel instantly if they were to trap the men they knew as yet as shadows with confusing names. Jacques' spine felt displaced, two fingers of one hand were dead, and his head bled profusely, but these were useful allies in the one overwhelming purpose of the Gestapo—answers; quick, useful answers; nothing else mattered.

"Where is Jean?"

"I do not know Jean."

"Where is Norbert?"

"I don't know Norbert."

Very soon the beating began. There was a monotonous regularity in the techniques employed, and fear had a greater range than torture.

"You are Jacques the Englishman?"

"I am English but not Jacques."

He made a long deposition full of falsehoods. The inevitable check revealed its lies and evasions and the next interrogation began with a more vicious beating. His nose became a bloody mess, his teeth were broken, his face swelled grotesquely. The Gestapo did not soil their own hands. French criminal types carried out the beatings; toadies given sadistic sanction for the first time in their lives.

The injuries from Jacques' double fall had received no medical attention; he had eaten nothing, drunk nothing, and as new blows descended, feeling in the normal sense reached a state of agony where any further pain was meaningless.

"We must know your part in all this."

"I am not Jacques the friend of Achille. . . . I am Jacques the interpreter. . . ."

It went on for eight days. The threat of slow death was continuous. Once they fitted a strange electrical device to his body. When they pressed a switch his genitals seemed to burst. Once a man came to his cell with a revolver and said that in half an hour he was to be executed, and Jacques fell on his knees and prayed; but he was not executed. Frequently they came back to the same questions:

"You are the chief in Normandy? Who do you know there?"

"Nobody."

A great blow in the face which seemed to break his jaw. "What were you doing in Normandy?"

"*J'allais voir mes maitresses.*" Another blow.

For Normandy always the same answer, but he was approaching that point where body and spirit parted and in the black, wet cell, sleep became difficult. His injured back made it hard to lie down. The final hell was closing in.

When Jean de la Olla went to the Café Dupont to meet Jacques and Costa Dimpoglou he already had news from Rafarrin which utterly dismayed him. It said that Pat had been arrested in the south, and it seemed unbelievable. Stopped in the doorway of the Dupont by Jacques, Jean left immediately and sought out Sebastien, another agent in his group. Sebastien was given instructions to proceed at once to Toulouse to warn Albert and Françoise Dissart against Roger.

Jean then hurried back to his hotel, met his wife Marinette, cancelled their rooms and took a bus towards Levêque's flat in the Avenue d'Orléans. Roger in touch with the Gestapo meant that Levêque was in danger, and particularly the small package which they had handed to the concierge the previous morning must be removed from the premises. It contained forged papers, seals, cards, photographs, a whole apparatus for changing identities.

Arrived at Avenue d'Orléans, they were met by a disturbed concierge who asked: "You were with Monsieur Levêque this morning?"

"Yes."

"You are going to him now?"

"Yes."

"Don't—the Gestapo are there."

They hurried away. Making towards an old Paris rendezvous the Café Ulysse, they found Norbert Fillerin, calm and self-possessed despite more bad news. In his mad rush before the Gestapo, Costa had warned the owner of the Café Ulysse of Jacques' arrest. Jean's heart missed a beat as Norbert told him. Jacques, the round, jolly, droll

Jacques, in the hands of the Gestapo. Louis gone, Pat said to have been taken, Roger a traitor, and now Jacques arrested . . . an appalling holocaust. Costa had left word at the café that he would call at Levêque's flat at two o'clock in the afternoon.

"We must stop him," Norbert said, and all three left at once. With the Gestapo already in possession of Levêque's flat, Costa would be lost if he so much as rang the bell.

Turning into the Avenue d'Orléans they at once saw a Gestapo man pacing up and down. Deploying at different approaches to the Avenue d'Orléans they waited, ready to head off Costa. Every five minutes they changed places to avoid becoming conspicuous. Half an hour later they were still manoeuvring around the flat unaware that Costa had gone to Levêque's workshop, not his flat, gasped out his news and dashed off as the Gestapo arrived.

When three o'clock came round and there was still no sign of Costa, Jean, Marinette and Norbert realized that he would not keep the Levêque rendezvous. They held a quick conference in a back street. One urgent mission remained to be carried out at once. Paulette Goubert, a close friend of Roger, had in her possession a list of people connected with the Organization. This must not fall into Roger's hands.

It was four o'clock in the afternoon. Paulette would still be working and Marinette was deputed to call at her dress-shop and warn her while Jean and Norbert waited in a nearby café. At a quarter to five Marinette returned. Paulette was not at her job and no one knew where to find her. All attempts to reach her that evening failed and they returned to Norbert's flat to spend the night. The flat telephone was probably tapped by the Gestapo and the following morning Jean hurried to the nearest Metro station and telephoned Paulette. She sounded cross and sleepy but when she heard what Jean had to say she was immediately awake. *"Je ne peux pas vous croire. Vous me faites mal."* She simply did not believe that Roger was a traitor. "I want you to destroy that list at once," Jean said.

"But this is absurd."

"Where can I see you?"

Paulette suggested the dentist's in the afternoon, but Norbert thought any delay dangerous, and urged that Marinette should fetch Paulette to a certain café at once. Marinette went off, but instead of entering the café named, Norbert and Jean went into the one opposite. They had hardly ordered an aperitif when four men came in, drew their revolvers, and they were thrust against the wall.

Marinette returned to the original café, with Paulette, and found no one there. Paulette said, "You must have mistaken the café,' but Marinette was very sure and very worried. "I'm certain they have been arrested," she said. She made discreet enquiries without avail. The rest of the afternoon she spent walking alone in the Metro, afraid that she was being followed. Twenty-four hours later, a distraught and lonely Marinette took the last train towards her home in the country outside Paris, but dare not approach the house itself for some time. She had to go back; her children were there waiting for her; but she felt very sick and was desperately afraid.

The torture began for Jean de la Olla with the whip. It was brought down twenty times until his naked back had great raw weals criss-crossed over it. The first blows spun him round and he felt as if his back had split open, but after the first six strokes a curious numbness ran over his body. They whipped him everywhere and the scars were to remain on his body for seven months. Then came the underground cell where jets of cold water were turned on him. They brought him from the cell into a warm room for interrogation and four men drove questions continuously at him, only to throw him back into the icy cell when he did not answer.

On the third day they put the chain round his neck and when he would not speak, two men took the ends and pulled it in opposite directions. He almost choked. Presently his eyes were bandaged, he was put against a wall and everything made ready to shoot him; but they did not shoot. Once he travelled to an unknown destination in manacles, lying on the floor of a van, with a Corsican guard's feet on his body; once it was said he astonished his guards by reciting the Ave Maria as they tortured him; once they found him praying in the black, wet cell, communion with his God giving him new strength.

It was the beginning of a long battle between spirit and body which still did not stop when final brutalities caused two mutilated fingers to fall from his right hand. It was possible in the end to understand why the slight, frail person with the beautiful eyes was regarded as a saint in the Organization.

Jean, Jacques and Norbert were aware of one another's presence in Fresnes but they did not meet for some while. Time lost its sequence and whole drifts of days seemed to run together. They suffered the same alternation of torture, agony, hunger and growing despair, and then at last, one day, they were dragged from their different cells, taken into the prison hall, and confronted with one another. Perhaps the Gestapo thought that the sight of their handiwork on another man's body would have a salutary effect. Alternate beatings, torture and interrogation had reduced them all to a state of near collapse. Jean could only talk and walk with difficulty.

Then the torture began again. For Jacques it lasted from eight-thirty in the evening until three the next morning, for Norbert until five, for Jean until ten.

Presently came the final warning: "We are going to give you one last chance. Speak or you will be shot."

They all refused to speak.

16

It was still early March 1943. A sudden burst of spring brought sunlight pouring down the streets of Toulouse on the morning when Paul Ulmann came to Pat and said: "Roger wants to meet you. I don't know whether you want to see him?"

Pat had never met Roger. He regarded him as a minor agent of not very great consequence and he glanced at the notebook where he noted the times of each rendezvous, but never the real name of the person. There was Vidal at midday, lunch with Renée Nouveau at half-past one, and another meeting early in the afternoon. He had set in operation plans to counteract the mysterious forces which threatened to crush them on every side and there were so many vital and complicated things to do; meeting Roger seemed unimportant, but since he said he had the full story of Louis' arrest in the north, Pat at last agreed.

Pat left Françoise's flat at ten minutes past twelve and joined Vidal in his gloomy kitchen where the old welcome awaited him. Pat piled six pistols and a cosh with a spring steel centre on the table and Vidal was beside himself with delight. Weapons were to him the breath of life and now they drank three aperitifs in quick succession to celebrate what was made to seem like a minor victory against some unseen enemy.

Pat left to meet Ulmann half an hour later. At ten to one Pat saw Ulmann standing outside the tailor's shop where he once worked, and as he strolled past, Ulmann joined him. "He's in there already," Paul said, indicating the Americanized Super-Bar. "But you know, Pat, I have an odd feeling. . . . Those two men outside—see? I don't like the look of them very much."

Warned that their raincoats and pork-pie hats were far too distinctive the Gestapo agents had lately taken to wearing clothes as close to the French as their Teutonic bearing permitted, and now they were not nearly so easy to detect. Pat looked closely at the two men, saw nothing suspicious, remembered his gun strapped under his armpit and his eagerness to hear Roger's news and shrugged his shoulders: "I think it's all right." They strolled over and entered the Super-Bar.

The bar was as small as its name was grandiose, consisting of half a dozen tables and a few stools with six or seven customers sipping ersatz coffee. At the last table, with his back to the door, sat Roger. He rose and greeted them with a scarcely perceptible nervousness. Paul sat next to him and Pat opposite. Immediately Pat plunged into business. "How did you manage to get down?"

From March 1 the Germans had changed the rules for crossing the demarcation line. There were no more special permits. A difficult and complicated stamp on the actual identity card had been substituted. "Can I see your card?" asked Pat. He glanced at it and momentarily slipped away to the lavatory. When he came back he noticed that the two men who had been lounging outside the café were now inside. He sat down, studied the stamp on Roger's card more closely, and reflected that one of their engravers could easily copy it. A moment later he said: "Now tell me quickly. Do you know who has been giving us away in Paris?"

"Yes!" said Roger. "I know the man perfectly well."

Something cold and hard was pressing deeply into Pat's neck and involuntarily he jerked a little forward. A voice said: "Don't move." A second later: " Get up—don't turn round and put your hands up."

His heart was beating in long, slow pulses, an extraordinary sense of shock and surprise restraining the full flood of fear. Of all days this was not the time or place he had expected an attempt at arrest.

There were other men already covering Paul and Roger and another voice said, "You too!" Once on his feet Pat realized that most of the customers in the café must have been Gestapo men. Six revolvers now covered them from all angles.

The man who searched Pat was quite small, but tough and ruthless. First he found his pistol and instantly cracked Pat across the jaw with his hand. Then he found a cosh in an inner pocket, and this justified a second blow.

There were only two neutral spectators in the café, with the proprietor white and petrified behind his bar. Pat's mind was now racing. Admit nothing, behave like a normal customer, gain time to escape. "I have to pay for my drinks," he began, and one Gestapo man smiled ironically. "You are coming with us at once," he said.

Separated from Paul he was pushed into the street and taken handcuffed down the road to the Grand Hotel, almost next door. Thrust into a room on the second floor, two German soldiers stood guard over him while a Gestapo man turned and said: "Now we're going to drink a bottle of champagne to celebrate. We won't be long."

The soldiers wore green uniforms with the insignia of the Security Service on their black collars. Pat looked at their faces and knew it was hopeless to expect anything from them.

The two Gestapo agents came back, bundled him into the car again and said nothing while they were driven to a second Gestapo H.Q. Once more the Gestapo men disappeared, German soldiers took over and a civilian secretary began a routine interrogation:

"Name?"

"Joseph Cartier."

"Born?"

"Paris."

"When?"

"1910."

"Profession?"

"Engineer."

"When did you arrive in Toulouse?"

"Yesterday."

"Where were you coming from?"

"Lyon."

"Where did you sleep last night?"

"In the station."

"Why in the station?"

"I arrived too late to get accommodation."

"What were you doing in Toulouse?"

"Oh—some business."

"What kind of business?"

"If you must know I am a black marketeer."

"In what?"

"Coffee."

Steadily it went on with Teutonic thoroughness. Pat examined the room as he answered. It was a large, airy room with three big desks and armchairs, and one low table. Not much chance yet of escape from it. When the two Gestapo men came back, one took up the questionnaire, glanced down it, tore the paper in two and said, "And now I hope you are going to tell the truth."

"I haven't lied yet," said Pat.

"You really must not go on pretending that you are Joseph Cartier, an engineer, and in the black market. We know otherwise. What about your friend Paul Ulmann?"

"He's in the black market with me."

"I shouldn't be surprised at that. But what about your dear friend Louis Nouveau."

"I don't know Louis Nouveau."

"And you don't know Jacques, or Jean de la Olla?"

Pat's already dry mouth went drier and his whole stomach tightened. "No," he said, but he had allowed a flash of expression to appear in his face and the Germans were pleased at their small victory. Still without any suspicion of Roger, thoughts were racing through Pat's head as he tried desperately to think who had given them away, and how and where he could break out of this appalling trap.

"And what about your flat in Toulouse?"

"I haven't any flat."

"No flat?"

"No—and I don't know what you are talking about. I am Joseph Cartier."

"Stand over there in the corner. . . . Put your hands above your head." In the next twenty minutes men came and went from the room and each time they passed Pat they pushed his head against the wall with enough force to make him see stars, but he gave no sign of any discomfort.

It was then, from the corner of his eye, that he suddenly saw Roger, as the door opened and shut, sitting in the next room smoking and talking with a group of Germans. In a terrible flash he knew the truth. Fool—fool—fool! Why hadn't he seen it before? They must know everything that Roger knew, but when Pat tried to remember the extent of his knowledge he found that he did not know the true extent. . . . Think fast, estimate what could be saved from the wreck, find a method of warning Albert, Renée, Françoise, and take a quite new attitude. . . . Whatever they knew from Roger it would be useless to deny; his own identity for instance. He would pretend to be quite frank with them up to a point.

When they came back into the room again he said: "I'm going to tell you my real identity. I'm Pat O'Leary, a British officer sent out to do this job."

The effect on the Gestapo men was extraordinary. They burst into loud cries of joy, dancing round the room and shouting, "I'm a Preetish officer! I'm a Preetish officer...!" This was clearly no ordinary catch. Five minutes later they offered him a meal of cold meat, salad and wine. The talk ran easily enough about Churchill, Hitler, Imperialism and war policies, but as he talked, Pat tried to prepare for what must follow, reading these men from their eyes, their gestures and words. At seven o'clock the first change came.

"Well now," said a man with a long, lean face, scarred at the chin. "We can see you're a good boy. Tell us something about your Organization.

"What do you want to know?"

"Where does Françoise live in Toulouse?"

"I don't know Françoise."

"That's impossible. You visit Françoise and Renée. . . .'

"I knew Renée Nouveau, but she disappeared a long time ago. I don't know Françoise."

The Gestapo officer tapped with his pencil.

"I hope you are not going to be difficult. Where does Françoise live?"

"I don't know."

The level voice repeated: "We want to know where Françoise lives."

Pat remained silent. A second later, at a sign from the man at the desk, two men leapt on him. First the chin, the nose and cheeks were punched viciously; then the stomach kicked, one man holding him as he fought and another systematically pounding his eyes, stomach and nose until a red mist rose, the room turned sideways and with a final thunderous roar in his ears from a sledgehammer blow, unconsciousness released him.

When he recovered he did not think such pain was possible. Every part of his body felt broken. His eyes were open but he could not see. . . . Then he heard a familiar voice in the pitch darkness, a moment later a cigarette-lighter spluttered to life and he saw through a dream that it was Paul Ulmann. Slowly he made out that he lay on a straw mattress thrown on a stone floor, in a cell full of people, sprawling huddled shapes, some snoring, some talking. A strong smell permeated everything. There might have been twenty figures crouched in the darkness, and between them there were four baskets, from which the smell came. Some had been beaten up; some had already talked; others were trying to overcome pain in sleep with the knowledge that it would begin again tomorrow. Pat talked uneasily with Paul for a time. Inwardly he felt horrified. Paul was a Jew, and the rumours of the living death meted out to any Jew were too familiar. Pain made it difficult to talk normally, and towards three in the morning they sank into an uneasy sleep. Figures crept over them towards the baskets, the smell grew worse and the five-feet thick walls excluded all external sounds.

It was light again and a German voice was calling, "O-Lee-Arie—where is O-Lee-Arie?" As consciousness came to him pain stabbed from every part of his body, his chest felt crushed, and every breath sent fresh agony through his ribs. A terrible thirst assailed him, but there was no water to drink, nothing to eat, nothing to clean his battered face; only the big German guard propelling him down the stone corridor.

They were back in the same room and the man with the

186

scarred chin was waiting. In his hand he had Pat's diary and the questions began at once. "Now, bastard—you have an appointment here today for ten. Who is it with? Beside him was a French interpreter, one of the band of semi-criminal types who collaborated with the Gestapo. Pat had decided to delay the next beating up as long as possible. It was now seven-thirty. If he faked his information about the rendezvous there might be peace until ten.

Slowly, as if afraid, he said: "it is with Monsieur Benoit."

"Where?"

"At La Frégate."

"Where at La Frégate?"

"In the buffet."

This was necessary because the entry in Pat's diary read: "10 o'clock Buffet—Frégate." Buffet was in fact the cover name of Madame Piccabia, the woman he had to meet. To prevent the Gestapo discovering Buffet to be a name at all, he used it as a place, but the Frenchman at once intervened. He knew the French only used the word *buffet* in relation to a station. "What do you mean, *buffet*?"

"French-Canadians talk of a restaurant buffet as well as a station buffet," Pat lied.

"You are a French-Canadian?"

"Yes."

"Where were you born?"

"Quebec."

The Gestapo man broke in: "Describe Monsieur Benoit." Pat now built up a detailed picture of a purely imaginary man he had no possibility of meeting anywhere. A long pause followed. Dirty, hungry, thirsty and in extreme discomfort he was kept in the office for the next two hours, unmolested and in the interval his pain diminished.

At ten minutes to ten, four husky plain-clothes men left for La Frégate and cold fear came back to Pat. He had already prepared a quite convincing explanation of the non-appearance of M. Benoit, but doubted its reception by an enraged Gestapo.

At half-past ten, the four men came tramping back again

and the fury burst. The Frenchman spoke first in fluent, maddened French. Then the Gestapo chief said, "You have three minutes to tell me the truth!" He glanced at his watch. Pat burst out passionately. "It's not my fault if he's not there, is it?"

"What do you mean?"

"He must have heard of my arrest and stayed away." Madame Piccabia had, in fact, kept the rendezvous, and while the Germans circulated in the lounge looking for a tall, dark man with a moustache and horn-rimmed spectacles, she passed and repassed them looking for Pat.

The Gestapo man hesitated, thinking.

"All right," he said at last. "We'll try one more. God help you if he isn't there." He opened the diary. "The next note is for twelve o'clock. Who is he and where shall we find him?"

Solemnly, elaborately, Pat once more described an imaginary person. Another two hours without fresh pain would almost completely restore his strength, but as he carefully added details of the café, the table and the password, a sudden chill struck him. This time there would be no excuses, no escape, but there were other reasons why he must at any cost delay the Gestapo until the last possible minute. Underground intelligence usually spread the news of an arrest within forty-eight hours, and if he could keep silent for that time, scores of agents would have been warned.

The second appointment was duly kept by the Gestapo and when no one resembling the description given appeared, they returned in a cold fury. Without a word they leapt on Pat. They battered him from one to the other and when he showed signs of fighing back, an iron ruler was brought down several times on his head. The pain was worse than any he had known and as he fell to the floor they kicked him on the head, the groin and on the shins until blood came. Semi-conscious, he could hear the thudding of their boots beginning to dull, and then a wave of blackness came down.

When he recovered consciousness they were asking questions about another appointment at noon the following day, but red balls seemed to be swelling and bursting rhythmically in his head, and he knew he had to meet Albert but could not speak of it. The questioning seemed to go on for hours.

That night the cell stank more than ever and Paul Ulmann had gone. Pat did not sleep very much. In the early morning came the call again: "O-Lee-Arie—O-Lee-Arie." This time, extraordinarily, he was driven back to Gestapo Headquarters by an agent known to him. He had sat opposite Schweitzer one day in a black-market restaurant and described himself as an engineer. Now the same Schweitzer drove the car with one hand, his other buried in the pocket of his trenchcoat.

"If you move," he said, "you are a dead man." Pat said nothing. Schweitzer was driving a Mercedes-Benz and suddenly exclaimed:

"It's a nice car, isn't it?" Still Pat said nothing.

"I travel all over France looking for chaps like you," Schweitzer went on, without drawing response. Pat was thinking—if I had a knife, I'd risk the gun and try to cut the bastard's throat.

That afternoon there was a new man waiting in the Gestapo office. A tall, pleasant-looking person who received him politely, offered him a chair and began by saying: "We know far more about your Organization than you imagine. I talked to Louis Nouveau and Jean de la Olla in Paris. They told us a great deal." Pat said nothing.

"Tom Groome too—but he, I'm afraid, has been shot."

Was it true? Was any of it true? Was Tom dead, finished, already? The thought sent a shiver through Pat. Presently the questions began with an almost casual air. It was some time before Pat discovered that his new inquisitor was a doctor of philology brought into the Gestapo because of his fluent French. Touching the civilized sensibilities which he saw were still below the surface Pat suddenly said: "What would you think of a German officer who gave away information?" The question led to a brief philosophic discussion. Filthy, tired, in pain, Pat tried to sustain the thread to gain more time, but the doctor of philology quickly became impatient. Sitting in the room were four German Security Service soldiers impassively watching the proceedings. Presently the questions sharpened. Pat tried to answer obliquely, and anger broke up the pleasant lines of the doctor's face; abruptly he got up and left the room.

A big, dark man with a square face and scarred cheek, wearing a glittering uniform, now burst in and came to attention. The soldiers leapt to their feet, saluted and remained standing, stiff as ramrods.

"I am Rittmeister Redzeck, the commandant of the Gestapo of Toulouse. I am told you don't want to talk. You have two minutes to make up your mind to speak."

He strode out of the door again and the four soldiers relaxed. Two minutes later, precisely to the second, the doctor appeared.

"I hope for your sake that you are going to talk."

"It depends on your questions."

"Tell me the names of the men in Toulouse you were in touch with."

"I cannot do that."

The doctor sighed, slipped out of the door and the Rittmeister returned at once. Pat stopped breathing; terror had him in its grasp; he felt hopelessly afraid. There was an animal look in the Rittmeister's eyes as he snapped his fingers. The four soldiers advanced upon Pat. All over again his body was broken, the blows dislodging teeth, mashing his gums against his jaw, covering his face in blood, blinding him, the pain growing to that pitch where consciousness began to slip away.

The Rittmeister came in. "Are you ready?" he said. At first Pat was almost ready—he could stand no more—and he felt he would have to talk. Then, through a red mist he saw the brutal face drawing nearer and nearer and the features seemed to enlarge with evil. "Are you ready?" the thick lips hissed, close to Pat, and Pat spat out "No!" with blood and venom.

The Rittmeister snapped his fingers. Pat's body whipped backwards and forwards convulsively under the pain and he felt he must scream, before the black and grey waves overwhelmed everything.

When Pat recovered semi-consciousness he could not see. Pain tore deeply into his body, but his arms were tied to something and he could not see. The sudden thought seized him that he had gone blind from the blows, but it was probably just the blackness of a cell. He could feel that his face was one swollen mass, his eyes puffy slits. He could just move his hands and his fingers felt what must be the legs of a chair. Struggling with the mists in his mind, he thought, from the pressure of one leg against another, that he must be naked.

Half-dead senses did not at first notice the increasing cold, but the air, drunk in icy draughts, stimulated feeling. An avalanche roared in his head and he drooped into unconsciousness again. Conscious once more at what seemed a moment later, he opened and shut his eyes, straining to see, and in the dead, still blackness a star seemed to glow, vibrate and burst. There was an odd, dimly heard whirring like a motor, shaking the walls of whatever dungeon held him trapped. Presently there was no feeling in his feet and legs, but a curious sense of blood freezing in his veins sent barbs of pain to every part of his chest. Frost settled on his lips, his finger tips went numb, and one by one, it was as if the fingers were falling off. As the icy net of cold was drawn through the last warm remnant of his vitals, pain and drowsiness fought with one another, and consciousness came and went.

Then he knew at last what had happened. He was in a refrigerator; he was tied naked to a chair in a refrigerator. Darkness flowed in again. A bloodless snowman frosted over with white sat in crucifixion within the metal case, feeling nothing, hearing nothing, slowly freezing towards death.

It might have been one, two, three hours. They had dragged him out again and a great blow-lamp was boring a hole deeply into his bowels. The steadily growing pain, the sense of a knife splitting open every limb as it sprang back to life, was only possible to the white heat of a blow-lamp. But as the frost melted from his eyelids, water poured out of his hair and his whole body dissolved from iron into fire, he saw with slowly recovered sight that it

191

was an ordinary electric fire burning close to him. There was a moment when he thought he might scream, and at that moment they forced cognac between his lips and another pain stabbed inside his chest.

The questioning began again. At first the words were dim. Then he knew that they were asking about the money, and Françoise, and the appointments and addresses. He slumped sideways in the chair and they propped him up and began again. There was a pool of water round the chair and everything dripped.

He had learnt something now. Before the torture began, fear drove one towards the words which should never be spoken and at the very threshold, abject fear found them on the lips, the one way out of the unimaginable nightmare. But when the beating and the torture began, a mighty fury broke, a fury that one man could induce in another, these animal grunts, a gathering of all the forces of that heritage which gave man self-respect, and a tigerish power to fight barbarians capable of such things rose with a force momentarily greater than pain itself. It did not last. Pain won in the end and the raging weakness of the senses overwhelmed the splendid moment of self-annihilation, but perhaps by then one was on the verge of unconsciousness. . . .

The refrigerator door had closed again. He was tied in the chair. The black frost settled on the senses. His blood began to freeze and he reeled deeper and deeper into nothingness. Time ceased again.

Someone was saying: "We're not as bad as that—here, drink this." It was hot coffee, beautiful, rich, brown, steaming coffee, but he could not feel the rim of the cup when they first put it against blue and swollen lips. "It's awful to see a British officer in this state—here, drink."

The room moved in waves. He drank. It was indescribable. A dry, rasping throat, and pain, leaving weakness in every limb, could not come easily to the act. "And try some cognac, too." He wolfed it down, like an animal. It burnt fiercely and the room still moved in waves.

Behind his pain he was thinking. . . .

Tom Groome

Three airmen on the Line in September 1942 pose with members of the Organization before a poster offering rewards for information of their whereabouts. On the left is Mlle Fillerin, who carried on with underground work after the arrest of her parents

Pat O'Leary at Baden-
Baden, 1946

"We keep in touch." On the left, Jacques Wattebled, next to him Bob
Sheppard, then Pat. On the right, Fabien de Cortes and his wife

Now for humanity, the appeal to reason, the knowledge of so many ill-defined borderlines between one loyalty and another which made it possible to twist logic in the service of betrayal, to rationalize, to deceive oneself. They knew every trick in this elaborate trade. There was a towel blanket rubbing his back, a smell of camphorated alcohol and the face of the doctor coming into better focus.

The questioning began softly, deftly, and Pat understood why men talked. Fierce enough agony brought the desire for death, the release from agony the desire for life, and it would be impossible not to talk soon. Deliberately he conjured up the faces of Jean de la Olla and Louis and Eddie. They had believed in him. He was their leader. If he behaved like a weakling, everything was deceptive, worthless, sordid . . . but he must find some way out. He did not want to die and he did not want to speak, but if this went on. . . . Already he had achieved one thing; he had kept them at bay for forty-eight hours and the warnings to agents must have gone out.

He was alone in a separate cell that night. It had no light, heating or water. A handful of straw covered a wooden bed and there was the inevitable bucket. Food was restricted to a few pieces of grey bread and cups of ersatz coffee, and now whatever position he took on the wooden bed, there was agony. Especially the great shooting pain which stabbed deeply and slowly up the back of his head distressed him. This would go on day after day. The beating, the refrigerator, the questioning, and slowly his physical strength would dwindle, his will collapse. He must find some way out before it really happened.

That night the door of the next cell opened, a man was thrust in and fell down groaning. The not very thick wall did no more than muffle his groans and at three in the morning, Pat learnt by tappings and shoutings that he was a police inspector who had been savagely beaten up, and was due to be shot within twenty-four hours. Death by shooting seemed the inevitable end for Pat, too. He tried to face up to death and it was to become a steadily developing ritual. Whatever he did now could only delay death. Death would always be waiting at the end of the line. Perhaps it didn't so much matter what intervened. But death at thirty-two . . . death in the prime of life. . . .

Two days later a guard came into the cell and said, "You leave for Marseille tonight—get yourself cleaned up." At midday he was given his first reasonable meal for days. A shaving brush, some soap and a razor arrived, and he made an attempt to cut away some of the bristle on his swollen face. Momentarily nausea kept him from the food. Then he wolfed it down. Late that night, two Gestapo guards took him through the back entrance of Toulouse station straight into a specially reserved compartment. Walking freely in the air again was a wonderful experience and a small sense of life returned. As the train drew away thoughts of escape began to stir for the first time in days. A piece of bread and jam and a glass of water was the sole meal on the train and even that had to be eaten and drunk in handcuffs. The inevitable need arose in the morning and one agent accompanied him to the lavatory, still hand-cuffed, undid his flies and assisted his relief.

Pat learnt later why he was transferred from Toulouse to Marseille, instead of going straight to Fresnes, the famous transit prison near Paris. Fabien, Dr. Rodocanachi and Dijon—owner of the Petit Poucet—had all been arrested in Marseille and from small details it had sud-denly dawned on the Marseille Gestapo that Pat might be connected with these men. Ironically the Gestapo Head-quarters in Marseille now occupied a tall, modern, white-painted building in the Boulevard Rodocanachi. Taken to the sixth floor, Pat was thrust into one corner of an office with his hands above his head; thirty minutes later, his arms numb, he heard footsteps, a hand touched him on the shoulder and a pleasant voice, speaking perfect French, said: "Are you Patrick O'Leary?"

Pat swung round. "Yes," he said.

A tall, fair-haired man, wearing a light blue suit, spot-less white shirt, check tie and suède shoes of the same sky-blue colour as his suit, smiled at him. Brutality wore many guises. This was quite a new one.

"I'm very pleased to meet you," the man said. "My name's Dunker Delage. Come this way. . . ."

They went by lift to the ground floor and paused at the door. "Don't try to get away," Dunker said. "I can shoot as well as I understand you do. I kill my man at fifty yards."

Something in the way he said it, some dash of boasting not usual in Gestapo agents, gave Pat his second clue to the odd nature of Dunker Delage. The first had been his clothes. They crossed a courtyard, climbed the stairs to what was obviously Delage's office on the second floor, and he greeted his German secretary elaborately.

"Take your coat off," Delage said, "and sit down."

The warmth of the building, the lack of food, the stiffness and pain from his injuries, and the terrible exhaustion, brought a passing sense of faintness. Pat sat down and dragged his senses back sharply as Delage pressed a button, a man entered, an order was given and a big file presently appeared on Dunker's desk. "This," he said, tapping it, "is what we call the Acropolis file. It concerns your Organization."

He proceeded to give a fairly good picture of part of the Organization and suddenly said: "Would you like a Pernod from your old friend Dijon at the Petit Poucet? Champagne if you like. We have quite a lot of drink from his bar. . . . We have that little bastard Fabien, too. Tough —very tough—he hasn't talked yet—but he will. We'll get him to talk all right, have no fear. . . ."

Again the note jarred. This was no normal Gestapo agent. He was talking too much for one thing and he seemed far too anxious to make an impression. Pat watched Dunker closely, observing the long thin neck with the prominent Adam's apple, the pale face, the beautifully fitting clothes, the carefully manicured nails.

Later he thought that inspiration came from these oddities in Dunker's character. Now the talk ran on easily enough until the door opened and there lounged into the room an extraordinary apparition. Once again beautifully dressed, with a neglected tie twisted to one side, his reddened face unshaven, his breath reeking of drink, and shreds of tobacco clinging to his lips, the young man sat down on a corner of Dunker's desk, lit a cigarette and talked away, disregarding the presence of Pat. He must,

Pat felt, be a very important person, but when five minutes later, with a cheery nod towards the prisoner, he left again, Dunker said: "That gentleman is a Jew. He has given away a lot of his compatriots. But once there are no more Jews to give away—it's his turn."

Late that afternoon, Pat was driven to St. Pierre prison and pushed into yet another cell. The same mattress of straw, very dirty and with lice crawling over it; the same bucket left all night and removed in the morning; but there was more light in the cell, and light had become very precious. Lying on the palliasse, Pat examined an idea which had come to him watching Dunker talking to the Jew, an idea capable of delaying the beatings and torture which could break his spirit very soon. Detail by detail he unfolded to himself the story he would tell and then he swung away in his mind and examined the whole narrative from a distance. Imaginatively, he deduced the questions which would follow, the chain of interrogation, stringing together every possible answer. Sleep came with difficulty. He was suddenly anxious to know whether it would work, whether he could stop the torture and preserve an interval of peace between now and the inevitable death which he knew awaited him.

On the second morning Dunker remained so charming that he did not execute his plan. He asked politely about the British representatives in Spain, Switzerland and Geneva, and Pat as politely invented a number of highly original characters selected at random from fictional counterparts. The secretary solemnly made notes.

In the afternoon it was different. Remote questions vanished, the threats began and at last Dunker said: "You *must* tell me what I want to know. Otherwise. . . ."

That night in the cell old wounds awoke, the pain from past torture came back, an agonized mind twisted and turned knowing that it was going to happen again, that it must happen again before his collapse and confession would ring quite true. One more bout of torture, and then the words would spring convincingly from his lips. But he must bear it once more to make the alibi complete.

The following day it came. Each time it seemed that the

final intensity of pain had been reached and each time it was worse. Pat awoke on the fourth day with lice crawling over him, the bucket stinking, his clothes greasy, the bristle on his chin growing into a beard, his face swollen hideously, and every limb in his body raw. The guard unlocked the door, gave him the mess called coffee and the regulation piece of grey bread.

Ten minutes later he left the cell with a curious exhilaration, for today the experiment would begin. In the office on the second floor a big bull-frog of a man was waiting. Dunker had vanished and Pat's heart missed a beat. "You are going to talk today," the man said. "You have *got* to talk."

Watched by three German soldiers he took Pat's fingers and began to bend them backwards. The stab of pain was mild but it opened the long imaginative chain, which at its extremity could end in madness.

"All right. I've decided to talk."

Five minutes later he began to unfold a long and detailed story to the smiling Dunker, while his secretary tapped at her typewriter. He began by saying that any British underground organization put the emphasis on security, and every cell was counterchecked against another to meet the known weaknesses of the strongest men. The cells of Organization Pat were built on the principle that what one did not know, one could not say, and none of the key men in the Organization were French. Half a dozen agents sent over from England had each taken charge of a separate cell. Radio communication was one cell, finance another, Spanish guides a third. Intercommunication was carefully sealed off by means of passwords. Pat knew that it was an ideal which he unfolded to Dunker. He knew that if their haphazard Organization, which grew so lopsidedly until control at the edges slipped from his hands, had been brought within such a discipline, he might still be a free man and something in the knowledge gave conviction to his words. He was telling Dunker what they *should* have done with something of the force of anger and regret.

"Where did you meet the agents?" Dunker demanded.

"In cafés."

"Which?"

"Sometimes the Super-Bar. Sometimes the Café de la Paix. But it's useless going to any of them."

"Why?"

"They know I'm arrested."

"How do they know?"

"If I didn't turn up for three rendezvous in a row it was understood that I had been arrested."

"Where did they live?"

"I don't know."

"Bastard—you're lying."

"The whole basis of security was to meet them in cafés only. I passed on instructions. I knew nothing beyond that."

"Nothing? You know what they look like!"

"Yes."

"Describe Albert."

This was the key to the whole elaborate system of duplicity. For Albert, who was dark and powerfully built, Pat gave the description of a tall, blond and fat man. The secretary took down every detail. Several invented descriptions followed. Suddenly, one hour later, Dunker picked up an early page.

"Just repeat this stuff about Albert," he said.

If Pat had invented his story it would have been useless to try to recall what he had said, but now he had only to conjure up the real man and describe his precise opposite, to get complete accuracy.

When he went back to the filthy cell again that evening, Pat felt encouraged because the threats had diminished and the thugs had not been summoned. The following morning a new and extraordinary character came upon the scene. When the cell door opened there stood a short, powerfully built man with a distinguished face and fine eyes, considering Pat expressionlessly. His flawlessly cut Wehrmacht uniform carried the three silver pips of a captain, but aristocratic assurance seemed to add considerably to his rank. He looked at Pat's brutally beaten face, permitted the slightest expression of distaste to cross his features and said: "That won't happen again. My name is Hans." Pat ignored the proffered hand, and shrugging slightly, Captain Hans said: "You need a razor, soap, towels, shirts . . . they will be sent."

To Pat's astonishment, one hour later every item which Captain Hans had named was delivered to his cell. The luxury of washing, of trying to shave, of wearing a clean shirt and fresh underclothes, was wonderful, but somewhere at the back of his mind he knew that this recovery of the small amenities must be a deliberate trick. The aristocratic officer returned two hours later. "Come with me in my car," he said. It was a beautiful car and as they drove off towards the Gestapo office, Captain Hans said he had come in on the night train from Paris. He glanced at Pat. "We've known about you for months," he said, "and we've been after you. Now you're caught. That's sport—the luck of the game."

Slowly it became clear to Pat that this man, with his flawless manners and beautiful clothes, his concern for the humanities and serene self-confidence, was a member of the Secret Service of the German Army.

Dunker had clearly met him before and as they greeted one another, showed him respect. The day's questioning began in a different atmosphere. Presently Dunker put a question and Pat said: "That's difficult to answer."

"Difficult!" Dunker roared. "What do you mean? Answer it!"

"It's not easy to remember . . ." Pat began.

"*Schweinhund*—answer!"

A smooth, calm voice broke in: "I quite agree with the gentleman—a most difficult question. . . . May I . . . ?" Captain Hans slid into control of the interrogation with almost imperceptible persistence. He conducted it in a classically correct manner. Dunker listened and grew steadily more sullen. Pat now knew that this was the greatest piece of luck. Optimism had always been tempered by the knowledge that deceiving the Gestapo at any length was generally a forlorn hope, but now . . . Dunker's own character combined with the unexpected appearance of Captain Hans to reinforce an atmosphere in which the elaborate duplicity he had begun to practise might conceivably win an interval of peace. No other combination of circumstances could have produced quite the right effect, and presently a third factor appeared which divided the enemy even more effectively.

The three men met again at precisely the same hour on the second day and Pat became aware that he was witnessing a battle between the Abwehr who despised the civilian thuggery of the Gestapo, and the Gestapo who regarded the Abwehr as just another branch of the Army, incompetent to interrogate spies. It went deeper than that. Clearly Hans regarded the Nazi Party's intervention in Army affairs with extreme distaste.

There were moments, during the six days which followed, when Pat felt himself an unimportant pawn in the game, and any flaws in the elaborate fictions he produced were overwhelmed by the bitterness of other rivalries, while the secretary continued to pour down page after page of notes.

Then one morning the Wehrmacht officer wasn't there. Dunker settled back in his chair with venomous pleasure. "Now that your friend has gone we can get down to real business," he said, "and no more kid-glove stuff." Yet something of the atmosphere remained. For the moment there were no more beatings up. Several long days of depositions, covering seventy-five typewritten pages were at last completed, and one morning the usual summons from the filthy gloom of his cell in St. Pierre prison did not come.

At first all that Pat heard in the cell set deep in the dungeon walls of the old fort was a blurred and very faint voice. Then, straining his ear against the wall he suddenly made out his own name. At last he realized that the voice he could faintly hear was the voice of Françoise Dissart. The words were echoing round the walls in the outer courtyard. *"Mon Pat! Ou es-tu? Mon cher Pat! Pat! Pat!"* The impulse to hammer on the door became overwhelming, but he knew that she must not be connected with him in any way and sat there, feeling very strange, as the dim echo of her wailing voice came down to him again and again.

"Pat! Pat! Mon cher Pat!" Somewhere outside the prison, recklessly disregarding her appalling danger, the old lady with her pile of grey hair must be striding about throwing her voice against the wall in an effort to make him hear. Pat prayed they would not take her, prayed that the guards, unfamiliar with the English word Pat, would regard her as a crazy old eccentric possessed with the idea that someone was falsely imprisoned in St. Pierre.

No one knew why they did not arrest her, and it was years before Pat learnt how Françoise Dissart, with bitter determination, carried on one section of the Organization throughout the remainder of the war. Broken up it might be, ill-fated and the victim of appalling treason, but many fine spirits rose in the ruins and parts continued to function until the very end. Only when Mifouf died did Françoise's courage and determination waver. By then over six hundred Allied airmen and soldiers had found— the way back.

17

THE train moved steadily towards Paris, and looking round at the faces of Fabien and Paulette Gastou, Pat marvelled afresh. Slender, dark, Spanish looking, Fabien de Cortes seemed little more than a boy, and for him to have stood out against the full brutalities of the Gestapo seemed impossible. And Paulette Gastou . . . there was nothing more than apprehension in her beautiful brown eyes.

That night, on the long journey to Paris, it seemed absurd that Paulette should ever be standing for twenty-four hours in a barrack square with scores of other scarecrow women, deliberately prevented from going to the lavatories; should witness women fouling themselves, and when one slipped away to the lavatory, should see The Panther, a woman S.S. guard, beat her to the ground, kick her head and jump with full force on her stomach until blood came from her mouth. . . .

Three Gestapo men lounged in the corridor of the train against the sliding door, looking in at regular intervals. They did not seem particularly brutal. The carriage was an ordinary passenger carriage, and they were not even handcuffed.

Presently the roar of the wheels and the rush of a tunnel covered their voices and they talked. As they talked, two possibilities were in Pat's mind: escaping himself or covering the escape of Fabien to convey messages to key men still at large.

There was no food or drink on the train, and hunger and thirst steadily mounted. As the hours wore on, the guards relaxed in the corridor and a plan began to form in Pat's mind. Presently he conveyed it to the others in whispers. On the rack above his head was his coat, and if he made a great show of taking it down and struggling into the coat, as the train ran into Paris, he could spread it over the door and limit the Gestapo agents' view for a few seconds. In those seconds Paulette was to open the opposite window, Fabien drop to the ground and dash away. There remained the question of judging the highest speed at which it was possible to leap from the train and a system of signals to co-ordinate coat and leap. It took time to brief Fabien in scattered whispers on the whole affair of Roger, to stress the importance of trying to tell London exactly what had happened through Gibraltar or Geneva. They must know that Roger, like Paul Cole, was a complete, vicious and highly dangerous traitor.

The journey seemed very long. To three people who had been in the Gestapo's hands for ten weeks it was exhausting. At last the familiar landmarks came up, the brakes began to grind, the train slowed and, watching the flashing poles and houses, Pat saw them slow to that point where he rose to his feet, signalled to Fabien and began to pull down his coat. A moment later, he turned his back on the doors, spreading the coat to the full extent of both arms, and struggled to find an invisible armhole. The click of the window was not noticeable, the slight figure of Fabien had vanished and Paulette pulled the window up again, before Pat succeeded in getting into his coat.

The sliding door sprang open, the Gestapo guard looked in and gave a violent exclamation: "Where's the little chap!"

"I don't know," said Pat.

"What do you mean, you don't know?"

It was absolutely vital to give Fabien two clear minutes.

"He went to the lavatory."

The train was moving very slowly. One Gestapo man dashed down the corridor to the lavatory. Another said: "I didn't see him go."

Pat remained silent. The train shuddered to a standstill. Gripped by the lapels of his coat, a voice demanded: "Come on, where is he? Where?" Reprisals on prisoners who permitted another to escape were sometimes worse than on the prisoner himself and that was one reason why Pat did not go instead of Fabien. More important, he hoped to be able to save some of his men by taking all responsibility on himself.

They never found Fabien. A French railway worker told him how to get out of the station unobserved, and he slipped away and reached some friends. In Paris, a hairdresser changed the colour of his hair, a tailor his clothes, and he succeeded in reaching Françoise Dissart in Toulouse. From there he made his way to Farrell in Geneva and at last the story of Pat's arrest became known in England.

As the dismal dawn light came up Pat could make out the furniture of the cell. This, he knew, was Fresnes prison outside Paris, a stepping-stone to Germany, concentration camps and death. The cell had an iron bed with a straw palliasse, a lavatory pan, a flap-table and a chair; a luxurious cell comparatively, with a real window of frosted glass permitting some light to enter.

A sound destined to become very familiar filled the air as the steel food trolley rolled along the steel rails in the corridor. It was six o clock in the morning, a key jangled in the lock, the steel door crashed open and there was a little Frenchman in rags waving a big ladle. "Your mug— quickly," he said. Pat sought swiftly for the mug.

"Quickly, blast you, or Fritz will start bellowing."

Pat found the mug, held it out, and a portion of black steaming swillage was poured into it. Somewhere above, another key grated in another lock and a big German voice roared: *"Schweinhund! Schnell!* SCHNELL!" The ersatz coffee tasted bitter, slightly sour and was lukewarm. There was no bread. Later he found that lunch consisted of a small bowl of watery soup and a piece of bread, and supper another cup of ersatz coffee. Twice a week a piece of meat two inches square was included in the lunch. Taken together it was barely enough to sustain life.

On the first day, a man who was to become appallingly familiar limped into the cell. "Keep it clean—behave yourself—and there won t be any trouble," he said. He was a short, disabled German soldier. Dark, strongly built, he had an air of brooding melancholy. He said little and he could obviously be very tough, but Pat quickly found that brutality only occurred at the orders of his superiors. He was desperately afraid of his superiors.

There now began a routine which was to run on for many months, and every fresh day Pat knew might be his last. There could be no other penalty than death for what he had done, and quite isolated in his cell, he tried again to reconcile himself to the final act, the moment when the firing-squad would level its guns and shatter his body.

In one sense he knew that he had a tremendous zest for living, but always underneath, from very early days, there had been deep qualifications. A lack of meaning, a sense of frustration, an awareness that no satisfaction could ever last, and deeper conflicts still had constantly troubled him. The doctor's life had only reconciled him to living for intervals, and he had known times when he understood those men who said that they wished they had never been born. Depths of awareness below the surface had never made ordinary life entirely acceptable. Death by shooting shouldn't mean so much to a man conscious of all this. But it wasn't death. One could accommodate obliteration. It was the way of death, the fear that the animal inside him, craving life, would break and destroy the dignity of the last moment; the fear of spoiling the last act of domination over death; of not finishing the story as triumphantly as these last three years had seen it grow.

He could see it all clearly: The hour before the dawn, the clamp of heavy feet, the silence of the guards, the cold air, and the men waiting as they led him to the wall. If he had to die this way, let him die with dignity. In the many long weeks of solitary confinement, the words came frequently. . . . Let me die with dignity. Once in the middle of the night, with the airless silence of the prison broken only by snores and groans, he came to the sentence again, and it was as if he spoke to someone. Brought up by the Jesuits and deeply imbued with religious thought, Pat O'Leary, as an adult person of thirty-two, did not easily turn to God, but in the long black nights there were times when a fresh desire for communion arose. Next to death the superficial layers of living were stripped away. Back in touch with primitive life, the stark realities of super-stition, the beating of ancient drums, rose all over again. The instinct to pray became urgent. Sometimes at night voices rose from other cells above and below him, praying aloud: "Lord, hear me—save me." "If there is a God—hear me." And sometimes a man began solemnly to chant the Lord's Prayer in a strange sing-song voice as though he didn't quite know what it was he sang.

A struggle took place in the third week. Deep reassur-ance lay in appealing to that God whose powers were so much greater than the Gestapo's; but prayer had been absent from Pat's life for ten years and to turn now to the ritual of a God he had neglected, seemed a spiritual opportunism which no worthy god would tolerate. Yet the need was overwhelming. When other men's voices rose calling on their God, the effect could be paralysing. Isola-ted, solitary, waiting for death, the temptation to com-municate in prayer with that presence said to be eternally on the edge of life, to receive once more His benediction, grew every day. Yet he did not pray. He resisted the strongest temptation. He acknowledged his God but did not want to exploit the acknowledgment, and in the end there was no prayer.

Not that isolation remained complete. There were times when singing swung through the prison like a wave, and the German guards rushed from place to place trying to quell the tramping glory of the "Marseillaise", only to have it break out in fresh places. Or the morning would bring a strong voice echoing down one line of cells:

"Pierre vous dit bonjour à tous! Courage et confiance!"
And another voice took up the message until it swelled into a roar and the German guards came bursting into cell after cell beating the prisoners brutally.

More subtly there was the air-pipe. By placing the chair on the bed, climbing on to a small shelf, and taking off the cover of the hot-air vent, Pat quickly found that he could speak to the men in the cells above and below him.

One morning a hollow puffing came through the pipe—the preliminary call sign—and a thin, ghostly voice said: "Hallo—hallo—hallo—what is your name?"

"Joseph," Pat answered. "What is yours?"

"d'Harcourt," the voice said. "Why are you here?"

"I was caught working for an escape organization. And you?"

"Resistance work"

"Your name is familiar to me—are you Pierre d'Harcourt?"

"Yes—how did you know?"

Pierre d'Harcourt—who had known Garrow and the Reverend Donald Caskie far back in the early days; d'Harcourt, the son of a distinguished French family; d'Harcourt whose life was said to have been saved because the Pope interceded with Hitler on his behalf—in the next cell. It was somehow cheering.

"I shall be sending you a present," the voice later announced, and then there was silence. Two minutes afterwards a single woollen thread unwoven from a prison blanket appeared through the air-pipe with a cigarette tied to its end. More followed, and then, supported by several threads, came a book. Pierre d'Harcourt had been in Fresnes for eighteen months and his long sentence and distinguished heritage had earned him a number of privileges which he did not hesitate to share.

Presently the blowing began from the opposite end of the pipe where it joined the cell underneath and this time a very American voice said: "'Allo, 'allo there. Say—who are you?"

The formulas were repeated. This was an American pilot named Ball who had been shot down, tried to escape in civilian clothes and was taken to Fresnes as a possible spy.

Pat unwound a woollen thread from his blanket and passed down two cigarettes sent by d'Harcourt. "Say, that's wunnerful!" a voice shouted up the pipe and Pat cautioned him immediately. The prison picked up and dangerously echoed every word, the peephole in the door was liable to be opened at any moment, and an eye sweep the cells, and no one must be caught using the air-pipe.

Twice, sometimes three times a day, short whispered conversations took place, and the picture of each person filled out until Ball and d'Harcourt seemed like old friends Pat knew by sight.

He met Ball by accident one day. Escorted to the showers he found the last party still busy washing and among them one big, tall fellow with an American accent. "You must be Ball," Pat said swiftly.

"Well—whadderyerknow—you're the marvellous guy who sends me presents."

They talked for a few seconds before the guards silenced them.

In the second week, a young man was thrown into the cell next to Pat's and within a few minutes Pat was tapping on the wall.

"Who are you?"

A subdued voice said: "I am Jean—who are you?"

"I'm Joseph. Why are you here?"

"I haven't done anything."

"Steady, here comes the Barker." A heavy tramp went down the corridor and a German guard bellowed for silence. A minute later Pat said: "Watch out, they sometimes come sneaking up in slippers. What did they get you for?"

"Nothing! Nothing!"

"Don't worry, it's not so bad."

"I'm going to be shot."

"Why?"

"I haven't done a thing, not a thing. It's terrible."

The last words were almost a sob. Slowly the miserable story emerged. The boy had indeed done nothing. His name happened to appear by accident in a notebook found on a Communist and he had been arrested and flung into jail on entirely false charges. Now he was sure that he would be shot. As he finished his story a faint shuffle came down the corridor again, and they fell silent. A moment later the peephole on Pat's door slid open, an eye watched him sitting motionless on the bed. He waited some time and the cover slid up again. He was still sitting on the bed. He gave the guard two minutes to move away, knocked on the wall and said: "Take heart, I've done far worse things than you, and I haven't been shot."

208

He felt sure it would not happen to the boy. But one morning soon afterwards, the young man came back from interrogation and his voice was hardly a whisper. "They sentenced me to death," he said. Pat tried to comfort him. It was useless. The still air, the sullen glare of the electric light bulb, the eyes swivelling in the door, all told the boy that there was no escape.

A week later, at four in the morning, while the whole prison slept, heavy boots came down the corridor, the cell door was thrown open and the boy made a strange animal noise. In the hush which precedes the dawn it was a terrible sound. He was fighting as they led him away. Five minutes later the peephole in Pat's cell was swung open. He lay wide awake on the bed, full of a great anger at the stupidity which could destroy innocent people for a formula, fighting with bewilderment that he who was guilty of every crime in their calendar should remain alive. Why hadn't they shot him when they so easily shot the boy? Why? Why? The question persisted for days.

Sleep was often fitful and interrupted. The heavy tread of the guards came down the corridor intermittently, the air was always heavy and sullen, and three or four times in the night the guards switched on the electric light, peered through the peephole, switched off the light and passed on. The unshaded bulb with its harsh beam left a dazzle in the eyes when the guard had gone, and once awake, a torrent of thoughts began—sometimes looking back over the past, a slow sense of detachment from life giving clarity to thoughts usually clouded, and sometimes an extraordinary feeling of lightness and lucidity.

One's brain had been washed clean. Small distractions no longer mattered and the tiresome machinery of eating, talking and earning a living were pushed into the background. It had been a full, rich, convulsive life. The drives of an early Jesuitical education still ran deep, the disciplines, the powerful conscience, the need to add something to life bringing continual dissatisfactions, a sense of guilt. . . . Parts of the record left a deep distaste . . . until these last few years. Something worth while had been accomplished now; something over the past three years had been forged at great pain and risk and now, in the isolation of this cell, it could be measured in redemption against the rest.

In the morning there were the physical and mental exercises; the physical to keep the body taut, and the mental to keep the mind alert; a whole series of small disciplines to hold the personality together. And then one morning he found an old nail between the slats in the floor, and began boring at the window-pane, spending two long hours softly turning and turning, watching the minute indentation deepen. He gave two hours to the window every day. It was hardly more than a blemish on the window after two days. Simultaneously the bent handle of a spoon was twisted into one shape after another. In the morning the nail; in the afternoon the spoon; one slowly penetrating the window, the other twisted and kneaded through infinite shapes until at last it began to slip easily into the lock on the window.

He had no watch. All his possessions had been taken from him. His suit was shabby and stained, his beard long, but he knew from the movement of light round the cell wall the approximate time of the day, and no longer cared about the name of the day. Or if the desire to know the date suddenly became overwhelming he climbed to the shelf, blew on the pipe and asked: "What day is it today? Tuesday?" And a swift conversation with d'Harcourt and the American airman destroyed another small stretch of time while they tried to establish the date.

Every fresh prisoner from the outside world contrived to pass on news of the war; every day someone amongst the thousands of cyclists who pedalled to work past the prison walls suddenly bawled a fragment of news from the B.B.C. Memorized, the news was bawled or tapped from one to another, the air-pipe, the tappings and shoutings keeping the prisoners aware of what was happening in the outer world. Three days after the Allies pushed the Germans out of North Africa, the prisoners knew. When Italy was threatened a wave of excitement ran through the cells, shouted conversations reached fever pitch and the guards dashed from cell to cell brutally silencing one after another. But the names of the Italian islands taken by the Allies were given; Sicily was said to be the next target and nothing could quell entirely the primitive drumming of intelligence.

After nine days' work with the nail, Pat had bored a small hole right through the window. Fixing his eye to this he could see the corridor downstairs along which passed prisoners who were permitted to exercise in the outside pens and it became a fascinating parade, a wonderful new interest. Suddenly one day Pat glimpsed Louis Nouveau moving down the corridor. He was only there for a moment but at once Pat began preparations to communicate with him.

An agent parachuted from London and captured by the Germans arrived and quickly recited every item of news to the three cells on the third floor, one of them Pat's. Listening casually, Pat suddenly pricked up his ears as he heard the name of Louis Nouveau's wife. The man had arrived back in London from France, and reported to the French headquarters where he found Renée Nouveau already at work. He spoke of her under her pseudonym Marquisette.

Excitedly, the next day, Pat pressed his eye to the window, waiting for Louis to appear in the corridor, but it was the wrong day. Three times he kept vigil for nearly an hour. Suddenly Louis was there and Pat put his mouth to the hole, shouting: *"Marquisette es bien, est bien arrivée à Londres! Marquisette est bien. est bien arrivée à Londres!"*

Louis stopped in his tracks. His head twisted in every direction, and then he was hustled on. A moment later a German guard burst into Pat's cell and for the first time in Fresnes he was beaten up. It was not his normal, limping, ex-soldier guard. This one was tall and broad with hairy fists. *"Schweinhund!"* he bellowed as his fist crashed into Pat's face. *"Schweinhund!"* as the boot cracked into his groin. Having no original blasphemy, he went on smashing and beating to the same word. Weak from lack of food and exercise, Pat suddenly felt very dizzy, sick and ill, and all over again old wounds reopened, agony came back and the heavy boots left his ribs feeling as if they had been gashed. In his clumsy fury the German did not stop to ask how a voice had been made to carry through the whole courtyard and the hole in the window remained undiscovered. Pat recovered the following day and a certain gladness filled his heart. Louis's mind must be at rest in one important sense at least. Another discovery followed. At his post watching the cavalcade some days later he suddenly saw a figure just like Fabien's—but his hair was blond. Then it flashed on Pat. Could he have bleached it? Was Fabien re-arrested and in Fresnes? At first Pat's heart sank. Then—patiently—he waited his chance to communicate once more, to find out exactly what happened.

The spoon-key now fitted perfectly into the lock of the window and the lock turned. Two nights later, waiting until 2 a.m., Pat unlocked the window, stealthily opened it, and felt something resembling fresh air enter the cell. It was glorious to look out through a wide space to another far bigger area, to feel the air brushing his face, and know that he could now, at will, extend the crushing walls of his prison. Every night the small imaginative flight into the courtyard took place and momentarily his personality expanded.

Then, one night, a voice came down from a higher window

"I give you the good evening of Mifouf."

"Who are you?"

"A Canadian airman."

"Where were you arrested?"

"Near the Spanish border."

"Did you have a blond man with you?"

"That blond man was me."

"And how is Mifouf?"

"Mifouf is in good health."

"And Marquisette?"

"She is very well."

It was Fabien. Fabien re-arrested and in Fresnes. In whispered bursts with long intervals, day after day, Pat pieced together the rest of Fabien's story.

Life now had some variety. A German padre came once a

week, read from the Bible and sometimes in the face of severe penalties, left one copy with Pat. He read it eagerly from cover to cover and at once began again reading slowly, the second time, to savour the full taste of print. In the five months that he was shut in Fresnes prison he read the Bible ten times.

A short, thin, fair-haired man, the German padre hinted that he served God before Hitler and could not condone the brutalities committed in the Führer's name The signs of Gestapo treatment on Pat's face distressed him, but a smile came into his eyes when he learnt that Pat had not spoken under torture and he said: "There's no more peace with oneself when one does." They talked of life, litera-ture, and the war, and it seemed to Pat that the padre was a very worried man, puzzled to know how the old Christian virtues could be reconciled with tyranny in any form. He spoke of Russia and the Russian front and Pat learnt that things were going very badly for the Germans there. The padre had a soft warm voice and beautiful eyes, and when he spoke of Germany, both were troubled. Poor Germany, he seemed to say. What in the sweep of history will all this mean to her; what inexplicable destiny has brought her to such a pass?

Three months dragged away inch by inch. Every morn-ing the steel wheels of the food trolleys came grinding round at six, and every evening sudden darkness descended on the cell at 9 p.m. The limping German jailer came and went with hardly a word, his basilisk eye swivelled regu-larly from the peephole, and the awful routine ran to-gether in a blur. Every day Pat did his physical exercises more slowly, tried to eat the choking scraps of food, felt the fatal lassitude creeping over him which would eventually find him lying in a sullen coma on the iron bed all day long. There were no longer keys to fashion, no longer holes to bore; every scrap of interest had been dragged from the walls of the cell, and an endless repetition of crushing habit had grown to overwhelming proportions. Sometimes the desire to run madly to the door and beat and beat until it burst open rose up powerfully. Sometimes the staring electric light bulb became intolerable, as though it had burnt up all the air in the cell and presently he must suffocate.

Then, one day, for the first time, he was allowed to walk in the open air cells with a trellis separating off a garden. His legs felt weak, his movements awkward, but the air was sweet and the sense of stretching cramped limbs delightful. After that it was better back in the cell. This brief spell waited just ahead, twice a week, one hour at a time, something different to anticipate. The open cells were lined with very old brick and into the brick a thousand messages had been scratched until the walls were a mass of signs, scrawls and symbols. The usual obscenities stood beside simple messages: "I shall be dead by the time you read this. Take hope. There is a God waiting. Jean Pierre. March, 1943."

It was customary to move prisoners from one open cell to another for the one hour's exercise twice a week, and it meant that the same cell might only be reached after two, three or four weeks. Thus the message Pat scratched on the wall with a nail for Louis: *"Renée est très bien— Adolphe"*, Louis did not read until a fortnight later. He replied at once: *"Merci. Roger est un salaud."*

Another month went by. Even the bi-weekly hour in the open had begun to pall. A sudden sense that he would be left to rot in Fresnes month after month until his own harshly sustained discipline cracked and he drifted into decay, swept over him. When he looked at the men in the exercise pens through the hole in the window and saw their thin, waxen features, their listlessness, he knew how easily prison life could undermine everything.

Five months after he first entered Fresnes, on a September morning, his jailer threw open the door, ladled out the black brew and said: "Be ready to move in half an hour." Pat felt his heart jump. "What's happening now?" he asked.

There were hells worse than the hell one already knew so intimately.

"I can't tell you."

Half an hour later he was marched down the corridor

into a double cell where another man already waited, a thin, haggard Frenchman.

"What's happening?" Pat said.

"I don't know," the man answered listlessly.

The key grated in the lock, the door opened and a third man came in. It was like an apparition. Pat had adjusted himself over the months to the death of Tom Groome, and suddenly here he was in the flesh, paler and much thinner, but unmistakably Tom Groome. They fell into each other's arms. "You!" Pat said, holding Tom at arm's length. "They told me you were dead.' "And you! Tom said. "The bastards! '

They embraced again, life flowed back into sluggish veins and as man after man was pushed into the cell they talked incessantly, sometimes laughing, both observing the other closely. It was wonderful to meet again like this. Company, and congenial company, had the power to divide hardship and men just back from the dead had special powers of fellowship. Presently the cell was hopelessly overcrowded, but still the prisoners arrived and found space somewhere.

Unmistakably the fourteenth prisoner to enter was an Englishman; big, tall, powerfully built, with melancholy eyes. He spoke to Pat and introduced himself. "My name's Hopper—John Hopper."

"R.A.F.?"

"No."

"Army?"

"No."

Hopper was nothing but himself and it was a year before Pat learnt in all its fantastic detail his astonishing story. Another Englishman appeared. Different from Hopper, Brian Stonehouse was thin, dark, aesthetic-looking. They greeted one another uncertainly, and Stonehouse said:

"I'm an Army man. S.O.E. What are you?"

Pat briefly explained. They exchanged a few more phrases.

"Looks as if we're for the high-jump."

"Germany?"

"Maybe."

215

Two hours went by. Twenty-five men were jammed into a cell made for two, and everyone talking in the restricted space made a deafening babble.

For all the talk, fear hung heavily in the air. Life had been hell in Fresnes but it could be worse in Germany, in the stone quarries where death came slowly and shooting was a luxury. The sound which seemed burnt into their consciousness suddenly quietened the talk, as the steel wheels of a food trolley came grinding along on the rails, but this was no ordinary meal. Extraordinarily, Red Cross parcels were distributed to the prisoners and the neat brown paper packages with the official seals seemed like an intervention from the civilized world outside. Fingers tore at string and wrappings, chocolate and cigarettes were uncovered with yells of delight. Someone suddenly said: "The last cigarette of those about to die. . . ." The words made a small silence. Then another voice said: "Ration it out—it's got to last a long time." Many ate only half the contents of their parcels, carefully wrapping the remainder for another day.

Five minutes later they were out in the courtyard surrounded by fully armed German soldiers shepherding them into a huge prison van. Up two steps into a dim, narrow corridor and each man was locked in a separate steel cell, the cells running down either side of the corridor. Narrow slits gave on to the corridor, but the outside wall of the van was blank. The journey seemed interminable and its direction uncertain. When they poured out of the van again, they were at the Gare de l'Est, the station for trains travelling east. As the last remnant of doubts disappeared and they knew for certain that they were about to enter Germany, the huddled group of prisoners, clutching old bundles and the remainder of Red Cross parcels, hardly spoke at all.

18

MARCHED into the train with iron-barred windows Pat, Tom Groome, John Hopper and Brian Stonehouse managed to keep together in one wooden compartment. They spoke very little. The carriage was unlit. In the half-light from the station, guards came and went on the platform and the hoarse cries echoed from the front of the train as a hiss of steam drowned conversation. "They could have shot us in France," said Pat. "Why take us all the way to Germany?" The logical deduction from his question should have been reassuring, but somehow it wasn't.

After dark, with tremendous joltings, the train began to move and Pat felt an appalling sense of helplessness. Nothing could stop this immutable passing from one country to another, from one code, where hope of civilized treatment remained, to another where anything could happen.

The train gathered speed. In the corridors the expressionless faces of the armed guards came and went, signals and an occasional dim light slipped by, the groups of prisoners muttered and talked. Pat and Tom exchanged war experiences with Brian Stonehouse. John Hopper remained aloof, revealing nothing. Gradually the talk fell away again. Hour after hour the journey went on, until figures sprawled against one another in half sleep, clutching the remnants of their Red Cross parcels.

Deeper and deeper they penetrated. There were long halts when the guards stamped about watchfully, talking broke out and Pat tried to see beyond the blackness of the window to the blacker countryside. Then the train jolted off again. From ten in the evening until five next morning the journey went on. It must have been just before dawn when the train drew into an unknown station. Pat started out of sleep and someone whispered, "God—listen to that." Harsh voices were shouting commands in German to savage, snarling Alsatian dogs. As the huddled prisoners all came to life there was a sudden sense of complete change. This was German soil. One could feel it in the foggy dawn which did not seem like dawn at all, in the lowering sky, the bleakly clean station and the shouting voices. Pat felt an emptiness in his stomach, a sudden sinking of his spirits and as he looked at the mass of concrete and corrugated iron which slowly slid to a halt and saw the S.S. guards moving up and down with their dogs, he heard Brian say, "Looks bloody awful, doesn't it?"

They made out the name of the station—Saarbrücken. Then they were ordered out and as they poured from the carriages, blows descended indiscriminately from many truncheons with cries of *"Raus!" "Schnell!" "Los!"* Remnants of Red Cross parcels were snatched away, one elderly Frenchman still half asleep was knocked flat on his back, and the dogs bared their teeth and bayed. "This way! This way!" There were big lorries waiting. They piled in and any man who showed signs of waiting his turn was beaten into greater speed. A vicious blow on the jaw set one man spitting blood.

The lorries lumbered away. Thirty minutes later Pat's lorry slowed down before a number of barbed-wire enclosures, lurched through a gate and jerked to a standstill. There were a number of wooden barracks, squat, ugly and grey in the light of a morning which never seemed to become day. Mirador machine-gun towers dominated the scene and in the central courtyard was a pond towards which they were ordered to run as they climbed from the lorries. For no reason at all everything had to be done at top speed, and truncheons came thudding down among the stragglers. As they reached the pond the order came in a great bellow: "March! March!" Twenty-five men were racing round and round the pond. Presently someone panted in a fierce whisper to the man ahead, "Not so fast," and a blow from a truncheon drove him on. Soon men were gasping, stumbling, trying desperately to slacken the pace as the dogs came baying at them, the guards struck again and again and a man staggered and fell into the pond. Crawling out, savage blows drove him back into the mad line again.

After the first hour the elderly Frenchman collapsed, a queer froth on his lips, and the worrying Alsatian dogs brought no response from him. Pat, his lungs bursting, his legs wavering, his eyes painful, tried not to look at the fallen man, but as he completed another circle, a guard jabbed him viciously in the ribs and it was his turn to collapse in the ice-cold water. Presently two more men fell semi-conscious, others no longer seemed to feel the truncheon blows and one man at least lay dead. For three hours it went on: and then abruptly stopped.

Immediately they were forced into line and marched to where a Ukrainian sat waiting with electric clippers. Sitting on a small stool Pat felt the first savage assault of the clippers on his head. From a long-haired, shaggy, tramplike figure, he was converted into a tonsured monk, bald except for a single ridge of hair running from the temples to the back of the head.

Then he was stripped and every remaining sign of hair removed from his body. It was a savage process leaving bleeding spots on head and groin. Next came the ice-cold shower baths. Then a man appeared with a large brush and a pot of brown disinfectant. It was sloshed over the crevices of the body and at once set up great raw stinging pains. The tonsured monk had now become a brown-painted savage.

There followed another spectacle of organized humiliation when everyone was ordered to rush to their wooden hut or *stube*, and the guards and dogs followed, crushing everyone into a pyramid round the small door, each man fighting his neighbour as the dog's teeth tore away flesh from any limb within reach.

The hut they at last scrambled into was a not very high wooden structure with three tiers of bunks built around the walls, each bunk having a filthy straw mattress. It was to become their home for the next three weeks.

Pat, Tom, John and Brian remained together, Tom tried to sleep in the bunk next to Pat s and Brian in the bunk above. They talked fitfully of what fresh horrors must lay in wait if they did not escape; but escape. . . .

They were awakened at one in the morning with brutal cries of *"Los! Schnell!"* and there were the guards prodding them with bayonets. They were rushed out into the square for a mad and meaningless roll call, some in pants, some naked in the panic-stricken dash to escape the bayonets and the rifle butts. They stood to attention for nearly an hour in the ice-cold and then were rushed back inside again. Immediately they had sunk shivering beneath the single filthy blanket the call came again "All out! All out!" and the roll call was taken once more, another spell of standing to attention leaving the men gasping with cold.

Within a few days they discovered the elaborate system of penalties. The slightest offence gave the excuse for "Twenty-five strokes!" This meant stripping a man naked, bending him over a chair with his feet and hands held by guards, while another prisoner gave the strokes with a cane. S.S. guards watched the punishment and as the first few strokes criss-crossed a man's backside with raw weals, they always shouted: "Harder! Harder!" and the blows always fell harder because the prisoner administering the punishment knew that he must satisfy his masters or suffer twenty-five strokes himself. From red the weals turned an ugly purple. The victim made no pretence of control, struggling and screaming because everyone quickly learnt that their tormentors preferred violent reactions. By the twelfth stroke the buttocks were raw and bleeding, by the twentieth they were beginning to swell and at twenty-five a man might have collapsed. It meant three weeks without being able to sit down, three weeks sleeping on one's stomach, and if one rolled over enough in the night, pains which broke up sleep and brought a man into an even worse state of exhaustion.

It was on the way to get a mug of soup which constituted supper that it happened to Pat. A prisoner in near rags stood beside a huge metal basin dishing out the mixture while the prisoners waited in a queue. Jackbooted, immaculately dressed S.S. officer Heinrich Hornetz walked up and down, watching. Suddenly it seemed to Pat that his eyes were fixed on him. Hornetz strode towards him. *"Schweinhund Englander!* Get to the end of the line!" From the middle of the queue Pat went to the end. It sometimes meant no food at all because the soup was exhausted. As Pat crept slowly forward again, Hornetz walked over to him and began speaking. "Your bastard compatriots bombed Saarbrücken last night—look what they bombed! Hospitals, women, children!" He thrust his face close to Pat's. "You bastard English slaughtering our children!" Pat moved another pace forward. Hornetz moved with him. Suddenly he spat, "What do you call that —eh—what do you call that?" Pat's face remained expressionless. He said nothing. "Answer me!" Hornetz shouted. "What do you call that?"

Moved to uncontrollable rage, Pat suddenly snapped: "I call that Coventry!"

Hornetz was too stunned for a moment to move. No one had dared to answer back for so long it seemed impossible that a prisoner could risk such arrogance. Then he began hitting Pat on the jaw, the eyes, the stomach. The first six blows were heavy and Pat staggered from place to place. Then Hornetz paused. "Attention!" he bellowed. Taking his wrist-watch off with great deliberation he began again. At the tenth blow it seemed a miracle that the stomach wall had not collapsed. Pat decided to fall down, faking unconsciousness. Hornetz now began to use his heavy boots. He kicked with tremendous force at the shins, the groin, the thighs and then turned his attention to the head. The first impact of the heavy boot on Pat's skull seemed to explode it. A great gash of pain blinded him. The kicking continued; the boot seemed to smash jaw and cheek-bone; everything reeled in sick pain, the light went dim and the sound and feel of the boot became muffled like a great drum being beaten in a large hall. Then there was silence. . . .

He was back in the *stube* and someone was sponging his face. Dimly he could make out two figures and hear voices in the distance. The outlines of the faces sharpened. They belonged to Tom Groome and John Hopper. "Try and drink this," a voice said. It was soup saved from supper by the prisoners. His face felt enormous, his teeth were broken, his nose so swollen he could not breathe through it, and pain tore at every part of his body. Waves of nausea and faintness came and went in the next twelve hours. But his head was the worst. There were times when it felt as if his head had burst and the sides of the skull were opening and closing over a great wound releasing a pain which no man could bear, and the roof span dizzily and he rushed into sick darkness again. It was only later that he knew how close to death he had come.

At first the talk of escape was theoretical as if it were a sort of exercise to relieve the distorted boredom which underlay the horror. Then, one day, John Hopper came back from the workshop and in his coat he had concealed a small saw. "I'll take care of it," said Pat and hid it in the straw of his mattress. He had not entirely recovered from Hornetz's attack, but despite the starvation diet, he was much better.

The day after Hopper had stolen the saw they worked out a firm plan. In the early morning a group of men had to empty the huge "dirt-basket" at one side of the camp. This was finished before roll call and the mass of prisoners usually waited, lined up outside the huts, while half a dozen selected men completed the job. Next to the huts stood the washroom. On a foggy morning it might be possible to slip from the huts into the washroom while the dirt detail was at work, out of the washroom towards the barbed wire, tackle a known weak spot with the saw, and while everyone stood in front of the barracks, slip away in the thick fog. There were amateur elements in the whole plan and everyone knew that it was a forlorn hope—but for the fog. The guards would shoot at the sight of a man near the wire, and one other stipulation brought the plan back into the theoretical class. The British, it was agreed, must all go together.

Twenty-four hours later it was known that a saw was missing. Prisoners were driven brutally out of the barracks, massed in the courtyard and brought to attention. Subtly sharpening the torture, the S.S. leered menacingly at one after another, without giving any indication of what was wrong. Hundreds of men were in an agony of suspense. What were the S.S. after? What had gone wrong? What had they done? The British alone knew, and felt very uneasy for bringing these threats down on everyone's head. Systematically the search began. All the limited furnishings of each block were first examined minutely and then, in threes, the mattresses brought out and opened up. Standing in the last rank of prisoners, Pat thought quickly. If they discovered the saw in his mattress it did not need much imagination to know the reaction of Heinrich Hornetz. He would probably be beaten to death.

As the second set of mattresses was brought out from the first block, Pat suddenly realized that the whole of their own *stube* was quite empty. If he could slip soundlessly back into it . . . . The plan needed great audacity and split-second timing. He chose the moment when all eyes were concentrated on the third set of three mattresses and edged, slowly at first, on tip-toe, towards the *stube* door. One false move and the guards would shoot, or if not shoot, know exactly where to look for the missing saw. The shadow of the door was within reach; he slipped in and ran noiselessly to his bunk; out with the saw and across to an unoccupied bunk, slipping it swiftly into a slender crevice between the bunk and the wall, pushing it deep down and returning swiftly to the door, pausing to see the guards opening another mattress; a few steps, another pause and he was back at attention in the line. The man next to him winked faintly.

It seemed certain that the whole camp would suffer if the missing saw did not turn up. In the end such a strange horde poured from one mattress after another, so many cigarettes, matches, trinkets, coins, letters, franc notes, crusts of bread, that the guards seemed to regard their search as well rewarded and nothing more happened.

Waiting outside the barracks for roll call next morning the chances of escape were watched more closely. The fog poured down over the wire, the men emptying the dirt-basket kept everyone waiting before the barracks, and the guards beyond the wire were not visible. It might conceivably work. They chose a day and the plan was carefully co-ordinated. On that very day Hopper received orders to join the dirt-basket party. The following day another Englishman found himself on basket duty and they cursed their luck. The third and fourth days there was no mist, and then on the sixth day, yet another Englishman was detailed to the basket. Before their chance came again orders were given to be ready to move out of the camp.

Approaching Mauthausen it was almost as if fairy-lights surrounded a holiday camp, so bright and sparkling were the tiny lights glimmering along the multiple lines of electrified wire, one touch of which meant instant death. The stumbling line of prisoners saw the lights in the distance without knowing what they meant. Three weeks in Saarbrücken had seriously weakened everyone and half the prisoners needed help as they were driven along, like cattle, for two hours, from an unidentified station to Mauthausen proper.

Entering Germany from France had been very bad; progression from Saarbrücken to Mauthausen deepened foreboding. There followed the same brutal reception, another bath under cold showers with no means of drying, and the hairdressers ruthlessly stripping off half-grown hair with woad-like stain daubed on bleeding patches. This was familiar enough, The grim, black, silent countryside was not very different, and even the bleak courtyards, the harsh blocks, dead still at two in the morning, the stark, hissing lights which bleached every barbed-wire exit with its cardboard guards, were no more bloodless and inhuman than those at Saarbrücken. But very soon they knew that life here was different.

Ordinary clothes vanished, and thin cotton "uniforms" took their place, "uniforms" deliberately designed to make a mockery of individuality. Pat's long thin cotton trousers ran over his "shoes", had no belt, and needed a large knot tied from surplus cloth, normally accommodating a paunch. His pyjama jacket was much too small, buttonless, and with a little string collar capable of closing it at the neck only. His shoes were flat, wooden blocks tied to the feet with strips of canvas. John Hopper looked quite absurd in a tiny jacket and trousers, but his long lean form dominated the uniform as he dominated everything. Tom Groome ruefully regarded a jacket, the sleeves of which came down over his arms. Gently they mocked one another.

They slept, first, on the floor of the quarantine block with no mattresses of any kind, and one dirty blanket each. Hopelessly overcrowded, they were jammed up against one another, head to foot, continuously struggling for more room. Literally they were packed like living sardines. And whenever they were making too much noise, the black apparation of the Kapo* burst in among the half-asleep forms and brought his whip down viciously on whichever body was nearest.

Pat became used to the nightly ritual. An indescribable smell arose from the mass of bodies, some so recently treated with carbolic, others carrying a week's dirt and the accumulated staleness of prison life, some smelling of urine, some of sickness and disease. At night the grey mass heaved and turned, and silent, ghost-thin men rose continuously to go to the lavatory, curses greeting every foot that struck a face. In the day everyone drank too much. Water allayed the pangs of hunger for a few brief minutes, and forced a continuous coming and going to the lavatory. And at night the snores mounted, groans came from bundles of rags, men talked deliriously in their sleep and still the silent traffic of stumbling men went to and fro between the latrines. The air grew heavy and foul; breathing became difficult; and sometimes a curious cold sweat broke out from a false heat and a man started up moaning for air. Pat was always glad when the light of dawn broke through.

They stayed in the quarantine block for six days. Slowly the fellowship of enforced community changed; sometimes there were fights for dirty remnants of food; sometimes homosexual overtures; sometimes sly plots to oust men from places away from the door.

* A "Kapo" was usually a German criminal from a jail or prison camp put in charge of a block of huts.

On the seventh day they went to the cold showers again and a strange rash appeared on Pat's back. He knew it was scabies. Transferred at once to the "Revier", variously known as the Hospital or Russian Lager, he found himself under the control of a Green-Triangle Guard, a German with a criminal record.

The Russian Lager—thus named because it had been built by Russians, half of whom died from beatings which drove them into inhuman bursts of work—smelt of death and disease. A long, low, wooden building with four rows of three-tiered bunks, the corridors between the bunks were narrow, and Pat, who had a top bunk, could kneel on the bed and touch the ceiling. So many bunks jammed together and each one occupied by sick and ailing people made the air foul, but its very foulness in the winter meant warmth, and warmth was the second god—food was the first—worshipped by the prisoners. Men lay with swollen glands and distended bellies, some emaciated into skeletons, some delirious and pouring sweat, some with carbuncles the size of footballs, some with suppurating wounds, some in their own ordure. Polish doctors under the supervision of an S.S. doctor were medically responsible for the Russian Lager, but they had little more than paper bandages and a handful of aspirins to treat major diseases.

The German Kapo lived in a partitioned space with some heating. A man of fifty, very tall and thin, he had a remarkable power of making his brutality even more sinister by never raising his voice or showing any signs of anger. He beat a man into unconsciousness with the detachment of someone driving a car. There were Yugoslavs, French and Russians in the block and every day one of them died. It passed unnoticed in an atmosphere where death was part of the air everyone breathed. At the slightest sign of stains on the mattress a patient was hauled away to special beds which simply consisted of wooden slats with a single filthy blanket and no mattress of any kind. Laid naked on the slats, next to the door, in freezing draughts, the patient could continue messing his "bed", but once or twice a day he was dragged off into the open air, where buckets of cold water were thrown over him and a scrubbing brush used to clean his body. Then he was dragged back to the wooden slats and thrown down without any attempt to dry his wet, shivering limbs. He was given no food and little to drink. By the third day the patient staggered back from the scrubbing board hardly able to walk. By the fourth he collapsed in a coma. Usually he died on the fifth or sixth day.

On Pat's fourth day in the Revier a Polish doctor came to him and said: "There's another British officer here—his name is Sheppard." It was a curious kind of shock to Pat. He wondered how a British-born British officer would react to the unexpected appearance of a Belgian-born British officer, whose knowledge of English was sketchy enough to render him suspect. He was suddenly afraid of their meeting. If his story did not convince the British officer. . . . But Bob Sheppard, a tall, blond Englishman, had himself been brought up in France, spoke English with a slight French accent, and at their first meeting both strove to be as British as possible with the comical consequence that each overplayed his hand. Presently the slight French accent put Pat at his ease, and he said, "You must have done secret work."

"I'm an S.O.E. officer," Sheppard replied.

Pat explained himself. When he spoke of being in touch with M.I.9, Bob Sheppard asked, "What sort of set did you use?"

"A Mark Five."

Technical jargon was better than any credential.

"I was parachuted into France," said Bob, "but I landed in the wrong place."

"The wrong place?"

"On the roof of a French gendarmerie!" Both laughed.

"Why are you in the Revier?" Bob asked.

"Scabies."

Bob Sheppard was clearly in the Revier because of the terrible skin disease on his face. "From a dirty razor," he explained.

At the end of a meeting which had to be brief, Sheppard said, "If you take my advice, it is better to listen and never say anything here. You will see appalling things. Don't say a word. One word may cost you your life."

Tall, determined and cheerful, as Bob Sheppard talked, Pat realized that this man was going to be a tremendous asset in prison-camp life. Only the cotton clothing, which reduced the most impressive human being to a clown, marked him down as a prisoner at all.

The routine of Mauthausen became appallingly familiar. The big bell shattering the silence of the camp at six in the morning, the rush to the washrooms and back to the *stube* to fold the blankets; 6.30, a cup of dark, slightly warm liquid; 6.45, massing on the "parade-ground"; 7, the interminable roll call; 7.30, those earmarked for outside work went off; 12, lunch—a litre of soup and if one was lucky a potato; 12.45, assembly to leave for work; 5.30, back to camp; 6, another roll-call; 6.30, dinner—a slice of bread, a two-square-inch piece of meat or cheese, a spoonful of jam and ersatz coffee.

In the evenings from half-past five to seven, prisoners from different blocks met in the courtyard. The English formed a group and there began that long, strange relationship between people whose chief common factor, a love for action, was now completely denied them. It was a life without civilized masks of any kind. Over the months they came to know one another intimately. Ultimate realities quickly struck through sophistication, class and profession.

Pat became friendly with the Polish doctors in the Revier. One day he asked about the strange phenomenon which took place at seven o'clock some mornings, when a number of older prisoners were called up to the operation-room to undergo minor operations, and never returned. At first the Polish doctors refused to talk. Then one of them said, "I have a great respect for British officers. Give me your word that you won't betray me. If you say anything, it means death to me."

Pat gave it.

The doctor then explained that a German S.S. doctor had come to him one day and said: "This block is overcrowded with quite useless men. You must get rid of them. I want them killed and you are going to do the job—you must select the men yourself and inject them with engine oil."

Every day the Polish doctors took someone sick and old, explained that he needed a minor operation and quietly injected engine oil, which brought death almost instantaneously. When Pat expressed amazement that they should carry out such an order, the doctors shrugged their shoulders. "If we don't do it, someone else will—and if it isn't the old ones it will be people like you." "You're murdering these men," Pat said. The Poles said nothing. Conventional values of life and death had come to seem suburban niceties, and the loss of civilized personality had reached that pitch where death was an order automatically obeyed without regret or any sign of remorse. The pattern of death extended everywhere. Pat became familiar with the gas lorries and the sight of prisoners loaded into them who died on the way to nowhere. He saw men kicked, strangled and beaten to death. He came later to the strange block where the slow extermination of seven Jews left a horror in his mind which remains as vivid today as it was then.

19

THE Kapo was over six feet tall and the epitome of brute force, with a low forehead, staring eyes, and a manner of speaking which produced as many grunts as words. A merchant sailor in private life, the S.S. had selected him as Kapo of Block 5 because he had murdered his mother. Recovered from the scabies, Pat had been sent as *Stubendienst* (cleaner) to Block 5 and found that this red-haired gorilla was relatively human towards him, because Pat had been a sailor and the tiny pig brain which directed the Kapo's activities dimly respected the camaraderie of the sea.

Block 5 had an echoing emptiness. Seven Jews were the sole occupants of the block and their plight was pitiable. With no other purpose than brutal destruction the S.S. had said that all seven must die by Christmas, but the emaciated skeletons were still dragged out every morning to work in the stone quarries. Silent, drooping, they set off, some with tears in their eyes, some talking to themselves, some with the furtive look of hunted animals.

The Kapo had put it to them bluntly: "You must all die by Christmas. You had better choose amongst yourselves who goes first."

When no one volunteered for death in the first week, he addressed them again. "If you don't choose, I will."

The following day, somewhere out in the stone quarries, while seven skeletons struggled to move stones weighing more than they themselves did, with heavy snow soaking their thin garments and tongues sucking the snow to quench their thirsts, the Kapo suddenly leapt on one man, dragged him down, and as his screams echoed round the quarry, beat out his brains with a pick-axe.

That evening the remaining six crowded round Pat. News of a possible Allied invasion had swept across

Europe and the mysterious drumming of intelligence had carried the message into the heart of Mauthausen. Was it possible that the invasion would begin soon, and once begun would break through swiftly? Was there, possibly, the hope that . . . or if not . . . ? Could they at least believe that the bombing raids might scare the S.S. or the Kapo into relaxing their sentence? Had they any hope if they hung on, tried to evade the death by pick-axe? Was there any point in struggling?

Pat spoke very carefully. Many things were possible. Hope sprang indestructibly for those about to die, and he did not wish to destroy a hope which might miraculously realize itself. They seemed to feel better after he had spoken.

In the second week there were still no volunteers for death. The ragged file of scarcely human men, who seemed tall because they were paper-thin, whose eyes were large in sunken faces, whose voices were sometimes whispers from weakness, staggered out into the ice-cold dawn, but no one volunteered to die.

Two amongst them were father and son, a boy of nineteen, frequently in tears, and the father aged forty-five, who looked seventy. He was a Jewish tailor who had deliberately withdrawn from political life of any kind to remain completely innocent, but he was a Jew and that was enough. The son had hardly begun adult life and if he possessed any coherent views of the world, they were scarcely worth exterminating.

They stayed together as much as possible, sleeping next to one another, and sometimes, far into the night, Pat heard the old Jew's slow, melancholy voice trying to soothe his son's fears. Or they talked to Pat and occasionally the great owl-like eyes enlarged in the thin faces, stared at Pat as though he had it in his power to save them, and would not save them. Always Pat encouraged them, helped them in their illnesses, tried to add scraps to their food; but what they needed even more than food was some re-affirmation of their right to live, and several times the old man turned away, tears in his eyes, and shambled back to his stinking bunk, while Pat cursed his powerlessness.

At the end of November the Kapo spoke to them again. "You're not dying quick enough. It's easy to do it. You can walk out in front of the wire and get machine-gunned. Or —you can run into the wire. You frizzle quick then. But get a move on—time's getting short."

No one died the next day; but on the following night when they returned from the quarry one of their number was again missing, and crowding round Pat, five Jews in terrible fear spoke of the cries they had heard. On the hundred steps which led down into the quarry, the berserk Kapo had torn another emaciated body to pieces with his pick-axe. There followed the same questions about the British, the Allies, the hope of an armistice before the year was out; but the Jewish tailor and his son were fatalistic now and the father said to Pat: "We may walk into the wire tomorrow." It was clean and simple. The flash which shrivelled life was better than a long death by mutilation and starvation.

Three days later there were still five Jews, each no longer interested in the fate of the others, and all fighting desperately with the cunning of despair to remain alive.

By the beginning of December the snow was very deep, the winds icy and the five Jews could not sleep very much because of the cold. One day in the second week in December another man did not return from the quarry. And on the 15th, Pat heard the Jewish tailor say to his son, "There's no hope. We had better die." The boy burst into tears. The tailor said again to Pat the next day, "We shall walk into the wire." But they did not. December 18 came and still the four Jews remained in a state resembling life. Still Pat tried to help them. Encouragement seemed the last indignity when hope had so long died, but Pat talked to them and sometimes they seemed stronger after-wards.

Sometimes, too, he looked down at his own fast wasting body and knew that he could not continue losing weight himself at such a rate without collapse. Originally he had weighed 160 lb. Now he was 90 lb. and still losing weight. His face had yellowed, his absurd cotton clothes hung on bones, a sense of deep lethargy very easily overtook him, and hunger pains sometimes brought him awake in the night as though a knife had entered his bowels. He drank more and more water. Everyone drank and drank.

Still he wondered why he remained alive, why they had not shot him, why the fate reserved for the Jews was not his also. If espionage against the religion of Nazism was a crime too simple to redeem by sudden death, this expiation, this long-drawn-out death by hardship and starvation was the kind of penance paid only for the most mortal sin; but why should he still be allowed hope while the Jews had none?

In the early morning of December 23 he began to clean the bunks of Block 5. Suddenly he saw the Jewish tailor leading his son gently by the hand towards the door. The boy sobbed and there were tears in the old man's eyes. Outside, with clumsy, fumbling steps, the old man began running, his arm around the boy. They could not run properly. They had not the strength. But they stumbled hopelessly towards the margin, and the shots which Pat expected did not come. They did not run straight and clean into the electrified wire. They blundered into it, and Pat felt the great blue flash as if it had seared his own body. And there on the ground were the two twitching bodies, entwined with one another, and presently still.

It was very silent and empty in the block that evening. The two remaining Jews were cowering animals. One shivered continuously. Tomorrow was the 24th and one must die. Neither spoke, and when Pat went to them and used whatever words he could find to hold their broken minds together, they stared back mutely.

The dawn was cold, grey, and misty. They could hardly walk as they left for the stone quarry, but one distorted drive remained: nothing mattered but the will to survive for another single day. The man who came back was a ghost, with fixed eyes and twitching lips, who tried to talk to Pat but could not articulate clearly. The last glimmering of the human spirit had almost gone. An animal looked out from the prison of shrivelled flesh and made meaningless whimpers.

On Christmas morning the Kapo almost carried him from the block. That night as the sound of a Christmas carol came across from one of the blocks, Block 5 was empty.

In memory some events have crowded together, one impression half obliterating another, but soon Pat's turn came to work in the stone quarries, and those days are still clear. Every day from seven in the morning till five in the afternoon, he heaved meaningless blocks of stone into futile shapes for little purpose other than his own pain. His hands bled, his muscles felt broken, his whole body ached. Large boils had developed from malnutrition and they were now damaged by the rocks, and every night, as the last tribute to his unseen lord and master, he had to carry a heavy stone up the hundred steps of the quarry from the bottom to the top. When he reached Block 9 at half-past five in the evening, he was often near to collapse.

Early signs of serious illness came with a sudden temperature. The first days it might have been malnutrition, exhaustion or prolonged overwork. Then a sick throbbing began in his head and he developed a cough. The cough grew worse and bloodspots appeared in his sputum. Presently sweat ran from his limbs as he set out for the stone quarry in the morning and his legs and arms seemed hopelessly weak. He felt sure now that he knew what was wrong with him and a sudden foreboding of death overtook him. If he was right, he would never survive such an illness under such conditions. He went to one of the prisoners, a Czech surgeon, Podlaha, once well known in Prague. The surgeon took his pulse and temperature, asked for the remaining symptoms and said, "You're right—you are walking about with pneumonia. Take this and go to the Revier."

But the Revier, with any serious illness, meant death, and Pat took the two aspirins which Podlaha selected from his hopelessly limited stock, and went back to his block.

It seemed impossible: a man who now weighed 80 lb. with great boils on his body, a temperature of 103, his head so dizzy he sometimes lost all sense of consciousness, hewing stones in a quarry, and at the end of every day, walking up a hundred steps, carrying a stone which he could only just lift. It was not normal strength which kept him going. Fear of certain death created an artificial life in his limbs when he should have collapsed.

At night he was often delirious. Sometimes in the day he seemed to be sleep-walking. A terrible battle between extreme weakness and floods of fear-driven energy racked his body in a way even worse than straightforward pneumonia. Every morning he struggled to rise from the bunk. How he left his block for the quarry he does not know. Day after day it went on, a fantastic, unreal mime. . . .

Then one day his temperature began to drop. If possible he felt worse. Reaction set in and papery legs seemed quite incapable of supporting him. Nervous energy was giving out, and once he fell, and had a prolonged struggle to rise again. Slowly, very slowly, he felt some semblance of half-life returning. His eyes ceased to swim, his limbs felt stronger, and presently one morning, he knew, with a melancholy sense of triumph, that he had won what seemed an impossible fight.

In Febuary 1944 Pat was sent to an outside commando —the word used when prisoners were employed for slave labour in nearby factories—at Wiener Neustadt. Returning one dark, snowy evening, he staggered exhausted into the lines of prisoners waiting on the square for roll call and heard the names beginning with sick distaste. This dreary routine had stamped itself in his mind as a mental torture, but tonight as he stood in his filthy cotton clothes, bare-headed in the snow, suddenly there was an unexpected silence. The *"Hier!"* answer did not come from someone. The grating German voice paused in astonishment. The name was repeated in a shout, but no one answered. Into the silence flowed a mixture of horror and incredibility. The roll call normally took half an hour.

Tonight it ran on for an hour, and at the end, *six men*, not one, were found to be absent.

At first the S.S. guard thought they were late and threatened horrible reprisals. Then the blocks were searched and at last the unbelievable truth dawned on him; they were missing. German prisoners speaking perfect German, they had slipped away from their commandos. An S.S. officer, his voice the snarl of a mad beast, bellowed: "Everyone will stand where they are at attention until these men are found!" It was then seven o'clock of a pitch black evening with the snow becoming heavier. Hour by hour they continued standing there while heavy-coated jackbooted guards strode amongst them bringing every slack figure to attention with vicious blows. The feet froze first; then the circulation ceased to reach the hands and a cap of ice formed over the head. From the extremities, the paralysis climbed up the legs to the knees, and from the head down to the shoulders. It was four hours before feeling vanished from the loins. An extraordinary sense of agonized disembodiment became complete. Each man was coated white from head to foot, and the whole massed array of 1,500 men had become as if part of the concrete square, statues without life.

Midnight came and went. The blazing searchlights showed the swirling mass of snow-flakes multiplying. By two in the morning the blood seemed to have frozen in the veins; by three thought had blurred, consciousness threatened to slip away and Pat felt the approach of a curious frozen sleep. It was towards four o'clock that the air shook to the brassy voice again. "Back to barracks!" Some had to be carried, some were unable to speak, some frozen to the point where they did not hear the command. In huddled groups the miserable mass at last settled down under their single blankets for what remained of the night. At six next morning, two hours later, everyone was brought out again to begin another day.

A few days dragged away and Pat was sent back to Mauthausen. With him went a very frightened man—one of the escaped Germans who had been recaptured. Together they entered the showers, and as they stripped, they saw two S.S. guards waiting. Naked, shivering with cold, Pat saw one of the N.C.O.s striding towards him, his face distorted. He was very afraid when the man thrust his staring eyes close to Pat's face: "Are you the swine who tried to escape?" Aping the enunciation with which the Germans mastered his difficult name, Pat came to attention and said: "No. I'm O-Lee-Arie, a British officer."

The man leered at him. "A Preetish officer—eh?" He turned swiftly away towards the German. "Are you?" The man hesitated.

"Are you?" the guard bellowed.

"Yes." The man cowered as he said it.

A look of ecstatic fury ran across the face of the S.S. guard.

"Attention!" he bawled. Instantly he launched a tremendous blow to the man's jaw. The prisoner's hand went up to ward off a second blow and the guard kicked him savagely in the stomach. As the man doubled up another sledgehammer blow hit his jaw. He fell down. "Up! Up!" The S.S. man kicked him to attention again. Then alternately he slogged his jaw and kicked his stomach, eight, nine, ten, eleven times, until one tremendous kick in the pit of the stomach brought blood gushing from the man's mouth; he screamed and fell down. The guard continued kicking him in the face, head, groin and legs. The twitching form at last lay quite inert and the pavement was quickly thick with blood.

"O-Lee-Arie! O-Lee-Arie!" It was five o'clock of a bitterly cold April day when the Kapo of Block 9 called for Pat. He was a slim, fair-haired German criminal who shut his eyes to the cruelty round him but was not cruel himself. "You are wanted in the Political Section," he said. "Get yourself cleaned up." Rushed to the *friseur*, for the thousandth time the spots on Pat's face bled and the ice-cold shower ran over his thin body. He tried to make the knot which kept up his ragged trousers less conspicuous, he re-adjusted the string which drew the collar of his shirt together, he retied the rotting canvas which held the blocks of wood to his feet. Once more he felt fear. If men came

237

back at all from interrogation by the Political Section they were often broken men.

In the offices of the Political Section it was warm, and a stout S.S. officer demanded at once: "You are O-Lee-Arie?"

"Yes."

"You know Paul Cole?"

"Yes."

"What do you know about him?"

Pat thought carefully a moment and then risked the answer: "I know he is a British traitor."

"He has been very useful to us," the officer said. Pat said nothing. "I said he has been very helpful to us." Pat remained silent. There were other men in the room now, all S.S. officers who began to crowd round Pat.

"You are a Preetish officer?" one asked in amazement. Pat nodded. They looked at him, astonished to see a British officer in this terrible condition.

"What do you think of Paul Cole?" the stout one persisted.

Control of words had become second nature in a camp where one false word meant death, but a sudden memory of all the misery and horror Cole had caused sent the words leaping from Pat's tongue: "He is a swine!" Involuntarily Pat stiffened to receive the first blow. It did not come. The eyes seemed to swell a little in the face of the S.S. officer but he went on with his questions. Five minutes later Pat was escorted to another room, and on the way a second S.S. man joined them, saying: "You are a Preetish officer?"

"Yes."

"Want an apple?" It was a full, rich, ripe, glistening apple such as they never saw in the camp blocks. Pat's mouth flowed with saliva as he shook his head.

"You have enough food?"

In the second room a big, red-faced man with enormous shoulders sat hunched over a desk. He proceeded to ask questions with some semblance of politeness.

"O-Lee-Arie—you are Irish. Wouldn't you like to go to an Irish camp?"

"What sort of Irish camp?"

The S.S. officer sighed. "What about working for us?"

"I cannot."

"Paul Cole has a very happy life in Berlin. Your conditions would change immediately if you worked for us. Our cause is very worth while. We are defending the culture of Europe." The S.S. officer smiled, and added, "And you would be on the winning side."

Every variety of argument was advanced over the next half an hour until at last, his strength fast ebbing in the warm room, his nerves raw from the expectation of violence, Pat said very quietly: "I prefer to die than to do that job."

Back in the block the news spread swiftly. The Britisher O-Lee-Arie had emerged from political interrogation without injury of any kind, and it was said that when the S.S. offered him a job he *turned it down*. In the eyes of the camp this was ultimate courage.

The Blockführer stood in the doorway regarding the thin prisoners, their arms and shoulders hunched against the cold, and pointed to Pat: "Who is that?"

The Blockältester came rigidly to attention. *"Der Stubendienst, Herr Blockführer,"* he said.

"Where from?"

"England, Herr Blockführer."

"Engländer!" In amazement the Blockführer came over and fingered the red triangle with the E on Pat's chest. *"Offizier?"* he said, and Pat nodded. Immediately he began talking about the war: "And who do you think is going to win?" Pat hesitated for a fraction of a second. Encouraged by his success in the Political Section he said, "England!" and the great fist came smashing down into his face knocking him to the floor. The boot was raised to begin kicking when the Blockältester said with twisted humility: *"Herr Blockführer—ein moment, Herr Blockführer!"*

Clearly he had something important to say and the Blockführer strode into his office. He must have told him of the interview with the Political Section, of the proffered job, and the good relations which seemed to exist between Pat and the S.S., because a few minutes later the Block-führer came back to Pat. He drew himself to attention and glared at him: "You insulted me," he said. "That's why I hit you."

So Paul Cole was living a luxurious life in Berlin with the Germans. Looking round at the broken hulks who drifted through the courtyard, the beginnings of a mad fury stirred in Pat, but somehow real anger had lost its edge, like everything else, from lack of energy.

20

FRESNES, Neuebrenn, Mauthausen, Natzweiler, Dachau. They had left Fresnes at the end of September 1943, spent three weeks in Neuebrenn, arrived at Mauthausen towards the end of October, remained there until after the Allied invasion of Normandy and reached Natzweiler in September 1944. Steadily the progression from one concentration camp to another carried degradation forward, and the long process of expiation approached its inevitable climax in the ritually correct way. The human personality must be humiliated, broken and destroyed fragment by fragment, until the will to live was gone and a skeleton of the original man lay down to die, another sacrifice to the Nietzschean gods.

The journey from Mauthausen to Natzweiler was made more horrible by typhoid fever. Crowded in the wagons, the four Britishers tried to nurse Tom Groome, already at that stage where he was almost unconscious. Still not one of the British knew that Pat O'Leary was really Dr. Albert Guérisse, and it needed considerable skill to convey by hint and innuendo what could be done, without revealing special knowledge. Not that treatment in the serious sense was possible until they reached Natzweiler.

Herded into a reception room, dozens of men stood, sat, or lay in groups. Suddenly a short, slim man came striding into the room and Pat stiffened. He glanced at the Englishmen surrounding Tom Groome, lying semi-conscious on the floor, and came straight towards them. Looking blankly into the eyes of Pat he gave no sign of recognition and Pat's face remained expressionless. This was a doctor examining new arrivals. . . . But what wonderful stroke of luck had chosen Boogaerts for duty that day; Boogaerts, another Belgian who had once studied with Pat in the same university, and was now himself a prisoner in the concentration camp. Presently they snatched a few words. "Albert!" Boogaerts whispered. Pat swiftly interrupted: "My name's Pat O'Leary and I'm a British officer."

"I see. . . ."

"Groome's very ill—typhoid fever—what can we do?"

"I'll get him into the infirmary."

They had not met since university days and now, here, in the middle of Germany, fantastic coincidence had brought them together.

"We must be very careful," whispered Boogaerts. "People are murdered here for nothing. I will try to get you into the infirmary as an orderly."

"What about the others?"

"We mustn't overdo it."

But for one reason or another during the next six weeks, with Pat's connivance, Boogaerts managed to transfer four of the five British from the filthy, overcrowded blocks where typhoid fever was beginning to spread, into the comparative quiet of the infirmary. Groome reached that stage where he lay on his back, his pupils contracted, his face a dusky grey, muttering deliriously. Pat kept his bowels cleared out, they tried desperately to sustain the classic treatment of regular doses of liquid food, and the milk soup which took the place of ersatz coffee in the morning at Natzweiler helped a little. Sometimes in the infirmary there was a drop of milk with rice, sometimes a very light porridge. It was all hopelessly primitive, but somehow Groome survived.

One morning, looking out of the infirmary window towards what was known as the jail, Pat saw an extraordinary sight. Marching down the main camp approach were five young women with a stamp and bearing which might have been English. It was a spring day with the first hint of sun in the air, and their graceful walk, still clean clothes and sheer femininity brought the first breath of civilization which Pat had felt for a whole year. They might have been a mirage and he stared fascinated. Female S.S. guards marched beside the girls and then, as the face of one turned towards the window, Pat's breath stopped. He knew this girl. It was Andrée Borrel, the girl-friend of the French officer Maurice Dufour. A desperate desire to shout, to hammer on the window, to communicate in some way with her, seized him, but it was dangerous and impossible.

Later that morning he noticed another woman's face looking out from one of the barred windows of the jail and he risked shouting to her. "Are you English?"

She must have been standing on a chair because she clutched suddenly at the window-frame as if about to fall, and then shouted back, "Yes."

"Do you need anything?"

"No, thank you."

"Why are you here. . . ?"

Her face suddenly disappeared from the window and there was no answer. That evening, the rule permitting prisoners to leave their blocks and gather in the court-yard, was suspended. The order came for all prisoners to stay in their blocks at risk of being shot. The camp was built on the flank of a hill, and staring out of the infirmary window Pat suddenly saw coming down the steps which were cut in a big alley between the blocks, a German doctor and a group of S.S. guards. They moved in the direction of the crematorium and ten minutes later one of the newly arrived girls was escorted from the jail across to the crematorium. Pat could not see her face. Then came a shot, followed by a long pause. Presently a gust of flame and smoke issued from the crematorium chimney. His eyes fixed to the window Pat knew that the great door of the crematorium oven had been opened and shut.

Five times in the next half-hour the signal burst from the crematorium chimney, and Pat shuddered not so much because a woman's body was being reduced to ashes, but because he heard only two shots for the five chimney signals, and the way of death of the other three remained unknown. Or was it? Many rumours circulated in the camp the following day. Intravenous injections, death by fire, by shooting. . . .

But why had these women, bearing no sign of torture, young, attractive and capable of serving so many purposes, been murdered out of hand while thousands of men like himself continued to drag out a living death in camp after camp? The illogicality was unbelievably brutal. No laws governed this nightmare world. Nor did human horror and pity long outlive the events which induced them. Five women had died mysteriously, perhaps brutally, but horror was soon overwhelmed by the increasing ravages of concentration-camp life. Everywhere grey skeletons were staggering about the camp, everywhere men were sickening and dying.

News of the Allied advance across Europe was confused. From outside commandos, from factories, from hints dropped by the S.S. to Kapos and Blockführers, contradictions multiplied. The Allies had been thrown back; were fanning out into France; were negotiating peace terms; were approaching Paris. The camp radio was quite clear cut. The advance had been broken up in complete confusion.

There were those amongst the prisoners who took no interest in any of it. They had reached a state where news no longer penetrated in rational form. A conviction that nothing could change the continuous misery which had become their lot made them regard talk of the Allies and invasion as something without significance. For Bob Sheppard, Brian Stonehouse, Tom Groome, John Hopper and Pat, it was different. The idea that they might even yet survive this prolonged nightmare no longer seemed absurd.

Within a few days came a serious set-back. All over again they were ordered out of Natzweiler to set off on yet another journey. Crushed into a train of steel wagons it seemed to them they must be penetrating even deeper into Germany. Each steel wagon was so choked with bodies that no one could sit down, the air stank and breathing was difficult. Bob Sheppard had been split away from the English in the confusion of leaving Natzweiler, but the others remained together.

In the steel box of the wagon, Pat and John Hopper quickly saw that the slightest sign of panic among the prisoners would be disastrous. Crouched against one another, jolting painfully along, they organized security men to stop any sign of quarrelling, fighting, or panic, at its source. As hour succeeded hour and the wagons lurched on, the smell of urine increased, the air became fouler and a sweating sense of constriction grew.

The few bits of bread and sausage they had with them were exhausted on the first day of the journey. There was nothing to drink. That night, after twenty-four hours crushed in the wagon, the train came to a halt and two S.S. guards armed with *schmeissers* forced their way in, kicked a space clear, and prepared to spend the night. The doors closed, the wagon jolted away again and the grinding of wheels swallowed up every other sound.

There was an element of unreality in the scene within Pat's view. The figures twisted into one mass, all the limbs appearing to belong to one convulsed grey heap. It heaved and moved, moaned and talked. Eyes flickered in a ghost face and a man suddenly clutched at his throat, talking in panic to his neighbour, looking with wild cunning at the men next to the steel slits in the door. Pat was still afraid of panic. The guards could shoot a man or two. But sixty men in animal fear beginning to fight for space and air would mean a crushed and mangled heap within ten minutes. Pat heard John Hopper whispering to him: "We could deal with those two bastards. Let's murder them and escape."

Pat thought for a moment. They were all very weak from lack of food and illness. Brian Stonehouse particularly was very weak.

"The British must stay together," Pat said.

"Of course."

"What about Brian?"

"You don't think he could do it?"

"I don't know."

"I can murder those bastards myself."

But John murdering the guards would be only the beginning of their troubles. No one spoke German very well, they had no money, no food, no maps, and whoever was left in the wagon—and many would be too weak to run —was certain to die horribly to revenge the death of the guards. At either end of the train machine-guns were mounted and guards waited to shoot down anyone who so much as showed his head. The odds seemed very heavily weighted. Perhaps, when the train ran down into the valleys, there would be mist.

"How can you get the wagon door open?" Pat said.

"I'll find out," John said and at once began edging his way minutely, determinedly, towards the iron door. With great stealth he allowed a long pause between each few inches of movement, sometimes waiting until he felt the guards could hear and see nothing, sometimes blaspheming in savage whispers for room to pass. They were all one grey mass in the wagon, shifting, swaying, changing pattern with its progress. A Frenchman lying near the iron bar which clamped the door into place woke up as John reached him.

"Quiet," whispered John. "How does this bloody thing open?"

. "Don't know."

"Move over and let me find out." With his back to the wall of the wagon concealing his hands, Hopper went to work, heaving, pushing, coaxing. The squeak of iron against iron was lost in the shrieking of the wagon wheels and presently he was throwing his whole weight sideways with the iron bar displaced. For a time nothing happened. Then he felt the door give and that was enough. Replacing the bar, it took a long time to manoeuvre himself back to Pat again.

"It can be done," he said.

"And one of those chaps is going to sleep soon. Look!" said Pat.

One guard was curling up on the floor while the other shifted his gun on to his knees. The rack-rack, rack-rack, rack-rack of the wheels quickened and through the slits in the steel wall it looked as though they were running downhill. Five minutes went by. One guard was asleep. John muttered: "It'll be pleasant to murder the bastards."

Once more he began his inch-by-inch pilgrimage towards the door and once again he reached it safely as the train slowed. Pat suddenly wondered what precise method he would use for the guards. Perhaps John would take the heavy iron bar from the door, make one step amongst the bodies, and bring it down with all the force which still remained in his big frame on the skull of the first German. . . . John was beginning to lift the bar with his big shoulders when suddenly a German voice bellowed: "What are you doing?" And a moment later, "Stand away —or I shoot!" For a moment Pat thought that John was going to take one tremendous bound straight at the barrel of the gun. Then, cursing, John stood aside.

It was the middle of the afternoon of the following day. A great crested eagle spread its wings, crouched on a swastika above a massive gate. As they limped through, a second steel trellis carried the words *Arbeit Macht Frei*— Work Makes One Free. They knew now where they were. Dachau. The very syllables made an ugly clash. The end of the line, the last living hell before they collapsed and the incinerator made a burnt offering of their bones.

There was nowhere to sleep that night. Built to accommodate 10,000, Dachau already had a monstrous population of 35,000, and the starving clowns in their ludicrous uniforms sank down that night amongst the ashes and sand of the main courtyard, without food or drink of any kind, trying to slip into that unconsciousness where misery could not penetrate.

Within the next ten days the full horror of Dachau was opened to Pat's eyes. This was a place where the rations of a whole block might systematically be cut down until eighty men died of starvation. This was a place where transports arrived with men deliberately piled like carcases, one on top of the other to the brim of the wagon, so they must die on the journey. This was a place where some in the wagons, the fortunate top layer, driven by the torture of starvation, ate the still warm flesh of their fellows so that carcases later thrown into the pits were incomplete, with a thigh gnawed away or a cheek. This was a place where men were beaten until the flesh broke open to the bone and if they dared to utter the single word "Stop!" they were regarded as insubordinate and were taken to a room where other "dangerous" characters were hanging trussed-up from the ceiling, their wrists behind their backs, feet just above the floor, and tied in a similar manner and left there. This was a place dominated by large white lettering visible from all over the compound: *Es gibt einen weg zur Freiheit. Seine Meilensteine heissen: Gehorsamkeit, Sauberkeit, Nüchternheit und Fleiss.* (There is a road to freedom. Its milestones are: Obedience, Cleanliness, Sobriety, Industry.)

The usual prison-camp hierarchy was brought to a pitch of disciplined perfection. As brutality increased, its systematization was made more rigorous. External control rested in the hands of S.S. guards, and internal control in those of the prisoners. There were the Lagerälteste (camp senior), Lagerschreiber (secretary), Arbeitseinsatzkapo (chief of labour allocation) and Kapos (foremen), Blockältesten and Blockschreiber, all drawn from the prisoners. Important prisoners wore red patches indicating political crimes, common criminals green ones, asocial elements black. An attempt to mix red and green prisoners in administering the camp had largely broken down. Internal terror and corruption were maintained by criminals carrying out S.S. orders in any way they thought fit. Daily routine had brutal echoes from the immediate past.

Dysentery, tuberculosis, malnutrition, boils, every kind of disease was at work amongst the prisoners. The growing mass of so-called patients justified the Englishmen continuing their work as orderlies. Hopper learnt to carry out injections, Tom Groome washed patients and carried corpses, Pat undertook multiple duties. Presently the work became much harder.

Pat does not clearly remember when the new outbreak began. Purple patches first appeared on emaciated bodies and men recoiled from one another, some crossing themselves as though the devil had sent a sign. Soon men were falling to the ground in fixed comas with pupils contracted and sweat pouring from their bodies. Pat realized that typhus had come among them, the dreaded rat-bred typhus. Within two weeks it spread savagely. The dark red blotches, the sordes on the teeth, the delirious men who had to be held down, became part of the everyday scene. Presently they were dying by the dozen every night.

In the infirmary there were few instruments, the tiniest supply of chlorethyl for major operations, substitute iodine and only the most uncertain means of sterilization. Feeling pulses, taking temperatures, climbing amongst bodies splotched with purple, watching men in wild delirium, seeing patients fouled by their own ordure, entering the makeshift surgery and helping to hold down men whose football-size carbuncles were lanced; these were routine matters. Sometimes malnutrition produced carbuncles which, when punctured, left great cavities capable of absorbing a human fist; sometimes patients were horribly swollen by localized dropsies, and oedema lay bare the bones of legs and arms; sometimes the typhus-ridden living were so close in colour, failing pulse and silence to the dying, it was easy to carry one away in mistake for the other.

The day came when Pat himself felt the signs of a high temperature. For forty-eight hours the dread of death by typhus obliterated every other thought, but driven to "bed" he remained there for two days only. Then his temperature dropped, incipient symptoms vanished and on the third day he was busy nursing, injecting, and cleaning up patients all over again. It seemed impossible. Wasting away from malnutrition, with a cavity under his ribs which made his abdomen drop inwards, the flesh along his thighs collapsed, his ribs projecting grotesquely, his weight reduced by half, his head sometimes dizzy from weakness, without medicine or proper treatment of any kind, he should have died in the first wave of typhus. But some cannon pulse in his extraordinarily vital body kept beating, a determination not to die sustained whatever it was in him which constituted spirit, and he overcame the early signs of typhus within two days.

John Hopper caught it next. Tall, gloomy, preoccupied, he went about the camp as if unaware that he walked amongst one of the most deadly diseases, and at last typhus attacked him too. Pat saw the rigor, the headache, the sleeplessness beginning to trouble him, but John said nothing, made no complaint of any kind. Pat had to insist on treating him. Even the giant strength of Hopper could not keep him on his feet while the disease ravaged him.

The death-rate increased. Soon there were times when it seemed like the plague in the sixteenth century. Within a month it was commonplace for fifty men to be found dead every morning. The smell of death, sweat, disease, dirt and urine, mingled with crude disinfectants to produce in the infirmary a nightmare atmosphere overwhelming to any newcomer.

Hopper recovered. With him, too, it was almost as if a dour determination to die in his own way and in his own time overwhelmed the bugs festering his body, and the gloomy giant shook them off completely one morning and there he was, walking a little uncertainly across the compound, where others might never have walked again.

A fully recovered Hopper told Pat his story. All these months had gone by and his history had remained obscure. He had never spoken of himself. Whenever anyone threatened to come too close he had withdrawn deeply into himself, but now, suddenly, one evening he talked to Pat, and in fragments this story emerged.

An engineer married to a French girl, he had been living in Paris when the Germans came, and at once he formed his own organization of underworld characters to shoot every Gestapo man on sight and deal with any German soldier foolish enough to venture into the lonelier streets of the capital after dark. A price, a heavy price, was put on his head. Twice the Gestapo shot it out with him and twice John routed them. He carried two guns and used them with the skill of the legendary figures from the Wild West. He could fire simultaneously from both hands with great accuracy, and he did not hesitate to ignore enemy bullets, standing up openly to take careful aim, shooting with a precision which made the Gestapo fear him; until one day they surprised him with his wife in a café, and four agents began firing before they had even entered the café. The bullets smashed round the table and instantly Hopper was firing back with both guns, but the bullets were coming from all directions and suddenly he saw his wife slump down. Still firing, he realized that she was badly wounded, knew the Gestapo would torture her if they took her, and in a moment of iron courage and decision, shot her dead through the head. In the end they caught him. . . .

He paused for a long time as he finished his story. His beautiful eyes regarded Pat sadly.

"Do you think that was right?" he asked at last.

"In the circumstances, yes," said Pat.

John nodded slowly. "Well," he said, getting up from a bunk, "see you tomorrow," and disappeared into his block.

The men came to know him in Dachau. The story of how he had routed the Gestapo reached the ears of the guards. Once, when one was about to strike him, a sudden expression came into John's face, a look which was called his "bad look", and some ultimate ruthlessness in it, some primal capacity to kill even if he himself died in the process, made the guard drop his upraised arm.

With no warning Pat was suddenly sent off as Stubendienst to an S.S. school at Bad-Tölz. From there he went out every day to help unload railway wagons at Bad-Tölz station. Handcuffed and escorted from the school by S.S. guards, every day the unloading was supervised with the usual brutality.

On the third day Pat noticed that the man working beside him looked like an Englishman. To be overheard talking would probably mean terrible punishment, but in between heaving coal, he whispered:

"Don't speak loudly, but are you British?"

"Yes."

"Prisoner-of-war?"

"Yes."

"Are you allowed to write home through the Red Cross?"

"Yes."

"Will you send a message for me?"

The man looked very suspicious. This scarecrow figure with a thick French accent who presently claimed to be a British officer must have seemed very odd indeed, but Pat slowly convinced him. The man said that he wrote to his mother in England every week. "Tell her," Pat said, "to call at Brook's Club and tell Jimmy that Pat's alive in Germany."

Extraordinarily, the man did not forget. He wrote to his mother in London and gave her the brief message. In turn, one afternoon, she sallied out, found with some difficulty Brook's Club in London, and told the porter that she wished to speak with Jimmy. Not prepared to identify members from Christian names alone, the porter at first wanted to turn her away, but she persisted and explained that she had a message from a prisoner-of-war in Germany. Jimmy was at last discovered to be Jimmy Langley and the first news of Pat filtered into London after eighteen months of complete silence.*

Back in Dachau typhus had reached new heights. Men were dying like flies, starvation had reduced scores of human beings to shrivelled, toothless skeletons, some wandering in their minds and no longer in touch with reality. The camp administration was weakening as news of Allied advances spread, but it did not weaken in favour of the prisoners. Seeing it all again, Pat suddenly decided that it was time the prisoners were organized on their own account and at once set to work.

Presently the I.P.C., the International Prisoners Committee, was born.

* M.I.9 did in fact know of Pat's whereabouts before this message was received.

21

STIMULATED by Pat, a Pole called Natlewski and a Belgian Haulot, word passed from block to block and each nationality was asked to put forward a candidate for the I.P.C. France, Holland, Poland, Czechoslovakia, Belgium, all nominated someone. The Russians put forward no less a personage than General Nikolai Michailow, the Belgians Arthur Haulot (now head of Belgian Tourism), and the English Patrick O'Leary. Times and dates of meetings were furtively whispered two days before, and at midnight, sixteen members of the committee slipped like shadows through windows into the compound towards the Polish block. Some came barefoot for greater stealth, some crawled the last few yards inch by inch, some flitted swift and sure, black flashes come and gone in a second. To be discovered at large after dark not only meant certain death; it meant the death of a committee which somehow held hope of challenging for the first time the brutal despotism which had dominated their lives so long.

When Pat crept into the Polish block for the first midnight meeting he could just make out the dim outlines of the high cupboards against the walls, the Altester's partition and the long wooden table with its stools. Blankets had been draped over the windows. Whispered directions, a hand guiding him, a small clash as he hit a stool, the hissed demand for quiet and then a match sputtered and three candles—stolen from the store—wavered uncertainly to life. Swiftly everyone positioned themselves round the table. In the dark corridor a guard had his head to a half-opened window watching and listening.

No stranger band of conspirators had ever come together. Gaunt skeletons, clad in clowns' clothing, they crouched in semi-darkness as Pat addressed them in German. His words were kept to a whisper but presently the

Russian general was interrupting to claim the right of the presidency over the committee since there were more Russians in the camp. The Poles strongly resisted. The French felt that their group was very important. Whispered exchanges became intense. In the end Pat was selected president.

Almost at once he began questioning the Polish members. They held camp jobs where information from the S.S. could be picked up. What was the mood of the S.S.——what were their intentions?—Which lead would the Lagerältester be most likely to follow in an emergency? From the French he wanted to know whether the Communists would take their orders. Each nationality reported on morale. A much closer picture of the precise conditions in the camp emerged. . . .

Suddenly there were two sharp taps on the door and a whispered exclamation. Everyone fell silent, the candles were snuffed out, and each man froze, quite still on his stool. Somewhere outside a distant sound of footsteps and voices. For seconds which seemed like hours the paralysed figures were rigid. The footsteps faded. The voices ceased. A minute later the guard gave the all clear. In the yellow light of the relit candles the faces seemed even more cadaverous and several men began whispering at once. Pat broke in asking for suggestions.

They might have been convicts with their shaven polls and sunken faces, but a grim concentration in finding some means of organizing against the Germans gave them complete unity of purpose. It needed strong spirits to overcome weakness, crippling inertia and sickness, to speak of organization, of emergency, of possible revolution in the camp, but these eighteen men now hammered out a plan. Time and again Pat led the discussion. Reliable prisoners were to be selected and appointed as police prisoners, the possibilities of getting arms explored, ways and means sought to save the lives of those condemned to death.

Breaking up after a meeting was even more dangerous than coming together. The candles were carefully snuffed out and hidden, one man scanned the camp alleys, gave the word, and one by one the men flitted back to their blocks again. The Russian general never came back to the secret meetings. Even in such extreme circumstances he did not mean to be compromised. Pat had to hold furtive consultations with him in corners of the compound. But the committee continued to function, its powers spread, and Arthur Haulot played a steadily more important part as vice-president.

Within a week each block had half a dozen men organized as policemen, armed, for the moment, with legs torn from stools. Presently the first identity-change was planned by Pat, the committee and a remarkable character called Bouboule. A man from the underworld of Paris, Bouboule's habit of flitting from one Parisian alley to another and taking casual shots at stray Germans had led him into five concentration camps. Incredibly, near starvation had not entirely obliterated Bouboule's girth and he rolled about the block spitting, at a reasonable distance, at the backs of the Germans, pouring gutter witticisms out in a thick Montmartre accent, ever ready with new ways of duping the Kapo or Blockältester. He seemed to bear a charmed life amongst every variety of horror, and broke into voluble talk on the slightest provocation, as if still in his favourite Montmartre *bistro*. He helped everyone. Ingeniously, he always had a possible "way round". Moving widely amongst the 35,000 prisoners, he always knew a man who could find a crust of bread, or could receive messages from the outside world, or perhaps get a better pair of "shoes".

One day he came urgently to Pat with the news that a Russian friend of his, already in the infirmary, was about to be shot. Underground intelligence from a drunken Kapo had warned Bouboule that Tutaieu, prisoner No. 14307, was probably next on the list. What could they do? Pat remembered the bodies carried away from the infirmary every day, the similarities which seemed to invest all men suffering from malnutrition, the indifference of guards to anyone carrying a corpse. Supposing the Russian was substituted for one of the men about to die, took on his identity and recovered in his place? Pat went to work at once and selected a man whose death would approximately coincide with the possible "recovery" of the Russian. He found an old skeletal Pole who could no longer speak, whose pulse was fluttering and who could not utter his name.

Later the following afternoon the pulse of 19027 ceased to flutter and the reflexes were gone. A signal came from the door that all was clear and Pat and Bouboule rapidly transferred 14307 into his bunk, exchanging their numbers as they went. Presently the body of the Pole, bearing the Russian's number, was carried out, and the records showed that another Russian had died. A whole week passed before they felt secure in their success. Then followed the tricky work of warning the Poles in Block 4 that a friend of theirs had been resurrected from the dead in the guise of a Russian and would shortly be rejoining them.

At the next midnight meeting of the I.P.C. someone pointed out that it might be possible to extend this falsification of the records. There was always the danger that the advance of the Allies would drive the S.S. into wholesale massacre of sick and mutilated prisoners to cover their appalling handiwork. Supposing the committee arranged to exchange scores of those condemned to death for those in the process of dying; Typhus was now killing people at a tremendous rate, and general deaths must be in the region of a hundred. Plenty of corpses could be substituted for the living. It was agreed to carry out fresh experiments.

But what the committee needed above all was weapons. Clubs from the legs of stools and one improvised knife were useless against machine-guns and revolvers. The appearance of a group of female prisoners one day, accompanied by half a dozen S.S. women guards, gave Pat his idea. The prisoners spent forty-eight hours in the showers and the female guards idled in the courtyard during the daylight hours. Watching through the window Pat turned to Tom Groome and said: "You're a good-looking chap. Why not persuade one of those girls to fall in love with you?"

"Good God!" cried Groome.

"They have access to the guardroom. They could steal some revolvers. Tell them it would look good when the Allies come if they could show that they had helped us."

The extraordinary thing was that one female thug was reasonable when Groome dared to speak to her, did seem attracted by him and was won over at the thought of having an ally who might speak for her as a war criminal. Twenty-four hours later she stole a revolver from the guardroom. Because she took this risk, Pat was enormously encouraged. The news from outside remained conflicting. The Allies were near, were far, were being thrown back, were approaching, were decimated by a new German weapon, were ignoring concentration camps in the rush to undermine Germany. Clearly this S.S. girl believed that the prisoners would be liberated at some time or she would never have taken the risk that she did. Pat hid the one revolver in his mattress. Now they must get more. A little blackmail seemed indicated. If they threatened to reveal to the Vernehmungsführer (Head of Security, Discipline and Punishment) that she had stolen a revolver, it might have stimulating results.

Presently the committee was in possession of four revolvers, many rounds of ammunition, a clear knowledge of guardroom routine and its internal layout. It would have been ambitious at this stage to allow the possibility of rushing the guardroom and starting wholesale revolution to become too tempting; there were those who dimly dreamt of the sweet possibility; Pat merely felt reassurance from the possession of four revolvers.

The arrival of the American, "Victor C", came like a breath of fresh and civilized air from an outside world long forgotten. A young man of twenty-four, he was an American major who had been dropped by parachute wearing civilian clothes in front of the advancing tanks. Equipped with motor-cycle, transmitter and perfect French, he was to discover what friendly elements the Americans could expect to meet. The epitome of American good cheer, short, dark, sturdy "Victor C", fresh from training in England, set off on his motor-cycle, but having briefed him on every small eventuality, someone in American Intelligence forgot to observe that people drive on the right-hand side of the road in Germany. Heading straight into the on-coming traffic he was immediately arrested. At least, that was the story told in the camp. It seems incredible. "Victor C" gave every sign of being far too intelligent to make such a mistake.

Now in Dachau, a healthy adult male amongst a population of spectres, what he saw appalled him, but he brought news which electrified the camp. The Americans were smashing holes in every German defence system and fighting was now taking place on German soil.

"Victor C" not only gave grounds for the wildest optimism. He also brought a new brand of humour into prison-camp life. His gentle boasting about his exploits delighted everyone. Pat would solemnly ask for some new highlight in his wildly adventurous life, listening with mock awe. Or Tom would say, after one recital: "That's wonderful, Vic. Let's have it again." Or perhaps it was the beautiful women in his life or his remarkable rank at so youthful an age. "Tell me," said Pat. "What rank are you born with in the American Army?" Vic was laughingly indignant. "You shouldn't say that. It takes something to be an American major, you know."

He saw through their leg-pulling and he wasn't angry or hurt. Immensely good-natured, he mixed with everyone and became a sort of mascot from the outside world who must expect a different race of men to guy him. Whenever "Victor C" was in session the horrors receded; death, dirt, typhus and brutality were momentarily forgotten.

Presently the substitution of living prisoners for the dead reached a difficult stage. It happened with an Austrian who told the I.P.C. one night that he was expecting to be shot at any moment. Escape outside the camp had proved impossible and danger-point had temporarily been reached in the number of substitutions which could be made without exposing the technique. Pat said: "If he cannot escape outside the camp, he had better escape *inside*."

Arthur Haulot, in charge of one of the Revier blocks,

258

played a considerable part in what followed. Planking which formed one corner of the block ceiling was removed, and the man was hoisted up into the roof and the planking replaced. At night, food saved and collected by prisoners was smuggled up to him. For the next three weeks he lived a nightmare life of near suffocation in the complete darkness of the roof cavity, unable to do more than crouch on all fours or lie down, gobbling his still more restricted rations. When he did not answer roll call a ferocious search began. Horrible threats were made and the search quickly spread outside the camp, but for reasons which the I.P.C. were beginning to understand, the search was not pressed home in its usual savage manner.

The I.P.C. met again by stealth of night. Political and national differences made security measures doubly necessary. A very limited number knew the exact composition of the committee, fewer still its meeting places. But the I.P.C. now had concealed arms, a shadow police force, two systems of saving prisoners condemned to death, a rough and ready method of checking the spread of typhus, and a growing intelligence of what was happening outside the camp.

New directions had evidently come from Berlin. Bouboule got wind of the fresh moves first. He reported to Pat who in turn reported to the I.P.C. It appeared that the Lagerschreiber (camp secretary-general) had definite instructions to organize death convoys. Attempts would be made to drag out the 35,000 prisoners in vast convoys, mow them down with machine-gun fire and burn the bodies in great pits, where the evidence of mutilation and starvation would be for ever obliterated. The Russians would go first. Always the Russians and Jews were subjected to the worst torture and the most horrible deaths.

Three representatives of the I.P.C. cornered the Lagerschreiber in the compound one night. He must stop these convoys at any cost. The Allies were coming one day soon. If he did not collaborate they would denounce him when they arrived and he would be shot out of hand—if a far worse fate did not await him.

It was a macabre scene. The tall, gaunt, calculating Lagerschrieber afraid to be thought "conspiring" with the prisoners; the whispered exchanges in the darkest corner of the compound; the mounting threats, and the counter-threat of exposure to the S.S.; the reminder that the I.P.C. represented 35,000 prisoners, some of whom would remain to denounce him whatever he did . . . and then the half-surrender, the questioning about methods, the offer to think it over.

The next night the threats were repeated, the same demands made. Already, Pat pointed out, they had revolvers. It was even possible that if the Lagerschreiber did not agree, his body might be found one dark night . . . somewhere beyond the wire. . . . But, how could he or any-one else sabotage the death convoys?

Some confusion was beginning to appear in the camp records. At the station, loads of men continued to arrive after completing a three-day journey locked in airless wagons, and many staggered away from their own defeca-tions to be driven to the camp. Wagon after wagon arrived. In the camp it seemed that as many died as arrived. Typhus, dysentery and starvation took a mounting toll. The records were not easy to keep . . . far easier to fake . . . far easier to mark off as dead those who were not in fact dead.

Intimidated by the I.P.C. and its hidden underground powers the Lagerschreiber at last agreed to co-operate. A subtle confusion began to spread amongst the meticulously correct entries in the records. Men who were dead were entered as living, the living given the identities of the dead. Agents of the I.P.C. moved around the camp warn-ing others earmarked for death convoys to report to the Revier on some pretext or another. There Pat had a list of the names and numbers of all dead people. Swiftly the living once more exchanged names and numbers with the dead, the list undergoing careful correction. A continual smuggling of prisoners into the great cavern of the infirmary took place while orderlies watched the dying men, waiting for the moment when Russians, Poles or French could take over their identity. It was a horrible, nightmare mime, carried out wordlessly.

Presently the S.S. could not help becoming aware that subterranean manoeuvres were interfering with the proper execution of their orders. By that time at least 5,000 prisoners had been saved from certain death. But some convoys did move out of the camp and silence settled on the tattered multitude as they watched their skeleton comrades stumbling out of the gate in ragged lines towards the hidden machine-guns.

In was Sunday, April 29, 1945. A hush had fallen over Dachau. The chimney of the incinerator was still and cold. Men huddled in their blocks, the guards were sullen, S.S. in the Miradors kept their machine-guns carefully trained, and a tall, blond, elegant second-lieutenant in flawless S.S. uniform was the only officer seen crossing the courtyard. For a whole week the wildest rumours had circulated. A sound at first like thunder had unmistakably become big guns; planes with American markings had flown low over the camp; bursts of machine-gunning indicated that Allied troops were far closer than anyone suspected. The committee had ordered everyone to stay in their blocks, to lie down if firing became intense, and everywhere the prisoner-police guards were watching for any sign of rioting or panic. But the afternoon of Sunday, April 29, 1945, was hushed and quiet. A grey sky held a threat of rain and the flat surrounding country was empty of life. The morning had dragged away full of tension, the afternoon brought restlessness and two attempts at violence suppressed by the police. But it was the unbelievable silence of this teeming hell, never without sounds of horror, which made for uneasiness, as though an unnatural vacuum was straining to suck something in.

At five minutes to four came three quick shots from a rifle. It was answered immediately by a long burst from a machine-gun. Tension approached breaking-point. Thousands of men, their eyes wild with excitement, fought to restrain the urge to burst out, to riot, to break and smash in a delirium of delight. And then, before their eager eyes, the great door of the camp suddenly burst open at the single thrust of a monster tank, and there was an American major in the turret, followed closely by a small jeep in which—astounding vision from a long-dead past—sat a beautiful young girl. The floodgates burst. Nothing could stop them. Wave after wave of starving bodies, in comic pyjamas, poured into the courtyard and tried to rush against, round, over the tank. A great roar of shouting rose. But the waves were halting, maimed, uncertain. Men were too skinny, too sick, too unbalanced to run normally.

According to prearranged plans the whole of the committee formed up and forced its way through to the tank, armed with its four revolvers. Simultaneously the elegant young S.S. officer arrived, drew himself rigidly to attention, cried *"Heil Hitler!"* and began an official statement. A great baying, which threw back from the walls in thunder, drowned his voice.

The American major was short, dark, and powerfully built. His open shirt was spattered with oil, his beard of four or five days' growth was ragged, his red-rimmed eyes tired, but he looked at the tall blond apparition in its beautifully cut clothes with something in his eyes which seemed to penetrate even the closed mind of that young officer.

The beautiful woman was walking freely among them. Men fell back in amazement. This silk-stockinged, uniformed, clear-eyed woman, moving without fear, carrying the faintest hint of perfume among the smells, the disease, the deformities of this mass, was a total miracle very difficult to accept as any part of reality. Pat never discovered which newspaper she represented. So many other things were beginning to burst all over the camp and immediately the American major demanded his attention. He winked at Pat and said to the S.S. officer, "Get up here!" The S.S. officer clicked his heels, saluted and climbed up. The major said to Pat: "You'd better come with me, boy!" Pat explained how much the committee had to do to maintain order in the camp. But the major was in a hurry. He had called at the station before bursting into Dachau and had seen the wagons packed with naked skeletons, dead in their own ordure. He had a peremptory sense of justice. The body of the S.S. officer was later found, five hundred yards from the camp, shot through the neck.

Back in the camp the committee and its police strove to keep control of 35,000 liberated men. Great waves broke in all directions. Notorious Kapos were chased, cornered and beaten, S.S. guards disguised as prisoners were trampled to death, private feuds broke into attempts at murder; one very vicious Armenian Kapo asked for Pat's protection and when the committee surrounded him to carry him off to proper justice, they were half-stunned by blows from the wooden shoes of thousands of prisoners trying to beat the Armenian to death. Men were suddenly wild animals, baying, tearing, screaming. It looked as though everything was running out of control . . . but the committee forced a passage through and the Armenian was safe for the present. Presently the committee restored order.

Some time later, with almost mechanical detachment and efficiency, another American officer appeared, set up a trestle table and began a religious ceremony in Hebrew. His rich voice rolled round the compound. Momentarily, awareness of a dimension long absent from life returned to some of the prisoners. Quiet descended. Religion had been banished with hope. Animals had no use for God. Now, on the hushed air, the deep, rich cadences re-echoed round the wooden huts, and the living and the dying paused in wonder.

    ·   ·   ·   ·

From the plane they could see, for the first time, the plan of the blocks, the outbuildings, the electrified fence. Everything looked quiet. The countryside slept peacefully in the growing warmth of the sun. From the air it was a harmless huddle of buildings and no one could tell its true nature. Pat, Tom Groome, John Hopper, Brian Stonehouse and Bob Sheppard sat silent in the plane as the outline tilted, slipped back, became a blur on the horizon and disappeared. They were headed for Paris.

Traffic poured into Paris from every corner and by every means, By train, tank, jeep, car, plane, bicycle, a multitude pressed in again. Circling over the city in the plane Pat could see the beautiful avenues, the great Place de la Concorde, the emerald Bois de Boulogne, the Arc de Triomphe, the Seine, blue, glittering, insubstantial in the afternoon sun, and there was a lovely unreality about it all.

He had come back at last but it did not seem real.

22

SOME months elapsed. A quite different Patrick O'Leary, in spotless uniform and with the beginnings of the great mass of decorations which were to crowd his tunic, was suddenly asked to go to the Paris police morgue to identify a body. There he confronted an apparition from the past. Lying on the slab, his red hair neatly brushed back from his brow, and an expression of fear still on his pale freckled face, was Paul Cole. A very strange chain of events had at last brought his extraordinary career to an end.

Trouble had begun for Paul Cole when the Allied Armies showed signs of winning the war, but not even this total reversal of the situation could quite outwit the adroit Cole. With the same twisted cunning which had saved his skin so often before, he successfully transferred himself— by what manoeuvres no one ever knew—from the German to the American lines, walked into an American Army Corps H.Q. one day, and represented himself as a British Intelligence officer who had worked behind the German lines, and had "got lost" on the way back. He told a fascinating story in such detail that everyone was convinced.

Claiming an intimate knowledge of those caches where the Germans had hidden looted art treasures, he was taken into the U.S. Art Recovery Section, presented with a car, and driven in state from one hideout to another which he located with extreme facility. He had now achieved the distinction of working for the British, French, German and Americans, steadily increasing his pay with every change. At this stage in the war, life in the American Army was comparatively rich, and at times unrestrained. The adaptable Paul Cole was once again enjoying himself, giving parties, regaling astonished American officers with exploits which would have seemed outrageous but for the details he was able to supply. He got drunk with some regularity, he talked unceasingly, he found fresh and willing mistressess.

But away in Paris an ironic little incident had repercussions exactly opposite to those intended. A person who shall be known as Audrey, one of Cole's ex-mistressess, had known him in his heyday in the south of France and had never lost faith in him since. Her love was not diminished when the Organization tried to persuade her that he was a traitor. Plainly and simply she did not believe them. For eighteen months she cherished her love and her belief in him, until one day he wrote to her from the American Army Corps H.Q., where another incarnation of Paul Cole was beginning to materialize. The first letter gave no address. The second, full of protestations of his innocence, brimming with ingenious explanations of his conduct, and plainly designed to provide an alibi, did disclose his whereabouts. Moved by the letter and anxious to confound those people who had said such nasty things about him, Audrey carried it off to Donald Darling. They had all lied about Paul Cole, she said. They were little better than malicious gossips. She had a letter which proved his innocence. Gently, Darling asked whether he might see the letter, and eagerly she gave it him. As he read, Darling memorized the address, and the following day wired Peter Hope, an M.I.5 agent then in Paris. Hope left at once with a French officer, travelled to Germany, traced the American Corps H.Q., and one evening called and asked to see Cole. "He's giving a party tonight," he was told. "Must you see him—now?"

"I'm afraid so," said Hope. At last they were shown in. There stood a flushed, happy Cole, surrounded by friends, drinking, talking, full of that superficial charm which had deceived so many. Hope and the Frenchman disclosed their identity. Cole went very pale. They asked to speak to him outside. At pistol point he was arrested, handcuffed and taken away.

It seemed that fate had at last settled his appalling account; but no. Taken back to Paris and imprisoned in the Cherche Midi, he lay there week after week while the French, English and Americans wrangled over the priority of their respective claims to bring him to justice. Each felt that they had the more serious charges, and each wanted to deal with the prisoner first. The wrangle became a bureaucratic duel. Presently it developed into a pitched battle.

At its height, news came through that Cole had escaped. Once more he had slipped through everyone's hands, and astonishingly, no one could explain how it had happened. Another month went by, and then one day there came to a local police station in the rue de Grenelle area a waiter from a café who reported that a man in the vicinity was behaving very oddly. He lived, he said, in a café owned by Madame X, never went out by day, seemed curiously suspicious of everyone and spoke with a thick foreign accent. "Monsieur," said the police inspector, "if we arrested everyone in Paris who fitted that description we should need to build another Bastille. Now go home and forget about it. . . ."

Two days later the man was back again. He insisted that this was no normal case, that something odd lay hidden behind the habits of a person whose behaviour had become even more eccentric in the past twenty-four hours. Largely to humour him two detectives accompanied him to the rue de Grenelle.

"Have you anyone strange living here?" they asked Madame X.

"No."

"No one at all?"

"No one."

"Not even upstairs?"

She shook her head. "Perhaps we'd better look." She led them upstairs, flung open a door, said "The police, darling," and there in his pyjamas was Paul Cole, his revolver already in his hand. The first bullet hit one detective in the arm. He spun round, recovered, grabbed the woman as a shield and simultaneously the second detective opened fire. His first two bullets penetrated Cole's heart. Cole staggered back, fired one more shot, and collapsed. Five minutes later the extraordinary career of a very ordinary British N.C.O. had come to a close. . . .

Looking down now at the pale face framed by the red

hair, Pat suddenly remembered, with the full force of the past, the Abbé Carpentier, Bruce Dowding, the beautiful nights when the boat did not come, and the Germans shooting from the Banyuls train. Mario Prassinos had vanished without a trace. Dr. Rodocanachi, M. Mongelard, Guy Berthet, all had died in concentration camps. Vidal, leader of the Spanish guides, was said to have been burnt alive. Dupré, Didery, Ulmann, Debaume, all were gone, dead, done. Over thirty men had not come back.

Down in the wastes of the Camargue at one of those desolate spots half-way along the southern line where illimitable sand dunes were continuously moving to the pressure of winds and sea, there was a rough wooden cross which bore the words: "To an escape worker whose way of death was not known."

Outside, in Paris, it was a lovely spring day.

EPILOGUE

APRIL 1951 in Korea, with the Chinese battering at the Allied lines and the American Third Division in serious trouble. News came back that a Belgian soldier lay badly wounded in full view of the enemy and Dr. Albert Marie Guérisse, an M.O. of the British 29 Brigade, then part of the American Third Division, went at once to the battalion commander. He wanted permission to go out and get the Belgian soldier. The battalion commander said it was madness. The man lay beside a dry river-bed in a plain commanded from all angles by the enemy's guns. Dr. Guérisse persisted. The commander said that the U.N. forces needed doctors and they could not afford to throw their lives away. Finally, Guérisse set off in a tank and as it edged out on the plain there was no sound of firing, no birds, no sign of life of any kind. They sighted the wounded man, a black speck by the river-bed, and as they nosed towards him all hell suddenly opened up, shells and bullets pouring down on the single, negligible target. The tank commander swung the turret round and fired back. Guérisse slipped out of the tank, and sheltering behind it crawled to the wounded man and began tending him. The tank was forced to move and the Communists concentrated their fire on Guérisse and the wounded man, a clear-cut target in the open plain, with nothing to protect them. Bullets whipped up the earth, dancing a mad pattern round and over them, while Guérisse literally tried to dig into the ground with his hands and feet.

Again the tank manoeuvred into position. Within its small shelter the doctor tried to carry the wounded Belgian towards it. Bullets were hammering on the armour and hissing splinters of steel shot in all directions; death was certain for anyone trying to climb into the turret. Unexpectedly there came something resembling a lull. The tank commander slipped out of the turret and together he and

269

O'Leary attempted to rush the Belgian into the safety of the tank. A member of the crew came to their help but was wounded almost immediately. Then, at last, both wounded men were dragged in. Presently the tank began lumbering back towards a Clearing Station. Three months later the Belgian Army made Guérisse an Officer of the Order of Leopold II with palm, and the Korean Government awarded him the Chung Mu, Korean equivalent to the British D.S.O.

With the second World War, over, the allure of Korea had proved too much for a spirit continuously in need of a purpose involving danger, action and adventure to absorb the fierce energy eternally renewed by some strange well-spring. One never knew the true depth of motive. All the surface signs could not plumb the hidden places where uncontrollable forces sometimes insisted on mysterious redemptions in disguises so complete that no one knew their real identity. To be a very brave man was one thing; to try to explain that bravery quite another. Perhaps the simplest explanations were best accepted; perhaps the hatred of someone with a gun trying to dominate one's behaviour was motive enough.

Today, Dr Albert Marie Guérisse is once again a doctor in the Belgian Army, the full circle of an extraordinary career having brought him back to his starting-point. His beautiful wife Sylvia and he have an eight-year-old son who bears a close resemblance to him and is named Patrick.

Dr. Guérisse continues in touch with members of his Organization and talks of them with that warmth and affection which a man might use about his family. He and Louis Nouveau have done many things to help those who came back. Fabien de Cortes is now employed in Louis Nouveau's business. Jean de la Olla, with one lung and a mutilated left hand, has been provided with a bungalow in the country where he lives, with his wife Marinette, on a pension granted by the French Government. Jacques Wattebled passed through a near breakdown and continues to run a library and theatre-ticket agency in Paris, bringing the old drollery to booking seats for the Folies Bergères. Robert Leycuras, grown even more dashing and handsome, is superintendent of a big French police station just outside Paris, apparently unaffected by war experience. Norbert Fillerin and his remarkable family continue to run their farm in Renty with tremendous success.

Leoni Savinos and Costa Dimpoglou now have businesses in London, Paula has married Francis Blanchain—now a distinguished photographer—and Postel Vinet is a director of a French bank. The same immaculate Louis Nouveau, with the beautiful English and flawless clothes, is sometimes to be seen driving through the streets of Marseille in a huge Bentley, his merchant broker's business now reaching into the remote corners of the earth. And also in Marseille, propping a new bar in a small hotel which sometimes caters for remarkable characters, it is possible of an evening to find old Gaston Nègre, his big form restored to its former proportions, the half-grin on his face, the cigarette screwed into his mouth and the inevitable gesture inviting one to join him in *pastis*.

Dr. Guérisse has revisited them all. Paulette Gastou, Chouquette, Françoise Dissart, and many others. It was Françoise Dissart who sat up in her sick-bed when Guérisse arrived with his wife Sylvia, and said to Sylvia: "You wouldn't have stood a chance if I had been a few years younger."

It was Gaston Nègre who chuckled when he heard that the Maquis had eventually trapped Roger, the traitor, and slowly brought him to a painful death.

It was Pat who told me of the day during the war criminal trials when he was confronted with Heinrich Hornetz, the S.S. officer from Saarbrücken, and asked whether he knew the man. Hornetz seemed reasonably at ease. Asked what he had to say when Pat described the attack which had nearly killed him, Hornetz said, "Look what he said to me—any man would have done what I did." But they executed Heinrich Hornetz.

It was Pat, too, who said to me in Paris, looking round a

lunch-table where twenty-five people sat, some gay and vivacious, some silent, some wearing decorations, some hilarious with reminiscence of how they had duped the Germans, some deeply lost in escape-route technicalities— "We keep in touch."